WATER INTO BONES

WATER INTO BONES

Birth Rituals, Ancestors, and Religious Pluralism
in Northern Madagascar

ERIN K. NOURSE

INDIANA UNIVERSITY PRESS

This book is a publication of

Indiana University Press
Herman B Wells Library 350
1320 East 10th Street
Bloomington, Indiana 47405 USA

iupress.org

First printing 2025

Cataloging information is available from the Library of Congress.
ISBN 978-0-253-07239-9 (hdbk.)
ISBN 978-0-253-07240-5 (pbk.)
ISBN 978-0-253-07241-2 (web PDF)
ISBN 978-0-253-07242-9 (ebook)

CONTENTS

Acknowledgments   *vii*

Introduction: Studying Birth Rituals and Ancestors
   in Madagascar   *1*

1. Birthing Babies in Diégo Suarez   *33*

2. Motherhood and Creative Confluences of Care   *68*

3. Bathing and Seclusion: Making Mothers
   Who Will Bless Their Babies   *105*

4. Turning "Water Babies" into "Real Human Beings"   *137*

5. Bearing Babies in Dynamic Religious Landscapes   *175*

Conclusion: Birth, Loss, and Competing
   Moral Cosmologies   *201*

Notes   *217*
Bibliography   *251*
Index   *261*

ACKNOWLEDGMENTS

This book is based on work conceived and developed as my PhD dissertation at the University of Virginia, where I had the great fortune of studying with Cynthia Hoehler-Fatton, Benjamin Ray, Jalane Schmidt, Adria La Violette, and Joe Miller, among others. I am most especially grateful to Cindy, my main adviser, who was always kind, meticulous, insightful, and extremely generous with her time, despite her extremely full schedule of professional commitments and engagements. I would have been lost without her guidance and breadth of knowledge.

I would like to thank the Graduate School of Arts and Sciences and the Society of Fellows for awarding me language fellowships that enabled me to travel to Madagascar to undergo language training before commencing research for this project and to spend a summer at the African Language Institute at Michigan State University in Lansing. I am likewise thankful to the Carter G. Woodson Institute for African-American and African Studies at the University of Virginia for granting me a predoctoral writing fellowship upon my return from completing this research and for all the fellows, and guest workshop readers, who read chapters that have since morphed and evolved many times to become the chapters that compose this book.

I am grateful to my friends and colleagues at Regis University who created space for me to focus on my writing by protecting me from taking on too many departmental and administrative responsibilities. Like other small liberal arts colleges, Regis does not always have the kind of funding or name recognition as some other universities, but the dedication of the faculty to students, research, community, and just being good humans is unparalleled. Many eyes read drafts of the chapters that compose this book, most of them colleagues at Regis, but friends and colleagues from elsewhere as well. I am grateful to all of you: Emily Gravett, Julia Brumbaugh, Russ Arnold, Kari Kloos, Chris Pramuk, Tom Howe, Erica Ferg, Laura Tilghman, Alison Castel, Sarah Puett, Sarah Adelman, Ethan Sanders, Alyse Knorr, Kate Partridge, and two anonymous readers. Thank you for your insights and also for your friendship.

The decision to study abroad in Madagascar nearly twenty years ago felt like one of those chance decisions that altered the course of my life in so many ways for which I am grateful. I am thankful to Anna Prow, the then director of the School for International Training's study abroad program in Antananarivo, Madagascar, in 2004, as well as the other staff of that program, for first introducing me to a country I have come to love. I made many friends that semester, American and Malagasy, whom I am still in touch with; several of the Malagasy I met adopted me into their families and continued to do so each time I returned. My continued interest in Madagascar is a result of relationships formed over that semester.

In particular, I would like to thank the Razafindratsita family, who have been my home away from home in Madagascar for the past twenty years. François, and Pauline, who is dearly missed; their children, who are like my siblings (Ianja, Tiana, Laingo, and Tolotra); their spouses; and their children all hold a special place in my heart. Thank you for taking me in time and again, for teaching me about your beautiful country, and for always making me to feel at home.

I am additionally thankful to my home away from home in Diégo. I have had far too many laughs with and learned so much from Madame Tamara, Vony, Hanitriniaina, Riza, and their spouses and children. They are funny, beautiful, down to earth, and infinitely generous. I also owe a debt of gratitude to Alex Totomarovario, who was chair of the English Department at the University of Antsiranana when I conducted this research, and to his wife, Laurette, for helping me find a place to live and for supporting me as I found my way upon first arriving in Diégo to commence my research for this project in 2011. Alex assisted so many students, American and Malagasy, in his too short time on this earth, and I am grateful to have had the opportunity to have known and worked with him.

I am also thankful to all the members of the English Department at the University of Antsiranana and the many students, some of whom have since become professors themselves, who provided me with not only help in learning

Malagasy but also friendships that have endured across time and oceans. I would like to especially thank Elodie, Martelline, Dahlia, Dorea, Danielle, and Yasmine. And there are many others. Of course, I am also deeply thankful to all of the women who agreed to be interviewed for this project. Thank you for allowing me a window into your lives, for your friendship, and for sharing your joys and sorrows, wisdom, and religious insights with me. I hope this book does justice to the stories with which you entrusted me.

My interest in religion, both as practice and as theory, has deep roots. I owe a debt of gratitude to my family—both the family I was born into and the family I married into—for nurturing the kinds of questions in me that led me to graduate school and to my field research in Madagascar. It is my hope that I have honored the gift of intellectual curiosity you all have given to me. Similarly, I wouldn't be where I am today without the religious communities that have shaped me. If this book is about belonging, about finding one's bones, then I am forever grateful for the religious communities that were a part of my growing up—communities that instilled in me a sense of worth, identity, and purpose. I am thankful, too, for communities of friends—friends from college and graduate school, friends from work, and mom friends. Your accompaniment through so many stages of my life—through schooling, travels, a global pandemic, the early years of motherhood, and the writing of this book—matters to me.

I am forever grateful for and indebted to my mother and mother-in-law, and more recently, my father-in-law as well, all of whom have provided so much support in the form of childcare. When my husband and I were first finishing our PhDs, applying for jobs, and trying to get our feet on the ground, our mothers were there every step of the way, providing childcare and words of encouragement that made sticking it out feel infinitely more possible. Likewise, they were there as we spun articles from our research and slowly, ever so slowly, crafted our earlier research into books. So many times, I came home to find that our dishes had been done, a load of laundry folded, a light bulb changed, and grandchildren mentored through art and garden projects. I could not have written this book without you.

I am perhaps most grateful to my husband, Ben. Your companionship, support, sense of humor, insights, and spirit of adventure made our time in Charlottesville, our travels in China and Madagascar, and our life in Denver infinitely richer. I sometimes shudder to think what my life would have been like had I not met you. We have climbed mountains, traveled the world, carried into this world our beautiful children, and wrestled out of our bodies these books that bear witness to the lives we used to live—students out there in the world. These days, our lives are much more drawn in, and I am grateful for all of it—the times out there circumambulating temples in Tibet, witnessing first haircuttings in Madagascar, growing vegetables in our gardens, singing in church together, being taken in by families all over the world, and, sometimes, more recently, doing our own taking in of those who needed shelter. Thank you for being my partner in all of it.

Last, I want to thank my children, my "water babies" (*zaza rano*), who are becoming more and more bone filled every day. Margaret, thank you for being my sweet, beautiful baby daughter, the one who first helped me understand the fragility of new life in the world as well as the simultaneous agency and determination that young babies possess. You came into the world a highly observant, sensitive, silly, and passionate person who has become a prolific writer, thespian, Rubik's Cube solver, and dog whisperer. I am inspired by your passions, by your care for the earth, by the ways you speak out against injustice and practice random acts of kindness, and by your love of story. Your coming into my life puts everything into perspective and makes this work feel far more important to me than it did before you entered my life. Henry, my snuggle bug, my love for you is all over these pages too. You have brought such tenderness into our lives and such joy. Your hugs, your love for and knowledge of animals, and your eagerness to chop vegetables with me in the kitchen is my daily consolation. And Julian, how I have loved watching you grow. You were the sturdiest of our water babies from the start—coming into the world with a tooth. What would people in Madagascar have said about that! You were born ready for the world—walking at nine months, scootering at a year, riding your own pedal bike to school at three. You are as bold and sure of yourself as you are sensitive and kind. I cannot wait to see who you will become.

Raising children is the weightiest, most important job. I am certain I would not understand the implications of the choices mothers were making in Madagascar had I not been faced with my own choices as a mother, about rituals and religious community and about discerning who my children are, what continuances exist in them, and what, if anything, has emerged in them uniquely their own. There is so much uncertainty in the world. It is my hope that I am instilling in my children some kind of sturdiness to face that uncertainty.

WATER INTO BONES

INTRODUCTION

Studying Birth Rituals and Ancestors in Madagascar

In January 2012, in the small town of Joffreville, near Montagne D'Ambre National Parc in northern Madagascar, a midwife named Bernadette showed me what she does to help premature babies grow strong. She indicated that sometimes babies are born at around seven months of gestation and that there is a traditional Malagasy medicine (*fanafody*) for this.[1] As we sat in the middle of her small wood-framed home, sunlight breaking through the wood slats, she picked up a clump of dirt from an insect nest, crushed it between her worn and sturdy fingers, mixed the dry dirt with honey in a small white porcelain bowl, added a silver coin, and stirred the mixture into a paste.[2] She then demonstrated how she encircles this medicine around all of the baby's joints, gesturing warmly on her own wrists, elbows and ankles as she spoke. She called this special medicine *fameno* and said it should be applied every morning for a week and then with each subsequent week another coin added and the procedure continued.

The mixture of medicines that Bernadette creates in a bowl is instructive when placed within the larger context of traditional practices in Madagascar. Honey is commonly used as an offering to ancestors; coins are symbolic of ancestral power, and healing powers are commonly transferred between generations through a person's inheritance of gold or silver coins. Moreover, spirit mediums paint their bodies with a special clay (*kaolin*) around their joints in the same way that Bernadette paints the bodies of premature Malagasy babies who are struggling to survive.[3] This material culture forms a complex set of beliefs and practices in which ancestors' life-giving power (*hasina*) is

channeled through the work of specialists, like Bernadette, and impressed on
the newly living so that hasina might continue in them.

Prior to traveling to Madagascar—initially in 2004 and subsequently in
2005, 2008, and 2011–2012—I had not paid much attention to ancestors. I had
rarely, if ever, contemplated my own lineage. Nor had I given much thought
to my own culturally prescribed white, American, Protestant responses to
death. Singing hymns, dressing the deceased in "Sunday best," and placing
the dead in caskets never to be unearthed again felt universal, even if I knew
otherwise. My glimpses into the ways in which Malagasy remember and relate
to their ancestors began in 2004, when I first learned about *famadihana*, or
the exhumation of the dead; witnessed a man channeling an ancestral spirit
at a tomb near Ambohimanga; and heard the nocturnal chants of those carrying the body of a would-be ancestor along a footpath that intersected a small
village outside of Ambilobe. Later in 2005, I witnessed the exuberant procession of an exhumed body through Anjozorobe and danced with drunken
commemorators into the wee hours of the night. However, it was not until
2008, after attending a haircutting ceremony for a baby of royal Antankarana
descent, that questions began to emerge for me regarding the relationship
between babies and ancestors. Within this ceremony, which included Muslim
and other traditional religious elements, one participant recited the names of
important ancestors within the lineage as a central feature of the welcoming
and blessing of this newest descendant.

This element of ancestral engagement, the kind that shows up around the
birth of a child, has thus far received little scholarly attention. Though scholars
of Madagascar widely agree that remembering ancestors is as much about
making futures and claiming belonging as it is about a preoccupation with the
dead or the past, the extent to which birth is involved, as an important rite of
passage for mothers and children, has been underemphasized. What I hope
to offer in this book is a window into these kinds of rituals, a window into the
lives of women whose life courses and engagement with ancestors are likely
to look different from that of men's. Moreover, in northwestern Madagascar,
the setting for this book, poverty and pluralism are material realities for most.
Thus, women's efforts to secure belonging, for themselves and on behalf of
their children, are not just about identity and meaning making but also about
establishing social networks critical to children's survival. Identifying the
sources of religious and ancestral influences in one's life is key in this process. In northwestern Madagascar, babies are being born into richly diverse

social contexts. In the small village where the aforementioned haircutting ceremony took place, Christians, Muslims, and traditionalists mourned the dead and welcomed the newly born among friends and family of multiple and sometimes hybridized religious and ethnic identities, thus offering a look into Madagascar's diversity and the ways in which parents navigate this diversity upon the birth of a child.

Other scholars attest to this diversity created by the Southeast Asians and East Africans who first settled the island sometime around the middle of the first century, followed by Swahili, Portuguese, Merina, French, American, and Chinese arrivals, all of whom have contributed to a unique and diverse religious culture characteristic of other islands and littorals in the western Indian Ocean. The people of northern Madagascar from village dwellers to the urbanites of Diégo Suarez, where much of the research for this book takes place, have incorporated a plethora of ancestries, ethnicities, and religious practices into their own, sometimes celebrating the hybridity that is their history while also performing rituals and traditions that set groups apart and create distinctive ethnic and religious identities. At the site of nearly every mountain chain, river or lake, and waterfall are stories Malagasy tell about landowners and new arrivals and about efforts to preserve sacred places and establish enduring communities in the midst of a never-ending flow of movement, migration, and environmental change. The birth of a child offers parents a pivotal moment to reflect on this diversity and the very particular ways in which they wish to engage with and craft their own place within it.

People engage with their ancestors in diverse settings—at birth and death and for aspirational as well as remembrance-oriented purposes. This book explores how Malagasy—and women in particular—adhere to ancestral practices at birth and in this kind of hybridized environment where children are often the products of unions between people of multiple faiths and ethnicities or the products of love between local women and the men temporarily stationed as dockworkers on Diégo Suarez's shores. It is the story of how women, charged with the task of observing ancestral *fady* (taboos) in their pregnancies, must listen to the voices of ancestors whose lineages span the oceans.[4]

The word *water* within the title of this book speaks both to the ambiguous, or watery, identity of newborn babies and to the pluralistic worlds into which babies are born, a pluralism resulting from the confluence of ancestries and religious traditions that have emerged in the port city of Diégo Suarez.[5] The word *bones* refers to the process by which babies find their place within these hybridized communities, their sturdiness if you will. This metaphor—water into bones—emerged out of my countless conversations in Diégo Suarez with women and men who shared with me many stories about bones and about water and the things that emerge from it. They described young babies as *zaza rano* (water babies) and how haircutting ceremonies and various other birth rituals are among the many means by which these young babies acquired bones, or their standing within their ethnic, ancestral, and religious communities. This book is my attempt to share these stories.

Ethnic, Ancestral, and Religious Worlds of Malagasy Babies

Madagascar is an ethnically diverse nation. In the island nation as a whole, there are roughly eighteen recognized groups though the identity categories that Malagasy use for themselves are far more numerous due to the existence of smaller subsections within many of these groups. As scholars have noted, ethnonyms, or *karazana*, emerged over the course of several centuries and for a variety of reasons—as a way to classify groups according to the occupations that some become known for, like the Vezo, who fish along the west coast; the areas of land that some are indigenous to, like the Antankarana, named after the famous *tsingy* rock formations in the north of the island; and the various forms of political organization that emerged during particular periods within Malagasy history that later became ethnicized, like the Merina of the central highlands, named for the Merina polity that became dominant in the Imerina region of the island at the dawn of the nineteenth century.[6] But perhaps more important than these ethnic distinctions are the ancestral histories that many share around figures within their families who left legacies that continue to press on, inspire, and shape descendants in profound ways, the latter of which is an important focus of this book.

These identities—centered on ancestral legacies—are typically inherited through birth but are also further cemented in individuals by way of their participation (or their lack thereof) in certain activities, for example, through family rituals that honor one's ancestors, through the observance of ancestral fady, through participation in religious communities, through one's occupation, through one's modes of speech and dress, and through ceremonies of commemoration in which participants are invited to reflect on their sense of communal belonging. Drawing on their research among Antankarana, Andrew Walsh and Michael Lambek argue that Malagasy identities are framed "less by categorization than by performance" and less by rigid boundaries of exclusion than by inclusion through communally enacted religious celebrations.[7] Though their research speaks to the formation of ethnic identities, I would argue that performance is an important factor within ancestral identities as well.

In the northern city of Diégo Suarez, where research for this book takes place, families perform these inherited ancestral identities in a variety of ways, both for themselves and for, and on behalf of, their children. Some of the more common actions performed for children include observing pregnancy fady; performing certain kinds of postpartum bathing rituals, like *ranginaly*, an ancestrally inherited style of cold-water bathing that is discussed in greater detail in chapter 3; and also blessing babies with haircutting, circumcision, baptism, and naming ceremonies, of which haircutting is discussed the most. In Madagascar, remembering ancestors in the lives of children is a twofold process that requires that parents instill within young children an embodied sense of who they are as members of a particular lineage *and* that parents discern which remnants from the ancestral past babies carry into the world by virtue of their special connection to the ancestors. Hence the notion that pregnancy is somehow "the ancestors' continuation" (*ny fitohy raza*).[8]

For many Malagasy, immersing one's children in the traditions of one's ancestors is a highly important act, for it enables children to be safely situated, and properly grounded, in the kinds of extended community that will give their lives meaning. This transfer of blessings involves the creation and passing down of hasina, a this-worldly life force that one must cultivate, maintain, and reproduce through right relations with land, people, and the divine. Maurice Bloch describes hasina as "the mystical force of primacy" and "a force of excellence, of essence, [that is] associated with high rank and even royalty, but also with the power of blessing in general."[9] But hasina is not just about who people and things are; hasina is also about what people *do*. As Jennifer Cole describes of Betsimisaraka, an ethnic group who live predominantly on Madagascar's eastern coast, "More generally, Betsimisaraka say that *hasina* is first produced through ancestors' mundane actions while they are alive, then simply by virtue of their death. In other words, through daily activities like farming rice, building houses, producing and raising children, and dying, ancestors imbue the land and village around them with their *hasina*."[10] Thus, the prevalence of hasina, in ancestors and in the world at large, is created as a result of human actions: when people impregnate the world with meaning by building houses, growing food, bearing children, and tending to the land on which they live. These actions are never exclusively innovative; rather, they always build on, and sometimes diverge from, the actions of one's predecessors—but they are always in conversation with them. Malagasy then maintain hasina by abiding by the customs (*fomba*) of their ancestors, by observing the inherited fady their ancestors followed, and by recalling their forebears' legacies through rituals of commemoration.

In Madagascar, ancestors have a pervasive spiritual presence. By insisting that their descendants abide by certain inheritable customs and taboos, ancestors, called *razana*, govern what land their descendants live on, how they pray, what foods they eat, and with whom they marry and reproduce. Malagasy understand ancestors to be temperamental, ever present, and actively involved in human affairs. Their spirits reside in tombs; in the soil their descendants farm and pass down to their children; in the forests where people hunt, gather, and mine; and in oceans, lakes and rivers where Malagasy fish, swim, and bathe. Ancestral presence is felt in the fires, floods, and droughts they sometimes cause; in the dreams and visions they inspire; and in the powerful words, revelatory actions, and healing hands of those possessed by their power. When the ancestors are pleased, their living descendants enjoy bountiful harvests and are blessed with multiple children who will be made to continue in their forebears' powerful legacies. Conversely, ancestral wrath can be experienced as hunger pangs, sickness, or an empty womb.

Outsiders have long been intrigued by the elaborate customs of Malagasy, who in differing ways, according to various regional customs, family traditions, and religious practices, viscerally venerate the legacies of their forebears. It would in fact be difficult to write anything about Madagascar without first mentioning the pivotal role ancestors play in the lives of many. Those familiar with these customs are likely to know something of famadihana, the exhumation ceremonies for which the Merina of the central highlands are famous; or about possession by royal ancestor spirits (*tromba*) among Sakalava peoples; or about the periodic mast-raising ceremony (*tsangantsainy*) of the Antankarana peoples.[11] Ancestors compose a central point of reference in all kinds of public and domestic rituals throughout the island.[12]

Yet while scholars have examined puberty rites, sacrifice, spirit possession, and funerary rituals as occasions for engaging historical narratives that anchor individual and collective identities and offer opportunities for innovation, much less attention has been paid to what this looks like at the most quintessential of new beginnings—the birth of a child—which is what I do in this book.[13] This omission exists despite the fact that many Malagasy understand children to be "the continuation of the ancestors" (ny fitohy raza).[14] Or as Gillian Feeley-Harnik once noted, in her research in northwestern Madagascar, "From hidden roots—the dead buried in the ground—the living grow up and out over the surface of the land like a tree, which they work to nourish. The deeper the roots, the greater the tree. Ancestors are that fruitful union: expressed in explicitly sexual terms in royal funerals; as a union between husband and wife in the relationships between a spirit and its medium; and as a union between parent and child in relations among the living. Ancestors emerge in the birth of children."[15] Similarly, Karen Middleton reveals that Hazohandatse infants, of southern Madagascar, are thought to grow best when they were connected to their primordial (or ancestral) roots.[16] Even if infants are born away from their ancestral lands, as many are, relics from the birth, specifically umbilical cords, were preserved and carried back to the ancestral lands, to the place where "the ancestors first settled." Dirt from these lands was then carried back to the child and mixed in an infusion for the child to drink. This practice of connecting the child with its ancestral origins is thought to root the child by connecting its umbilical cord to its most vital and generative source (the ancestors).[17]

In northern Madagascar, where research for this book takes place, infants are frequently dubbed water babies (zaza rano) and hidden or handled with extreme care until they have successfully made their transition from liminal beings bearing an intimate connection to the ancestral realm to fully arrived-in-the-world humans. As Robert Jaovelo describes, "L'imaginal *sakalava* semble suggérer que le nouveau-né n'appartient plus au monde des Ancêtres d'une part, et que, d'autre part, il n'est pas tout à fait intégré encore dans le monde des vivants."[18] In other words, the newly born exist in a space that is neither wholly of the realm of the ancestors from which they come nor wholly of the realm of the living into which they will one day integrate. When a baby's teeth come in, which represents a hardening of the bones and the beginning of the end of their liminal status, parents mark the occasion with a ritual sacrifice and haircutting and formally declare the baby a human, a new descendant among the living. Haircutting ceremonies, which are discussed more thoroughly in chapter 4 of this book, not only serve as occasions to celebrate the life of a new child but also offer parents and grandparents the chance to articulate through speech-prayers (*joro*) what it means to be a member of one ancestral family or religious community versus another and thus help children become rooted in or tethered to the traditions that will help them thrive.

The idea of "partial reincarnation," where aspects of the ancestral spirits are reborn in children, is more prevalent in West African societies and their diasporas than in East African societies.[19] In Madagascar, beliefs about children continuing from ancestors and about ancestors sometimes reincarnating in animals likely comes from combination of both Indonesian and East African influences.[20] This kind of understanding of babies as somehow growing from ancestors, or at least bearing a special connection to ancestors, can have profound implications for the ways in which parents care for children, evidenced by, among other things, the amulets and heirloom jewelries parents place around children's necks and wrists to both protect children from harmful spirits and link them with important personalities from the past. Malagasy mothers are heavily involved both in these protective measures and in efforts to facilitate important connections between ancestors and babies, whereby babies learn to separate from the dead in order to become more fully human and to connect to certain members of the dead so that their lives might be integrated into a greater collective.

Scholars have long recognized that "the work the living perform for the dead" is gendered in interesting and complex ways.[21] For example, in certain ritual contexts, women may not be allowed to perform sacrifices or invoke the ancestors, but it is also very clear that women are very much involved in other kinds of activities within these same ceremonies. Women are often the weavers of funerary shrouds for secondary burials, they cradle like babies the bones of exhumed ancestors in famadihana, and, as will be made clear in this book, they are heavily involved in the planning and performance of practices of ancestral remembrance that occur at birth—in the rites of blessing that ensure that the newly born will transition from the ancestral realm to the realm of the living.[22] Women's engagement with ancestors looks different from that of men's in part because of societal gender norms and in part because the life courses of women, for all kinds of cultural as well as biological reasons, are simply different from those of men. These differences are discussed in greater depth in chapters 3 and 4 of this book.

In Madagascar, as elsewhere, interest in ancestors can be said to be about many things. It is a means by which people remember the past and a means by which some family members ascertain authority over other family members.[23] Ancestral commemoration can establish belonging among relatives and can serve as a means by which to incorporate new kinds of kin into their communities, by way of peoples' relationship to a collective of spirits with which their lives conjoin. Interest in ancestors can be about claiming or reclaiming one's access to land, about labor, and about creating intergenerational (and often patrilineal) descent groups that give people an enduring sense of place within the community.[24] Interest in ancestors is also aspirational, a kind of hopeful imagining and reshaping of the past. Nowhere is this more evident than in the rituals Malagasy employ to remember their ancestors in the lives of the newly born.

According to my research assistant Édith, who was in her midtwenties and a student at the University of Antsiranana when we met, ancestors are not merely symbols of the past; they are a real presence of loss in people's lives. Moreover, the loss that people feel can sometimes be more pronounced when the next generation of babies are born with personalities and tendencies that remind parents and caregivers of those recently passed. Family and community are very important in Malagasy society, Édith explained, and that community extends beyond death. People believe that if you do not care for your ancestors properly after they die, they can become bad (*masantôko*). In our time together, conducting interviews and walking the city, Édith often spoke fondly of her grandfather in particular, of how she missed him, and of how badly she wanted to see him in her dreams. She complained that her relatives who were most afraid of seeing her grandfather were ironically the ones who more frequently received visits from him in their dreams.

Later in the year, Édith finally did see her grandfather in a dream, an experience she had wanted for the past fourteen years. She did not understand the dream, but there was a baby in it who was just learning to sit and who was wearing red clothes. Her grandfather was introducing her to the baby. Édith did not know who the baby was, to whom it belonged, or how it fit into her family. She remained puzzled by what her grandfather was trying to communicate to her and was overwhelmed by the revelation. When she woke in the middle of the night, she felt inundated with joy upon finally having seen him, but in the morning, she felt sad again and cried because she missed him.

The spirit that visited Édith in a dream had been her maternal grandfather. He had been very special to her and she to him. There had been other grandchildren born in Édith's family before her, including a boy cousin, but as Édith explained, her grandfather did not give the family's heirloom silver necklace to this cousin of hers; instead, the first baby to receive the silver necklace in a haircutting ceremony had been Édith. Tears welled up in her eyes as she recounted to me the dream as well as the special relationship she and her grandfather had shared. In Madagascar, ancestors have come to represent many things to many people, but what Édith's story reveals is that they are also more than mere representations. Ancestors were once beloved family members, some of whom were royal, others of whom were slaves, some of whom were gracious, and others of whom were mean (*masiaka*) and imposing. And their spirits and legacies continue to crop up, in both expected and unexpected ways, when families gather, when grandchildren dream, and when mothers give birth to babies.

In addition to observing rituals based on ancestral commitments, parents also observe other kinds of religious rituals, which are often, though not always, intertwined with ethnic and ancestral practices. These include Islamic birth rituals like *aqiqas*, whispering the call to prayer in newborn babies' ears, and Christian baptisms and dedications. Due to relationships established between the Merina monarchy and British missionaries during the early nineteenth century and the French colonization of the island from the late nineteenth to mid-twentieth century, the majority of twenty-first-century Malagasy are Christian and attend religious services at one of the many Catholic, Protestant, Pentecostal, or independent Christian churches that exist throughout the island today. This is especially true among Merina and other ethnic groups in the central highland regions. In northern Madagascar, however, due in part to that region's historical participation in Swahili trading routes, fewer Malagasy claim a Christian identity. Most Sakalava peoples, for example, who inhabit western and northwestern Madagascar, are non-Christian.[25] And among Antankarana groups, who inhabit the northern region of the island, the majority are Muslims. There are also sizable Muslim communities among Antemoro, Antanosy, Antalaotra, and Anjoaty ethnic groups.[26] Additionally, there are a very small number of Hindus and Buddhists, most of whom are more recent immigrants from China and South Asia.

Despite the prevalence of Christianity and Islam in the central highlands and northern regions, respectively, the Indigenous spiritual traditions of Madagascar, including all of the ancestor-focused practices described in the previous paragraphs, abound and are observed by Muslims, Christians, and the nonaffiliated alike. Of course, it is also true that there are a growing number of Christians, mainly of the charismatic and Pentecostal variety, who want nothing to do with Indigenous religious practices on the island in part because they view such practices as idolatrous and in part because they fear becoming possessed by a demonic spirit perhaps posing as an ancestor.[27] Nevertheless, for the vast majority of Malagasy, Indigenous religions centered on the remembrance of one's ancestors, often called *fombandrazana*, or "the customs of the ancestors," figure prominently in most people's lives.[28] They borrow from African, Asian, and Arab traditions and form the foundation for the acceptance of, conversion to, or rejection of all other relatively newer religious beliefs on the island (e.g., Christian and Muslim traditions) and thus have a pervading influence across religious boundaries.

Tangible evidence of all of these various religious traditions was evident throughout my time in Diégo Suarez. I heard the sounds of people of faith everywhere I went. The calls to prayer were amplified five times daily from the city's mosques. Religious messages on radio stations broadcasted the prophetic words of Christian evangelist Pastor André Mailhol, a Pentecostal pastor who was predicting the end of the world and the demise of the West during my time in Madagascar from 2011 to 2012.[29] I read about religious events in newspapers, in the tracts that missionaries distributed, and on the billboards and flyers that organizers posted around the walls of football stadiums announcing upcoming revivals. I saw evidence of people's varying beliefs on the decals and icons that decorate the taxis and *taxis-brousses* (bush taxis) that bus people to and from work and school and in the framed pictures storekeepers posted on their shop walls—images of various Muslim clerics or Christian iconography.

I experienced the religious fervor of Malagasy in the sanctuaries of Lutheran churches where shepherd-healers (*mpiandry*) offered services of healing and renewal. I experienced similar religious fervor in the lively Christmas Eve pageant performed by children at an Anglican church and in that same church's exuberant installation of a new bishop, greeted ceremoniously by congregants, who paraded up the church aisles dressed in regional clothing performing the customary songs and dances from their respective districts. I rose early in the morning to discover the Indigenous religious commitments of those making vows to their ancestors by bringing offerings of honey and rice and bathing in the waters of the ocean near the sacred site of Nosy Lonjo. I more than once confronted religion in the streets—witnessing funeral processions and wedding parades.

Last, I was invited to share in numerous funerary and birthing ceremonies performed by Muslims and Christians alike—occasions where friends and relatives gathered to feast and remember, to mourn the loss of lives gone and celebrate the lives of the newly born, and, sometimes, to remember the connection between the two. Madagascar is renowned for its practices around caring for ancestral legacies, for swaddling and cradling exhumed ancestors like infants, and for dancing with corpses. What this book also makes clear is that both death *and* birth require ritualized forms of care—rituals informed by the diverse ancestral and religious customs of Malagasy families—and that these rituals are one of the ways that families, and mothers in particular, ensure that the newly born make their transition from zaza rano to bone-filled members of their communities.

Why Diégo Suarez?

The northwestern coast of Madagascar, once part of Swahili trading networks, a place where the country's first mosque was erected and home to several important port cities, is an especially diverse and historically rich region of the island. Archaeologists estimate that from the eleventh until about the middle of the fourteenth century, the northwestern part of the island was a highly urbanized and religiously diverse place, with both a high participation in Indian Ocean trade, especially the slave trade by peoples living along the west coast, and significant numbers of Muslims, who built mosques and were very much a part of the Islamicized Swahili culture that existed at the time.[30] Madagascar is renowned by nearly everyone for its rich biodiversity, but alongside its biodiversity is likewise an impressive story of cultural and religious diversity, which is especially showcased in the northern city of Diégo Suarez. There are two main compelling reasons to situate this study in the city of Diégo Suarez. First, it's an especially diverse place—religiously, culturally, and socioeconomically—and second, which is related to the first, it is a place where marriage has historically been very fragile and thus offers a particularly good place to explore how it is that women, who themselves have diverse ties, build up the social ties of their babies through religious and ancestral practices.

Diégo Suarez is the capital city of the northernmost province of Madagascar, named after two Portuguese explorers said to have "discovered" the island of Madagascar in 1506. As provincial capital, it is a heterogeneous city with many regional lures, including a large university, a teaching hospital, an operative port, an enormous naval shipyard, a fish processing plant, and several administrative centers. Archaeological evidence reveals that Diégo Suarez has a long history of enticing people to its shores—certainly longer than is implied by the so-called Portuguese discovery of Madagascar in the sixteenth century.[31] What most attracted me to the northwestern shores of Madagascar nearly two decades ago was the religious and cultural diversity of the region. I was drawn by the sounds of the calls to prayer wafting from the mosques that lined the streets of Diégo Suarez, struck by the aesthetics of the colorful Asian-imported sarongs that women wore, and intrigued by the sound of the language, full of Swahili borrowings.

The diversity and at times hybrid identities of Diégo's residents—which I describe more fully later in the book—come together to create a vibrant city full of all the tensions and harmonies one might imagine. In 2011, when I arrived for the third time since my initial visit to the city in 2004, its streets were busy, full of pedestrians, cyclists, motorists, yellow Renault taxis, children in uniforms on their way to and from school, chickens, stray dogs, and street vendors selling fresh mangoes, oranges, pickled mango chutneys, *sambos*, and other fried treats.[32] Diégo Suarez was a place full of life inhabited by Malagasy and foreigners alike—the permanent home of many northern Malagasy and the temporary home of many southern Malagasy migrants, from as far as Toliar, who come for months at a time to make money as rickshaw drivers or as able bodies willing to break up bits of concrete on the side of the roads.

Diégo Suarez's history as an urban economic and religious center—first for Muslim merchants and later for Indo-Pakistani immigrants and Yemeni Arabs, who were brought to Diégo Suarez by shipping companies to labor as dockworkers during the first half of the twentieth century—is well established. Some residents discuss this history openly. For others, these histories of the peoples, animals, and goods that were brought to, and also displaced from, the northwestern coast linger on in the myths inhabitants tell about the cows (*aomby*), pirates, and "mermaids" that emerged from the ocean waters and about the "ancestors' spirits" who reside in the bodies of the "jewelry-wearing crocodiles" that reside in nearby sacred lakes.

The unbelievably beautiful turquoise waters that surround the port city of Diégo Suarez have made it possible for the arrival of vast arrays of foreign peoples, animals, foodstuffs, and ideas. Residents continue to relish these waterways as sources for the arrival of new things. Families of all income levels and backgrounds enjoy a walk to the port to see the large vessels that dock in Diégo Suarez. More recently, people enjoy greeting the enormous cruise ships that arrive during tourist season. Diégo Suarez's residents draw deeply from the waters that surround their city, both literally and metaphorically, as the bay serves not only to bring foreign peoples and goods to the area but also as a wellspring for the emergence of new myths, religious customs, and cultural traditions that form the rich fabric of Diégo Suarez residents' way of living.

In addition to its highly developed religious and cultural diversity, Diégo is inhabited by people from a range of social and economic circumstances. It is a city that has attracted migrant workers and settlers from all over the island and from around the world, some of whom have managed to create sustainable livelihoods, but many others of whom, for all sorts of systemic and personal reasons, have not. To put it bluntly, Diégo is poor, like many cities in Madagascar, but more typically so than the capital, for example, and therefore more indicative of the kinds of material states many urban Africans find themselves in with respect to access to resources for giving birth.[33] As an American researcher, living there for almost a year, I was very aware of my own relative wealth compared to local friends and acquaintances, but I nevertheless felt at home and welcomed into people's lives.[34] Diégo is beautiful and vibrant and rich with tradition, but it is also hot, depressed, and sometimes dangerous. Despite the fact that temperatures do not cool down very much at night, almost no one I knew slept with the windows open unless their windows were fitted with security bars, which was true for a very limited number of people.

Residents blamed crime on multiple factors, citing political instability, gangs, and economic depression. Whatever the reasons, residents of Diégo did not always have access to the kinds of resources that kept people safe and well, socially and physiologically. As will become clear in the body chapters of this book, the relative poverty of some of Diégo's residents meant that people sometimes did not always have enough food to celebrate holidays properly, and more gravely, it also meant that mothers were not always able to secure the medicines they needed in time to prevent or manage severe illness in their children. Parasites that cause diseases like malaria and diarrhea and respiratory viruses are dangerous to babies everywhere, but in places where people sometimes have to make decisions between buying food or medicine and where clinics and hospitals are not themselves well resourced, these kinds of illnesses are even more dangerous. In Madagascar at large, the under-five infant mortality rate is around 50.2 per 1,000 live births, which is nearly ten times higher than the under-five infant mortality rate of the United States.[35] Moreover, according to data from UNICEF, "more than two in three children (67.6%) are multidimensionally poor in Madagascar, meaning they suffer material deprivation in at least two different dimensions of well-being."[36] The stakes for integrating children into social and religious communities that connect people to vital resources are higher in a place where nearly five out of every hundred children will not make it to their fifth birthday. For all of these reasons, Diégo felt like an important place to study birth and its associated rituals.

For reasons related to the religious, cultural, and socioeconomic diversity described previously, marriage is fragile in Diégo. It is a place where social norms are less fixed, probably attributable to the fact that in Diégo, encountering difference is a centuries-old practice, due to the region's historic participation in Swahili trading networks and more recent reputation as a kind of industrial and educational hub. In regions such as this, there are fewer single narratives about the "right" way to worship God, engage with one's ancestors, or incorporate children into religious and kin-based communities. There are of course common practices and common traditions around which people orient, but the decisions of mothers are less prescribed than they might be on other parts of the island, especially as compared with the cities of the central highlands, whose populations are more predominantly Christian and thus more religiously homogenous.

For example, in Diégo, interfaith relationships and marriages across various ethnic groupings are more common than in other regions of the country. It is also more common for women to marry late and sometimes after they have had children with other partners. In northern Madagascar, marriage is often reserved for couples who have settled into their lives and careers, not just for the young and in love. Thus, blessing and incorporating children into social and religious communities looks different in Diégo than it does elsewhere. It's a more creative process, and when parents do *not* remain a couple, belonging is not always guaranteed or fostered in the same way. As Gillian Feeley-Harnik documents, sometimes rites of incorporation for babies, like haircutting, are as much about trying to get the father's family involved as they are about contests over childhood affiliation, a point I discuss again in chapter 3 of this book.[37]

Given the city's history in attracting migrants, though I conducted the majority of my interviews in and around the city of Diégo Suarez, the vast majority of my informants did not consider themselves to be from Diégo. As is true of many Indian Ocean port cities, Diégo is sometimes composed of more newer migrants than long-term Indigenous residents (*tompon-tany*). Moreover, in Madagascar, being born in a city does not make one "from" that place. Instead, many of my interviewees, some of whom were born in Diégo Suarez, named other towns and villages throughout the northern province of the island as the places they were from. My dear friend and research assistant, Zafisoa, lived in Diégo Suarez all her life but did not consider it to be the place where she was from. Her mother, Madame Serafina, who had been living in Diégo Suarez when she conceived Zafisoa, observed the common custom of returning to her natal village to give birth. And Zafisoa did the same when her own daughter, Sera, was born because where one is from has less to do with where a person lives and more to do with where one's ancestors are from, the place where one is rooted and tied.[38] Thus, families can reside in Diégo Suarez for multiple generations without considering themselves autochthonous to the area, which is not to say that migrants never become ancestrally rooted in new places but rather that such anchoring takes a long time.[39]

Those who did not grow up in Diégo Suarez migrated to the city for numerous reasons, primarily educational and financial. Some young women came to work as maids in wealthier families' homes; others to attend school at the University of Antsiranana, the largest and most reputable university in the northern province of Madagascar; and still others to live with relatives while attending secondary school. Last, some came to find work in the naval shipyard or the fish processing plant or to work in the informal sector of the economy. Viviane, a neighbor of mine, came to Diégo Suarez for this final reason. A single mother, she arrived with the youngest of her five children several years prior to my meeting her in 2011. She came with nearly nothing in the way of savings but quickly found work as a maid. She cleaned a woman's house in the mornings and sold popsicles for another woman outside a secondary school in the afternoons.

Viviane explained that in the beginning she earned only enough money to pay for a place to sleep and to buy two cups of dry rice per day, which she and her daughter shared. When Viviane first arrived in Diégo Suarez, she worried she would find no means by which to take care of herself and her children. However, she soon discovered that she could make money very quickly in the city. When I interviewed her in 2012, she was living in a small makeshift house near the university where she sold raw vegetables in front of her house. Migrant or otherwise, the women I interviewed for this project both helped create and are created by the religious, cultural, and socioeconomic diversity of their city. Navigating this diversity upon the birth of a child provides valuable insight into the ways in which families, and mothers in particular, access the spiritual, cultural, and medical resources they need to raise their children well in these contexts of religious and cultural pluralism and material poverty.

Concepts and Themes

The concepts I use to frame this book can be broadly grouped into three categories: (1) pluralism and hybridity, both as concept and as practice; (2) ritual and the relationships of reciprocity that ritual often engenders; and (3) identity and belonging. In many ways, pluralism is the water in which northern Malagasy swim. That said, following Diana Eck's lead, I make a distinction between "pluralistic environments" and "pluralism," where the former is the atmosphere in which most of us find ourselves and the latter is the practice of making sense of, and engaging with, that multiplicity.[40] Hybridity is then what results from pluralism. It is the outcome of our intentional efforts to engage meaningfully with the diversity that surrounds us or the means by which we construct ourselves as coherent amid and in relationship with the tangle of connections and experiences that shape us.[41] Hybridity is also a means by which we understand ourselves given our ongoing and multiple relational encounters. That said, hybridity is not always intentional work; sometimes, it is a process that simply happens to us by virtue of our being shaped by diverse encounters.[42] Whether intentional, inadvertent, or both, I find Eva Spies's framing of hybridity most useful—"the temporary result of multiple relational processes," a momentary snapshot of who we are, and how we understand ourselves, given our varied and evolving experiences with people, things, beings, and memories.[43]

In the context of the stories presented in this book, hybridity is a useful concept as it highlights that what it means to be Malagasy is always changing. The same applies to some of the more distinct and particular labels Malagasy use to describe themselves with regard to ethnicity, ancestral lineage, or religious orientation—all of these categories are also always in flux. This can of course be said about most identity categories, though it might be truer for some than others, perhaps especially true of cultural groups within Indian Ocean port cities like Diégo where identities are born out of centuries of cross-fertilization. This history of diversity and cross-fertilization is the backdrop for the stories that women shared with me on the northern coast of Madagascar in the early 2000s, and it highlights that their efforts to make bones (something enduring) from water (something ambiguous and hybrid), in a part of the world more historically complex than is often recognized, is a relational and ever-evolving project.

The social and cultural worlds that Malagasy babies enter are diverse and evolving and further hybridized by the coming together, and persistent reconfiguration, of the families who produced them and remain charged with their care. As I have already insinuated, mothers in particular are charged with the task of drawing together, or sometimes redirecting, the rich tributaries of influence in the lives of their children that they might grow up with a strong sense of self as well as a strong connection to those sources of influence. In this way, mothering decisions in Madagascar have the potential to help further elucidate hybridity as both an intentional process and a phenomenon that simply "happens" to us by virtue of our living in a world where we are connected to, and influenced by, people with a wide range of cultural and religious inheritances.

So much of what we inherit, and of what we learn, in terms of habits, beliefs, and cultural and religious customs come to us by chance or as experiential knowledge that we do not always even recognize as something we have received. This is certainly true for Malagasy mothers, whose passage into motherhood begins long before parenthood is even on the horizon. It begins when young children are themselves mothered and thus learn to receive and later embody the behaviors associated with being mothers in their communities. And this cycle continues for the babies who are raised in these communities who, when held, carried, fed, comforted, and sometimes ignored, are taught something of who they are, if and why they matter, and of the kinds of cultural and spiritual things of value within their society. This book investigates the processes by which these messages are inscribed on Malagasy women's and babies' bodies as well as the agency that women and babies have to participate in, and cocreate, these ritualized worlds, which brings me to another important concept in this book: ritual.

I use the word *ritual* to refer not only to rites of passage that take place within formalized religious communities but also to the kinds of meaning-laden ritualized activities that Malagasy orchestrate, and sometimes unconsciously participate in, as part of the perpetuation of certain religious/familial/cultural values that when enacted have the capacity to transform participants. My definition borrows heavily from Robbie Davis-Floyd's definition of ritual as something that is repetitive, patterned, symbolic, and transformative.[44] Though this definition could be critiqued as excessively broad, my intention is not to apply it to virtually any human activity but rather to see certain taken-for-granted human activities, like birth, as activities that are not just physiological but also culturally constructed in ways that matter for mothers and children. As Pamela Klassen notes, "Ironically, given the fruitfulness of the idea of birth to many religious systems in terms of divinely wrought immaculate conceptions, being born again, and enduring cycles of death and rebirth, in Western religions, women's actual experiences have been sorely ignored and underritualized."[45] Given the dearth of research on the topic, in this book, I privilege Malagasy women's stories of actual physiological birthing, and their activities as ritual orchestrators, as those who procreate meaning from the act of giving birth and raising children, as opposed to writing about women as mere symbols of birth and procreation.

I use the phrase *birth rituals*, in particular, to refer to the range of activities that precede and follow the physiological event of birth: blessings, naming ceremonies, haircuttings, baby showers, and so on. In the early stages of this project, I saw childbirth, postpartum rituals, and initiation ceremonies in largely separate spheres. However, Malagasy women quickly led me beyond my compartmentalized focus. Their stories of childbirth, following or disregarding pregnancy taboos, cold-water postpartum bathing, ritual "medicines" they placed on their children, their consultations with doctors alongside massage healers, taking their babies to church services where Jesus could "chase away the demons," and elaborate haircutting ceremonies where ancestor spirits were invoked to bless water babies that they might be transformed into "real human beings" led me to the conclusion that everything that happens before, during, and after the event of birth is interconnected. As Catherine Bell writes, "Birth rites are not necessarily celebrated when a child emerges from the mother's body" but rather "are an extended set of activities invoking fertility, the purification of birth pollution, the sexual identity of the fetus, the safety of mother and child, and the conferral of social status when the baby is named and introduced to the larger community."[46]

Alma Gottlieb was among the first to study the religious and cultural worlds of infants and to recognize that infants have culture. She argued that babies act as agents, that they make demands, and that they develop and behave largely according to cultural rather than biologically determined expectations.[47] According to Gottlieb, infants—no less than other beings—are shaped by those around them, cued into local systems of meaning, by way of rituals and other socializing actions, and physically trained to tune their

bodies toward certain kinds of social and spiritual awareness. In her pioneer-
ing ethnography, Gottlieb asked her readers to explore the question of where
babies come from. Are they newborn souls, or are they old souls? Do they
know something when they're born, or are they blank slates? Among Beng of
Côte d'Ivoire, where Gottlieb conducted her research, babies are understood
to be reincarnated ancestors. They come from the ancestral realm and must
be coaxed to stay in the world of the living. Thus, they are protected with
religious charms, given daily baths, and their desires for food and comfort ap-
peased. In Madagascar, the connection between babies and ancestors is a bit
different. Babies are not so much reincarnated ancestors as they are blessings
from the ancestors, who carry within themselves remnants of those who lived
before. But like Beng, Malagasy also create rituals of care around the newly
born that are as much cultural as biological—rituals that encourage babies
to remain among the living and these rituals give us insight into the creative
ways in which mothers are continuing the legacies of their ancestors in the
lives of their children.

The third concept I use in this book is belonging, or the process by which we
establish close relations and affinities with people in order that we might feel
included and grounded in larger social and/or religious collectives. Closely
linked with belonging is identity. In this regard, I take seriously Kwame Appiah's assertion that identities, while flexible and fabricated, matter to people
and make it possible for people to belong.[48] According to Appiah, taboos are
central to the process of identity making, as they help forge bonds between
people who observe them, but of course other kinds of ritual and communal
practices, including many customs and rituals surrounding the birth process,
do this too.[49]

In Indian Ocean port cities like Diégo Suarez, the processes by which people establish identity along racial lines and across other social and religious
categories are constantly in flux as a result of the continuous migration of
peoples and goods in and out of these cities. This ever-in-flux kind of cosmopolitanism engenders processes of identity making that are always shifting
and emerging in relation to the flow of peoples, spirits, and things in and out
of the area. Moreover, urbanization compounds this movement and flow of
people in and out of cities within the Indian Ocean, thus increasing possibilities and potentialities with regard to identity and belonging. M. G. Vassanji
describes identity in another such Indian Ocean port city, in Dar es Salam,
Tanzania, as "a confluence of many streams, a multiplicity of identities; a

palimpsest."[50] Or as Mauritian writer Ananda Devi describes of the Indian Ocean island of Mauritius, "being Mauritian is exactly that: belonging to all these worlds, and through a process of synthesis and syncretism being able to extract something new and authentic."[51]

On Indian Ocean islands, like Mauritius and Madagascar, and within port cities like Dar es Salam and Diégo Suarez, there are many confluences that flow into people's understanding of both their particular and overarching identities. Moreover, islands are both insulating, a point made by Ritu Tyagi, and expansively interconnected, which means that people sometimes feel "islanded"—straddled or stuck between various worlds—but also open to many different possibilities.[52] As a result of the migration of people from Africa, Asia, and the Middle East into northern Madagascar, through different waves over time, the region enjoys a reputation as a very nonessentializing kind of place where identities are constantly being constructed through various processes that enable people to find a sense of identity and belonging. In this book, I argue that women play a central, perhaps foundational role in these processes by organizing and participating in birth rituals that mark themselves, and their babies, with particular kinds of religious and ancestral identities that grant belonging. As Pamela Feldman-Savelsberg has argued, "The process of creating and maintaining group membership—belonging—for oneself and for one's dependents is an important part of reproductive labor."[53]

Belonging is forged through many means, including by ritually acknowledging the "natural" affinities that grant children and others membership within a kin-based community. Belonging can also be achieved when people elect to participate and/or be initiated into certain types of religious and/or kin-based communities. Rituals are important in each case by marking people with particular identities and by ritualizing the processes by which people come to belong, but another way that rituals help establish belonging is by fostering relationships of indebtedness or reciprocity.

In Madagascar reciprocity is extremely important. It is the process by which Malagasy build social networks by creating indebtedness between themselves and other relatives, spirits, and religious specialists important to theirs and their children's care. In this book, I especially highlight the relationships of reciprocity established between mothers and caregivers or between mothers and the family members and specialists who help them navigate pregnancy, birth, and motherhood. One example of this is the practice of giving midwives, and other kinds of specialists, material gifts, instead of set payments for their services. In Madagascar, these gifts to religious specialists, are called *hasin-tanana*, which Andriamatao Rakotosaona has translated as "the customary money given to a massage-healer."[54] They can come in the form of money (an unspecified amount) or other material goods like chickens, rice, food, or soap. Gift giving, as opposed to transactional kinds of payments that often close out debts or terminate relationships, ensures that mothers have the kind of ongoing support and social capital needed to address all of their children's spiritual and social needs. Since midwives, for their part, often understand their work to be "a gift" bestowed on them by their ancestors, many do not charge for their services but rather offer their services voluntarily, or as a gift in the Maussian sense, where a gift is never freely given but instead embedded with the expectation of reciprocity.[55]

This kind of gift giving between mothers and the specialists charged with their care can be understood within the broader context of Malagasy relationships of reciprocity, which occur on the human-divine level, between royalty and their subjects, and, in a less hierarchical manner, between family members and friends. The Malagasy concept of *fihavanana*, which refers to many things, including friendship, a readiness to help, and what Marie Rakotondarmiadanirina refers to as "right relationships in consanguinity," applies here.[56] Though there is no perfect translation in the English language, fihavanana is an ethic of mutuality that undergirds many Malagasy relationships and ensures concern for the common good.[57] In this book, I argue that embedding children in relationships of reciprocity is crucial to babies receiving the spiritual, material, and medical support they need both to survive and to become firmly rooted in their communities.

Despite Malagasy efforts to bless, protect, and mark children with certain identities that foster belonging, Malagasy parents know all too well that not all children will survive the vulnerability of their infancy. Early in the course of my field research, informants led me to a hill where babies' remains were placed when they die at a very early age—that is, before they had reached the status of full-fledged human beings. Malagasy in the area reportedly explained that zana rano could not be buried in the same way as older individuals who die because they "don't have bones," a story I unpack in greater detail in chapter 4.[58]

In a country plagued by poverty whose social structures have been disrupted by colonial and neocolonial interventions, parents are struggling, perhaps more than ever before, to provide children with the kind of social support systems and spiritual stability they deem critical to their survival. As a result of punishing labor and tax laws imposed by an external colonial government in the early decades of the twentieth century, as well as more recent changes caused by structural adjustments programs and a move on the part of the Malagasy government to a neoliberal economy, many Malagasy families have been displaced from their ancestral lands or have chosen to migrate from rural settings to urban environs for monetary reasons, leaving behind the supportive social structures they may have enjoyed in the countryside.[59] Within these new urban contexts, parents were struggling to determine which religious communities and ritual practices best provided their children with "bones"—the sense of belonging and social worth that would ensure their thriving.

According to Feldman-Savelsberg, whose research focuses on Cameroonian migrants, reproduction and belonging are closely linked, such that when women's productivity goes awry as a result of infertility, miscarriage, or an unintended pregnancy, it sometimes constrains women's ability to integrate themselves into the kinds of kinship networks and sociocultural communities critical to their well-being.[60] If and when children do emerge, and this is especially true for migrant mothers, "the circumstances of birth create multiple layers of social relationships as a child is born into a lineage, strengthens its parents' conjugal and affinal ties, and gains citizenship either on the basis of genealogy or place of birth."[61] Gaining citizenship through birth is especially important to Cameroonian women migrants to Germany, the subject of Feldman-Savelsberg's research. In the context of my own research, I am interested in the ways in which children help mothers in Diégo Suarez, many of whom are migrants to the city, create multiple layers of social relationships across lineages and religious and cultural communities in order to navigate their contexts of reproductive insecurity and forge belonging.

Studying Birth Rituals and Ancestors as an Outsider

Research for this book comes from open-ended interviews conducted over a nine-month period (September 2011–June 2012), mostly in Malagasy with the help of research assistants, occasionally in French or in a combination of French and Malagasy, and rarely in English, from a sample of approximately fifty informants ranging in age from seventeen to seventy-nine.[62] My interviewees, nearly all of whom are given pseudonyms in this book, included primarily mothers, but also some fathers, elders within the community, religious

leaders, and medical professionals in the city of Diégo Suarez. The majority
were Christian, including Catholics, Protestants, and Pentecostals; a minority were Muslim; and an even smaller minority maintained that they "did not
pray" (*tsy mivavaka*), which in the context of northern Madagascar typically
means they did not participate in institutionalized religion. Of the people
who claimed no institutional religious affiliation, many still spoke of God,
or Zanahary, the now Christianized but originally Indigenous word for the
creator God in the Malagasy pantheon; the religious customs and taboos
(fomba and fady) of their families; and sometimes of their families' divination
practices. The women and men I interviewed do not comprise a representative sample of the people of Madagascar, nor do my interviewees' varying
individual perspectives speak comprehensively to the issues presented in this
book. Rather their personal stories give voice to the diversity of opinions on
issues of childbearing, mothering, and religion in Madagascar.

This project is an ethnography defined in the broadest sense of the word—
that is, I employed "a research process based on fieldwork using a variety of
mainly (but not exclusively) qualitative research techniques but including
engagement in the lives of those being studied over an extended period of
time."[63] Within this broad methodological category, my approach is historical, anthropological, and reflexive.[64] By reflexive, I am both aware of and
critical of my own presence in the field, and the knowledge presented on these
pages is tentative and relative rather than conclusive and universal.[65]

As an outsider, I had limited, and mostly observational, access to the religious and medical facilities Malagasy rely on in the birthing and parenting of
their children. I also had limited access to women's stories. As a foreigner, my
presence was like a filter that inspired my interlocutors to share some aspects
of their lives with me while hiding others. At the very least, the stories that my
informants shared with me were presented differently than they would be to
longtime family members or friends. But being a foreign researcher has both
advantages and disadvantages.

Foreigners in Madagascar, especially white foreigners, called *vazaha*, are
greeted by local people with a variety of emotions ranging from curiosity,
respect, and admiration to envy, hostility, and suspicion. In smaller towns,
Malagasy children welcome foreigners with friendly shouts of "bonjour
vazaha!" accompanied by exuberant jumping, waving, and giggling. In larger
cities, where income discrepancies are high and the presence of foreigners less
novel, vazaha are sometimes heckled by beggars, street children, and roadside

vendors. Moreover, even though I came from the United States, a place from which very few people visit Madagascar, my home country was often conflated with France and other European countries, as the place from which white foreigners come, especially vazaha men, some of whom might be looking for Malagasy girlfriends and wives.

This is not to say that Malagasy are unfamiliar with geography or are unable to have nuanced understandings of foreigners and the places from which they come. It simply shows that the global circulation of knowledge about other peoples goes both ways and profoundly influenced how Malagasy thought of me and I of them. Just as I have heard North Americans say on countless occasions, "I know someone who went to Africa, but I can't remember which country," Malagasy also sometimes saw me as coming from a rather vaguely conceived notion of the West. Despite the frequent conflations, it is also true that generally speaking Americans enjoy a more favorable reception in Madagascar as compared with, for example, French, which has to do with the fact that many Malagasy-American encounters occur primarily between Malagasy and Peace Corps workers, researchers, or missionaries, who are generally more interested in Malagasy language and culture than French tourists.

Given all of these circumstances, I tried to be extra aware of, and also sensitive to, the perceptions Malagasy had of me and me of them. This meant examining assumptions I had with regard to motherhood in Madagascar. It also meant that instead of automatically assuming that my American ways of behaving were appropriate, I asked my Malagasy friends for advice in certain social situations. I also tried not to flaunt my relative wealth, and given that my husband and I were at the time living on my graduate student stipend, this was not terribly difficult. We cooked at home with foods we bought from our neighbors' food stands and Diégo Suarez's outdoor markets and tried to limit our consumption of things like beer and pizza and supermarket foods, which are enjoyed by only a small percentage of Malagasy. We invited people over for dinner. I introduced myself to my neighbors, learned their names, had daily conversations with them, and attempted to reciprocate when Malagasy shared stories and meals with me.

Over time, these social investments bore fruit. As I was then a young woman of childbearing age, discussions of childbirth with Malagasy of childbearing age quickly became a topic of mutual interest and concern. Thus, despite all of the ways in which Malagasy viewed me as an outsider, there is no denying that my age and gender also afforded me a kind of insider status. Interviews among my peers rapidly took on the shape of conversational exchanges where fears and concerns were addressed, and issues of balancing motherhood with work and school came up frequently as several of the young mothers I interviewed were pursuing higher-education degrees. And the older women I came to know gladly took me under their wings and saw their relationship with me as a mentoring one. They understood my interest in childbirth as "natural" given that I was young and did not yet have children of my own. They pressed me to have a child as soon as possible and were quite elated when I shared with them news of my first pregnancy, which occurred during the latter part of my research period, just before I left Madagascar to return to the United States.

In the course of my fieldwork, formal interviews often gave way to more casual conversations on Diégo Suarez's busy streets, in the backs of taxicabs, at neighborhood vegetable stands, and at the crowded outdoor market where my husband and I shopped and became known by our neighbors. At its best, ethnographic research can draw attention to the often untold yet highly provocative life stories of ordinary people going about their lives, drawing us into people's personal narratives in ways that shatter and complicate the prejudices we previously had about them. Ethnography can change how humans see other humans and for the better. At the same time, ethnographic research can also be exploitative and collaborative with imperialist agendas.[66]

Collecting intimate stories from people of color in Madagascar in order to satisfy my white Western-inspired intellectual curiosities can certainly be understood as exploitative. Moreover, making sense of the stories women shared with me using theoretical lenses produced in the Western-dominant academy can lead to generalizations and misrepresentations. I have always felt both drawn to and wary of ethnographic approaches for the aforementioned reasons. Given these ethical considerations, I have tried to understand the Malagasy women I interviewed as humans and friends first rather than exclusively as spokespeople for certain traditions. I have also strived to understand them as co-interpreters rather than simply as informants with the hope that this style of fieldwork might lead to truer representations of their lives.

I had many successes during my research, but I also made some mistakes. One oversight was in the way I looked beyond my initial contacts for more and more people to interview. Often, I was looking for yet another story, consulting friends who would lead me to their friends, neighbors, and acquaintances. On the one hand, this method enabled me to reach a wide range of individuals and enabled me to compare and generalize in a way that a small informant pool would not have; on the other hand, after I began writing, I discovered that my interviews with the women I had known the longest offered me the best insights for my research.

A second mistake I made in the field was that I occasionally withheld my personal opinions more than I perhaps should have. In an attempt to offer a neutral listening ear, I sometimes found myself sharing less. When a friend of mine, Amélie, expressed disappointment that her doctor had written her baby a prescription for soda as a rehydration drink, I wish I had stood in solidarity with her and agreed with her wisdom as a mother that soda was not the best drink for her toddler. At the time, I did not want to be critical of what she was doing or of what her doctor had advised. I thought her doctor probably recommended bottled sugary drinks because these drinks were less likely to contain contaminated water as compared with homemade rehydration drinks, but I also knew that Amélie was careful about boiling the water her son drank and was right to be concerned about offering him soda. I wish I had simply said that. And when my friend of nearly ten years Fitahiana asked me if I planned to breastfeed my baby, I was surprised to realize that I had not shared more of my parenting plans with her.

The decisions I made in the field regarding who I interviewed and how much I shared were difficult decisions. I wore many hats. I was simultaneously a researcher, a white foreigner, an English teacher, a neighbor, a friend, an acquaintance, and a young married woman with no children. But I was also first and foremost a human being with questions, curiosities, and flaws. As such, I endeavored to share as much as I inquired (when appropriate), knowing full well that doing so would mean that interviews might lead in some cases to longer friendships, friendships that I trusted would enrich my research.

I experienced two major life events during my nine months of research for this book. I lost my grandfather, who was at the time my only remaining biological grandparent. I grieved that I was not able to fly home for the funeral. Greater still was the pain of not getting to introduce him to his great-granddaughter, with whom I became pregnant weeks after his passing. I still remember the visit from my research assistant, Édith, who brought fruit to my bedside when she learned of my grandfather's death, a token of consolation that meant more to me than she knew. Suddenly, both pregnant and grieving, all the efforts I had been hearing about to both remember and re-member the dead in the lives of the newly born, or some cases, the not yet born, began to make sense to me in a different, deeper way.

I began this project when the prospect of motherhood was barely on the horizon. I complete it having birthed three beautiful children and miscarried two. As a white American academic, raised in the Protestant Christian tradition, by a single mother, in the South Texas coastal city of Corpus Christi, I am in many ways a stranger to the religious and cultural worlds of the women of Diégo Suarez, Madagascar. As a woman who would one day bear children, and who like many of my informants, cares deeply about the social, cultural, and religious dimensions of what birth and motherhood can and should look like, I am also deeply and personally invested in the topic.

My investigation of pregnancy, childbirth, and its associated rituals in Madagascar began informally in 2008. I had traveled to Madagascar for a third time, this time for an intensive language study, in preparation for doing dissertation research. I lived in Diégo Suarez and studied Malagasy with a student from the University of Antsiranana. During that eight-week trip, I traveled one week to Antsiravibe, a rural community just south of the Ankarana National Park, because I wanted to both get out of the city for a while and learn more about a community-initiated ecotourism site. Tent camping at the foot of one of Madagascar's famous red tsingy mountain ridges, Tsingy Mahaloka, and incidentally reading Anita Diamant's *Red Tent*, a fictional life story of the biblical character and midwife Dinah, I spent most of the week sitting on *lamaka* (woven reed mats), peeling potatoes and carrots with women from the community. I listened to their conversations about the right way to water their vegetable and flower plants during the dry season so as not to splash up dust on the leaves of plants, heeded their advice about rubbing coconut oil on my body to prevent certain insects from burrowing into my skin during forest walks, and held their babies while they prepared food for me and another camper.

That same week, I was invited to attend a haircutting ceremony for a baby of royal Antankarana lineage, whose rite of blessing, as mentioned earlier in this introduction, included reciting the names of her ancestors while partaking in a common meal. This experience, together with the many conversations I had while peeling vegetables with women that week, made me realize that the very topic I found myself thinking about for pleasure (childbirth, midwives, and the story of Dinah) was pleading to be uncovered in a different context. That week I discovered that women were not merely willing to share their stories of birth and child-rearing; they were actually begging to be asked. This book is my attempt, through research conducted years later, to hear and share their stories.

Before conducting this research, my knowledge of birth was intellectual rather than experiential. I was nonetheless drawn to women's stories and women's wisdom, particularly the kinds of embodied wisdoms that mothers pass on to children—wisdom about plants, medicinal and otherwise, about gardening and mothering, and about family histories and certain kinds of spiritual awareness. This book is a testament to this kind of knowledge, the kind the body learns through experience and the kind that gets modeled for us and then sewn into our bodies such that we can perform certain tasks without even thinking about them, the wisdom our ancestors passed down to us through our grandparents, aunts and uncles, and our fathers and mothers. This book is about birth, the wisdom we acquire from it, and ritual—the experiences, and stories from our past that form us and get etched into our bones. Like most humans on the planet today, I live in a world that is urban, religiously diverse and hybrid in every sense of the word. In these kinds of contexts, our sense of place and identity is never guaranteed, but through the naming and blessing of our children, through rituals of blessing and incorporation, we work to make it as guaranteed as possible.

After the birth of each of my three children, I still remember how gently my sister pulled her stole around her neck and how gracefully she read the words she so carefully prepared, words that gave breath to the sacredness of the moment and expressed the theology of the task before me—that of raising a child. I remember the soft newborn sounds in the background and how at each blessing, my babies, who were only hours old at the time, were passed around, adored, and told that they were worthy, that they belonged, and that they were loved. I also remember how at my daughter's baptism, at our church in Charlottesville, the minister said it did not matter that she slept through the ceremony; she did not need to be conscious to receive the grace of God. I will also forever recall the first time my daughter received communion at a gathering of people around food at a farm in Charlottesville. What a perfect moment for a first breaking of the bread, made sacred by the story we told about it, of an earlier communion of people trying to love and heal the world.

It has always been my worst fear that my research, and this book, would reek of colonialism—be another example of an "us" trying to make sense of "them." The older women I interviewed in Madagascar knew before I did that this story was never just about me trying to make sense of a "them." They found it quite natural, that I, a young married woman not yet a mother, flew to another part of the world to seek wisdom about the journey of life on which I was about to embark. This research and this book was, and still is, my effort to make sense of us—the story of us mothers trying to make bones from water.

Chapter Overview

Chapter 1 describes the landscape of birth in Diégo Suarez, Madagascar: the options available to women, the history behind the medicalization of childbirth in Madagascar, the inadequacies of the current medical infrastructure, and the existential level of insecurity that women face as a result of poverty and political instability. I also highlight cultural and spiritual dimensions of childbirth and the importance of relationships forged between women and midwives who help mothers navigate insecurities and access the resources needed to welcome their children into the world in safe and meaningful ways. In this chapter, I argue that relationships of reciprocity, between mothers and midwives and between mothers and other kinds of caregivers, are critical to children's survival by helping mothers foster social indebtedness that ensures they have what they need in times of insecurity.

Chapter 2 focuses on women's stories of navigating childbirth and reproductive care. I demonstrate that the process of instilling bones in the newly born, of granting them their stronghold in this world, requires pulling together creative confluences of care. Much of this work is about belonging—about immersing children in the kinds of rituals that bless and protect and also mark them with the kinds of identities that grant inclusion within and across multiple different communities. By strengthening children's belonging within particular religious and ancestral communities, parents, particularly mothers, strengthen and reinforce their own belonging within these same communities, which ensures they have the social, financial, cultural, and medical resources they need to raise children through the fragility of their early years.

Chapter 3 explores the postpartum rituals that northern Malagasy women observe with special attention given to taboos, or fady, and the practice of cold-water postpartum bathing, or ranginaly. When postpartum bathing rituals are combined with a period of seclusion, women are afforded much-needed care and rest and also given instructions from elders within the community regarding how to raise their babies according to the religious affiliations and inherited customs of theirs and their husbands' lineages. I argue that while some of these rituals can feel empowering and can even be the means by which mothers assert influence over their children despite a father's more principal claim, it is also true that postpartum practices can be burdensome as women must learn to embody the fady and fomba (taboos and customs) not only of their own family but also of the baby's paternal kin. Women's bodies are contested sites. Women are often used as instruments in the perpetuation of both matri- and patrilineages and sometimes in the construction of competing religious identities within their families. And, the transition to motherhood can also be a time of discernment and choice, an opportunity for women to be guided and mentored, and a chance for women to negotiate and deepen their place within their families, and in the larger society.

In chapter 4, I examine haircutting ceremonies and the rituals associated with them that parents in Diégo employ to instill bones, or a sense of enduring social worth, in their children. I argue that the process of instilling bones in children is an incremental process that begins at birth or even earlier, when children are still in the womb, and then later as well, when children are first overcoming the malleability of their infancy. Moreover, what the stories in this chapter evince is that this process of incorporating the young into community is often taking place in environments of pluralism where, rather than passing down a set of unchanging traditions from one generation to the next, it is people's engagement with difference that helps them formulate their sense of who they are.

Chapter 5 highlights broader changes regarding people's access to, and relationship with, ancestors, ancestral lands, and the rituals that bind descendants of these lands together. The book as a whole highlights the importance of ancestors in Malagasy religions, and in particular, the unique ways that women engage with ancestors upon the birth of a child. By contrast, this chapter features stories of people turning away from their ancestors, and from ancestral commitments, due to urbanization trends as well as changes to the religious landscape. Ancestral communities are not the only communities in which mothers invest and seek belonging on behalf of their children. That said, alongside trends of turning away from ancestral commitments, or perhaps because of them, twin efforts to preserve traditional rituals and medicines also exist in the face of these rapid changes. Thus, despite the growth of Pentecostal and charismatic forms of Christianity on the island, which encourage a severing of ties with one's ancestors, ancestral customs pervade in unique and evolving ways.

I conclude the book with a discussion of what women's engagements with ancestors might look like going forward given urbanization trends, the pluralism prevalent in cities like Diégo Suarez, and growing interests in Pentecostal and charismatic forms of Christianity that encourage a break from, rather than a rooting oneself into, the traditions of the past. I discuss the competing moral and visions for a thriving Madagascar and suggest that mothers will be on the forefront of navigating these changes. Though it is not entirely clear what changes to the religious landscape will look like for women and babies, subtle shifts in birth rituals offer a preview as they both reflect and represent larger changes in the ways that Malagasy relate to their ancestors and seek various kinds of spiritual therapies and religious community.

ONE

BIRTHING BABIES IN DIÉGO SUAREZ

On a hot day in January, as part of my volunteer teaching responsibilities in the English Department at the University of Antsiranana, I began by asking the students where the rain was.[1] It was relatively dry considering we were well into what should have been the start of the rainy season. One student attributed the lack of rains to climate change. Another student, responding to this comment, declared, "It's because they're building big buildings" (*satria iro manamboatra trano be*).[2] Curious about her statement, I asked for clarification, "Are you saying that when people build big buildings, this causes climate change?" "No," she replied, "I'm saying there are people who think a construction company is the reason the rains have not come." More students chimed in to explain that some thought the builders of a new hospital in town might be using sorcery to delay the start of the rainy season so that they could continue their construction uninterrupted.

Diégo Suarez residents' concern over the construction of a new hospital in their city stemmed partly from underlying suspicions many had about the motives of the nation's then president Andry Rajoelina, who had ordered the construction of the hospital. Although Rajoelina enjoyed some support at the beginning of his presidency due to what had been a growing dissatisfaction with his predecessor, by the time I arrived in 2011, Rajoelina's popularity had decreased significantly. Coastal Malagasy are seldom fans of highland presidents like Rajoelina or his forerunner, Ravalomanana. Ever since the hegemonic rise and fall of the Imerina Kingdom (1750–1895), people living along Madagascar's coasts have been distrustful of highland political leaders whom they often accuse of funding projects in the central highlands while paying little mind to crumbling infrastructures elsewhere on the island where the majority of the population resides.[3] Many Diégo Suarez residents saw Rajoelina's promise of a new hospital as an underhanded, last-ditch attempt to regain popularity after failing to keep earlier promises. "Why doesn't he repair the already existent teaching hospital?" one student asked. "And how will we know that the hospital will ever be completed?"

One did not have to spend much time in Diégo Suarez to see that residents' concerns about Rajoelina's motivations were well warranted. At the beginning of his presidency, he had promised several new dormitories for students at the University of Antsiranana—only one of which had been built when I arrived, and even that one remained uninhabitable as those in charge neglected to finish the installation of water pipes within the building. The multistory pink concrete building sat beautifully as a tempting icon, nearly finished but without dorm beds or water. Meanwhile students were living in buildings that appeared to be remnants of something that once was. If it were not for the signs of habitation—clothing hanging from the balconies, stray dogs digging through the piles of trash behind the back of buildings, charcoal cookers on the porches, or lively music blaring from radios—one might have assumed that no one lived in the older dormitories. Students explained that many locals feared that the new hospital might have the same fate as the new dormitory, and they needed the season's rains more than they did a false promise of a new hospital.

In addition to the new hospital under construction in 2011, Diégo Suarez had two other large hospitals, one government dispensary with a maternity ward, and dozens of other privately funded medical clinics where people sought care, including maternity care. However, the sheer number of healthcare options did not always translate into an abundant supply of healthcare workers and resources for the northern coastal city. As is true in most urban areas, many factors influence accessibility to quality healthcare, including transportation, healthcare worker shortages, underresourced facilities, and personal beliefs about sickness and health.

During my nine months of research for this book, I visited as many medical facilities as possible in order to acquaint myself with the people who worked there and also to get a feel for the kinds of places where women give birth to, and seek therapy for, their children. In doing so, I discovered that Diégo Suarez residents' lack of interest in the new hospital, despite their articulated desires for medical facilities, is less paradoxical than it would at first seem, which I attribute to at least three factors. First, as I have described above, there's a healthy level of skepticism among coastal groups around the political projects of highland presidents. Second, the colonial circumstances under which birth was medicalized in Madagascar in the late nineteenth and early twentieth centuries have left some skepticism around the political motivations behind projects related to women's healthcare. And last, there's an existential level of insecurity caused by economic decline, political instability, and a rapidly changing religious landscape that can make accessing medical and cultural resources difficult.

This chapter is about the landscape of birth—the options available to women, the inadequacies of the current medical infrastructure, the importance of cultural customs, and the importance of the relationships mothers forge with midwives and other kinds of religious and medical specialists who help them navigate these insecurities and access important resources needed to welcome their children into the world in safe and meaningful ways. Relationships of reciprocity between mothers and midwives are critical to children's survival, not simply because midwives are knowledgeable but because reciprocal relationships, as opposed to transactional relationships, help mothers foster a kind of social indebtedness that ensures they have access to the care they need in moments of insecurity.

The Landscape of Care

Over the course of my research in Diégo Suarez in 2011–2012, the overwhelming majority of women I interviewed expressed an interest in more medicine during childbirth, not less. With a few exceptions, most embraced a medical model of childbearing, despite the fact that reputable US media sources consistently portray Africa's high rates of infant and maternal mortality as a result of women's refusal or resistance to giving birth in clinics.[4] Though some residents of Diégo Suarez expressed doubts as to whether or not a new hospital under construction in their city would ever be completed, most hoped that it would. In fact, as will become clear in the chapters that follow this one, most of my informants understood giving birth in a hospital-like setting as a "modern" option to be espoused. Thus, while some African women were initially reluctant to subject themselves to the experiments of the novice midwives and surgeons of the European colonial period, in the early decades of twenty-first century, when the Westernization of childbirth is well underway, we should not assume that women are taking a similar stance. Nevertheless, despite the fact that most of the women I interviewed expressed promedical stances toward childbirth, nearly 40 percent of my approximately fifty informants gave birth to at least one child at home or in the home of a trained midwife.

The conclusions we can draw from these stances are threefold. First, in Madagascar, the decision to give birth at home, or in the home of a traditionally or medically trained midwife, is not understood to be in protest to the medical establishment in the same way that such a decision might be in the United States. That is to say, Malagasy women are not choosing between homes versus hospitals; their options are both far more numerous and far more limited. Second, even though the majority of my informants expressed a preference for hospitals, not all of them could afford this option for every birth. Road conditions, proximity to health clinics, and other financial and social circumstances also played into their birth venue decisions. Third, women's decisions to consult with traditional midwives and specialists were not typically in protest of the medical establishment but rather a strategy of investing in multiple complementary approaches to increase one's chance of a positive outcome.

In Diégo Suarez in the early 2010s, the reality was that the very rich preferred to give birth to their babies in Antananarivo, the capital city of Madagascar, or even to leave the island to give birth in a hospital in France or Mauritius. For most of Diégo Suarez's residents, however, traveling abroad or even outside of the city by plane was extremely cost prohibitive. Traveling to Madagascar's capital by road via *taxi-brousse* (bush taxi), even though more affordable, involved a twenty- to forty-hour bus ride on bumpy roads and was thus not desirable either. As a result, most women in Diégo Suarez sought prenatal and maternity care either in privately funded clinics; at the large teaching hospital, Hôpital Be; or in the birthing room of the government-funded Dispensaire.[5] All of these options were decent. They were staffed by dedicated nurses and midwives, but many were working under less than ideal conditions with very little compensation.

The Hôpital Be and the Dispensaire, technically speaking, offered government-subsidized care as compared with the more costly private clinics, but patients at the government-funded medical facilities still had to pay extra for supplemental medicines or to have a doctor attend their birth, expenses that are quite hard for most patients to meet. Additionally, given the crumbling infrastructural state of the Hôpital Be and the fact that in both the hospital and the Dispensaire the birthing rooms contain multiple beds, affording little privacy, there were those who found giving birth with elder retired nurse-midwives in their homes a more comfortable option. For high-risk births and emergency situations, women opted to go to the Hôpital Be, as this was, at the time, the only facility in the city capable of providing cesarean surgeries. If one gave birth there, however, and did not have complications, there was no guarantee of access to what was then the single obstetrician who served that hospital. In sum, my discussions with dozens of women in Diégo Suarez in 2011 revealed that despite the efforts by both local and nonlocal governments and aid given by global health organizations, Malagasy women were still struggling to find safe, affordable places to bear their children.

Medicalization of Birth in Madagascar

In Madagascar, childbirth was medicalized as a result of measures enacted by French officials between the years 1895 and 1906 partly in order to ensure a large Indigenous labor force to supply the colonial government's administrative needs and partly in order to provide the medical facilities necessary to attract French settlers to the island.[6] Although it is safe to assume that the doctors, nurses, and midwives who assisted the first hospital patients did so out of a genuine desire to help women safely give birth to babies, the general impetus behind medicalization had more to do with the racially inspired pronatalist proclivities of the French governor-general Joseph Gallieni (1849–1916).

Governor-General Joseph Gallieni implemented his pronatalist program through a series of laws and decrees enacted in 1898 aimed at increasing the population of the Merina. The Merina, a lighter-skinned ethnic group living on the high plateau of Madagascar, were deemed by Gallieni to be a superior race and thus highly desirable recruits for the French colonial administration.[7] Through the program, Gallieni built the first ever medical school, as well as other hospitals, leprosariums, maternity wards, and orphanages throughout the island.[8] The presence of larger teaching hospitals in every province throughout Madagascar, including the Hôpital Be in Diégo Suarez where some of the women I interviewed gave birth to their babies, owes its origins to these late nineteenth-century colonial measures.

In addition to his efforts to secure a robust Indigenous labor force, something Gallieni considered critical to the successful establishment of French settler colonies in the African world, Gallieni was also influenced by fears that were circulating in Europe and North America at the time about the perceived decline in the population of the white race in general and the French in particular, the latter of which he understood in the context of France's "intense rivalry with a newly unified Germany."[9] In response to these fears, Gallieni and other French leaders during this period sought to increase France's population growth through a variety of means, including by establishing settler colonies throughout the French empire. This, he surmised, required the creation of European-style health facilities to assure prospective settlers that they would have a place to go should they contract any of the diseases rampant on the island during this period, including syphilis, leprosy, tuberculosis, smallpox, and malaria.[10] Although Gallieni was not the first to order the construction of European-style medical facilities on the island, he was the first to do so on such a wide scale. The first modern medical facilities, built by British missionaries several decades earlier, were subsequently acquired by Governor Gallieni during his tenure on the island in an effort to reform them from what he perceived to be their overly parochial nature.[11]

Thus, the medicalization of childbirth in Madagascar, though beneficial to most, was also beset with underhanded colonial motives, some of which had negative social consequences for babies, mothers, and their families. For example, in the late nineteenth and early twentieth centuries, during the French occupation of Madagascar, the colonial administration insisted that all infants be given a permanent name and be registered with the state immediately following birth.[12] This law disrupted the western Sakalava practice of waiting two weeks to name infants to ensure that harmful spirits would not have a name by which to call, and thus provoke, newly born children. While many surely welcomed the medicalization of childbirth, it is also true that the medicalization of childbirth—and, in this case, the Westernization of birthing practices—disrupted some of the more trusted customs around the birthing, naming, and welcoming of the newly born.

The medicalization of childbirth—in any society—comes with both benefits and tensions, as new medical and political agendas inevitably collide with more weathered and customary approaches to birthing and infant care. As expressed above, Gallieni's efforts to improve infant and maternal mortality rates were part of a larger scheme to encourage reproduction among certain groups of Malagasy whom he deemed racially superior and to increase the pool of human labor needed to support the French occupation of Madagascar. Nancy Rose Hunt documents similar motivations on the part of French colonial officials' construction of maternity clinics in the Congo during a similar time period, arguing that these projects were intricately tied to the goal of producing a healthy colonial workforce in the face of declining birth rates.[13]

The medicalization of childbirth, along the Indian Ocean, in Africa, and around the world, has a long and complex history, and it is not my aim to give a comprehensive account of it here.[14] Nevertheless, it's important to note that, while virtually all women have been in some way affected by the medicalization of childbirth, all women have not had equal or similar kinds of access to these medical advancements. Depending on social, geographic, and economic circumstances, some women have accessed the lifesaving advantages of obstetrical care with relative ease, while others have had little to no access. Some have been treated as bodies to be experimented on, as test cases, while others have benefited from the experimentations performed on the former.

More recently, interventions in women's healthcare have come from international aid organizations looking to curb, rather than grow, population growth. Some of the largest donors include USAID (United States Agency for International Development) and Marie Stopes International, a London-based organization that aims to expand women's reproductive choices in thirty-seven countries throughout the world, including Madagascar.[15] Organizations such as these support programs that provide training for medical personnel, for family planning education, and for more wide-scale distribution of contraceptives. While the motives behind these initiatives are many, including efforts to reduce poverty and ameliorate the lives of mothers and children, some initiatives to curb population growth are focused more on protecting the island's biodiversity than on improving the livelihoods of women and their children. This is evidenced by the fact that many environmental agencies are now implementing integrated health and environment programs that combine conservation efforts with family planning resources.

Some of these organizations are better about consulting with the needs of local populations than others.[16] As Eva Keller documents in her research among villagers adjacent to Masoala National Park, the efforts of conservationists to protect lands and limit population growth sometimes directly clash with the Malagasy efforts to anchor themselves in the land through the growth of many descendants. She writes, "To grow like the banana plant, or to imagine oneself as if at the apex of a conically shaped fishing net, not only means having many descendants whose births testify to the ancestors' blessing and project ancestry into the future but also means viewing life as a process of turning neutral soil into tany fivelômana ('land that enables life'), of growing ever deeper roots in the land over the course of generations, and of ultimately creating 'land of the ancestors' (tanindrazana)."[17] While Keller is speaking to the values held by rural Malagasy in a very different context than that of Diégo Suarez, it is still true that international efforts to either increase or curb population growth anywhere on the island do not always align with the values and needs of the communities on whom these agendas are imposed.

In virtually all of Madagascar, kinship is established through peoples' connection to land, lands that hold the bones of one's ancestors, lands that anchor families even as they grow out from the lands that retain their ancestral roots. In cities, where work and life look different than in agricultural locales, families sometimes *do* desire fewer children despite the principal value placed on familial growth. Many of these urban dwellers welcome the family planning resources that these international donor organizations provide. That said, programs aimed at either increasing or curbing population growth through the years have not always taken into account the particular social and cultural needs of the local communities they serve.

In addition to the infrastructural inadequacies of the current medical system, mistrust between coastal groups and the political projects of highland presidents, a tainted history of colonial medicine, and the sometimes competing agendas of locals and the international aid organizations that support them, when I arrived to conduct this research in September 2011, Madagascar was still suffering an economic depression as a result of a devastating political coup. In 2009, Andry Rajoelina, mayor of Madagascar's capital city, led a military-backed coup against then president Marc Ravalomanana. The coup culminated in the installment of Rajoelina as interim president until future elections were held. As a result of the overthrow, Madagascar's membership within the African Union was suspended, some foreign donors withheld aid, and some other would-be investors took their money elsewhere. Madagascar's tourism economy suffered as well, as fewer considered the island a stable enough place to spend a vacation. All of these circumstances left many Malagasy without work and dismayed about the nation's future and made it more difficult for women to access the kinds of support services needed during pregnancy, childbirth, and the postnatal period. These circumstances also made it difficult for midwives and other support specialists to deliver the kind of care they are trained to provide.

Midwives "Make People Living"

Midwives in Madagascar, sometimes called *matrons, sages-femmes, renin-jaza,* or *mpampivelona* (the latter two of which mean "mother of children" and "one who delivers/makes people living"), are deeply knowledgeable human resources, critical to helping women and their families access the medical, spiritual, and ancestral resources needed during the all-important early months and years of a child's life. They undergo medical training either through formal processes or through the informal process of apprenticeship. They also draw on a rich array of spiritual resources, sometimes even relying on powers granted to them by way of a transhuman source, which confers on them a special kind of legitimacy in the eyes of their clients.

Those familiar with Malagasy religions will likely have some knowledge of the role that specialists like spirit mediums, healer-diviners, and leaders of invocation (*mpijoro*) play in helping people maintain right relations with one another, with their ancestors, and with God (Zanahary). Spirit mediums (*tromba*) channel voices from the ancestral past; diviners help their clients discern appropriate courses of action with regard to illness or family grievances; and mpijoro (leaders of invocation) preside over all kinds of ceremonies including ritual sacrifices, birth rituals, and funerals.[18] Midwives, though less prevalent in the literature, also play a central role in many, if not all, of the aforementioned activities.[19] Midwives, together with other specialists, are vessels of cultural and spiritual knowledge, especially the kinds of rituals and customs that women observe to invoke ancestral blessings on the newly born. As will be evidenced in the following story—of Alicia—many of these traits are true not only of traditional midwives, who learn their work by way of apprenticeship, but also often of more formally trained medical midwives.

In Madagascar, this spiritual and cultural work is critical to the birthing process. Cultural practices are important anywhere, but in places like Diégo, where the biomedical infrastructure is lacking, cultural and spiritual practices can direct much-needed care and attention on the vulnerable in vitally important compensatory ways. Moreover, relationships with midwives tend to be reciprocal, rather than transactional, in nature, which ensures that women have someone to turn to in moments of insecurity, regardless of whether they have the in-the-moment means to pay for services. Despite the spiritual prestige associated with the job, in other ways, the work of a midwife is hard and sometimes underappreciated, especially in Madagascar, where midwives struggle alongside their clients to access clean water, sufficient electricity, training, and medical resources needed to support women and babies. Alicia's story, in particular, evidences this reality.

Alicia

Alicia, the young medically trained midwife (sage-femme) appointed by the government to serve in the small rural fishing village of Cap Diégo, exemplified the ambitiousness and vibrancy of Malagasy youth. She dressed professionally and stylishly, often sporting sundresses and heels. And she had a vazaha husband, a fact that offered her a much-coveted status among her peers. She spent weekends at her home located several kilometers outside of Diégo Suarez on the road toward Joffreville, but during the week, she worked and slept at the medical dispensary where she served residents of Cap Diégo, a fishing village with a population of about fourteen hundred just across the bay from Diégo Suarez's main shipping port at the north end of the city.[20] Each week when she disembarked from the boat that brought her from Diégo Suarez onto the shores of Cap Diégo, Alicia would quickly trade her heels and dresses for more casual attire. And when there was no work at the clinic, which was rare, she was known to take out a pirogue to do some fishing. As evidenced by the ways the villagers greeted and joked around with her, her neighbors seemed to appreciate the fluidity with which she moved in and out of the urban and rural environs of Diégo Suarez and Cap Diégo, respectively, a fluidity with which they themselves were also familiar.

After I first met Alicia at the main medical Dispensaire in Diégo Suarez, she invited me out to her clinic in Cap Diégo. She agreed to talk with me about matters of birthing and midwifery if I would provide her with some English language lessons. Out of this informal agreement, our friendship grew. I frequently visited Alicia at the clinic. On one particular occasion, Alicia was at the clinic with her mother, Josette, when my research assistant Zafisoa and I arrived to talk with her. Alicia showed us around the clinic, including the bed on which she sleeps, the bed on which her clients labor, and her desk, where she sits with women to provide family planning consultations. She spoke at length about her medical training and knowledge, while also disclosing her knowledge of cultural and customary practices.

Together, she and her mother shared with us some of the traditional customs women use to stimulate labor, including rituals of blessing that take place in doorways in order to symbolically push women into the threshold stages of childbirth. They also discussed some of the herbal medicines women use during labor and the postpartum period. She and her mother mentioned *rômba* (African basil) and *ravintsôha* (lemon leaves) as the most widely used herbal medicines by Malagasy women in the postpartum period.[21] Hearing them discuss so openly and matter-of-factly these traditional customs enabled me to see that the differences between traditional midwives—like Bernadette, whose story will follow this one—and medically trained ones are not always as stark as they are sometimes made out to be. Both midwives showed respect for, and had knowledge of, many traditional and ritualistic practices leading up to, during, and following childbirth, and both also took advantage of the medical training and resources available to them. Moreover, like Bernadette, Alicia also saw her work as a calling, though her discovery of this calling looked different than Bernadette's.

As she described, Alicia never intended to become a midwife. Prior to becoming one, she had studied law and was preparing to work in a courthouse. Her grandmother had been a very well-known and expert matron, but it never occurred to her to follow this line of work until a friend of hers casually suggested they go and take a test to see if either of them qualified for the midwifery training program at Diégo Suarez 's main hospital, Hôpital Be. Alicia agreed to go only to please her friend and because the salary was good. When they took the test, Alicia had the fourteenth-highest score out of nearly one thousand participants, which she understood to be fortuitous and evidence of a calling. The top scorers were then selected to go through the training at Hôpital Be. After completing the training, Alicia was placed by the government in the clinic that serves the fishing community of Cap Diégo. Thus, while Alicia earned her living and reputation within her community as a result of her medical training at Diégo Suarez's Hôpital Be, she, much like traditional midwives who gain their knowledge through apprenticeship, also saw her work as a vocation. She did not enter midwifery by way of a spiritual vision, as traditional midwives sometimes do, but she did believe her grandmother's spirit, in a roundabout way, had a hand in her career path.

After I had conducted several interviews with Alicia, she invited me to spend a week with her at the clinic in Cap Diégo. During that week, I learned that Alicia sees many clients every day, and if a woman gives birth at night, she has to work by candlelight as she has minimal access to electricity. She has solar panels and a boat battery that powers a tiny television and some adhesive circular red lights that resemble the lighting directing you toward the exits on airplane aisles, but power is sporadic at best. Moreover, at night, it is hard to sleep because of a bat infestation in the rafters of the clinic. A couple of nights, I awoke to Alicia banging on the walls with a long stick in an effort to shut them up. In addition, I observed that Alicia does many things for the people of Cap Diégo beyond the parameters of providing family planning services and labor and birthing support. Every day and well into the evenings, people bought phone credit from her because there was no place on Cap Diégo to buy phone credit for residents' pay-as-you-go cell phones. Toward the end of the week, a shirtless and brawny young fisherman came over to ask for credit. Evidenced by the conversation they had, about the day's bountiful catch and other aspects of life on the island, it was clear that Alicia took the time to try to understand what life was like for the villagers she served and that the respect she had for them was mutual.

Despite some complaints about the job, Alicia appeared to enjoy her work. She understood midwifery to be her mission in life and saw the hardships of her work simply as "le drôle de travail" (in Malagasy: *asa afa-afa*). Moreover, she liked spending time in the fishing village. She felt that Cap Diégo was calmer and safer than Diégo Suarez itself. She left the clinic windows open at night when she slept despite the fact that there were no bars. "It's too high for anyone to climb in, and anyway life is safer here," she said. She explained that Diégo Suarez used to be safer too, that it used to be that you could walk around at night, anytime of night, with little worry, but now things are different. When I asked her why things have changed, she attributed it to *faroche* (gangs) and corruption.

Alicia had her own perspective on why life is hard in Madagascar, and on why Diégo Suarez has become an increasingly dangerous city in which to live. Regardless of their accuracy, her descriptions spoke to the extreme poverty in which people lived and the existential level of insecurity many people experienced living in Diégo Suarez. According to statistics published in 2013, shortly after this research was conducted, 71 percent of the population was living at or below the poverty rate.[22] And, as recently as 2018, in the Diana Region of Madagascar, which includes Diégo Suarez, only 27.4 percent of the population had access to clean drinking water and 50.5 percent, access to electricity.[23] While these aspects are not always highlighted as a reason for Madagascar's relatively high infant and maternal mortality rates, they should be. Instead, reputable media sources, like the New York Times, often blame women's "preferences" for traditional midwives and "their stubborn adherence to tribal traditions."[24] Articles such as this perpetuate American myths about Africa—myths that portray poverty as consequences of the widespread observance of "regressive" cultural traditions.[25]

What such media sources do not always represent is that women are sometimes afraid to leave their homes at night; clinics are poorly stocked; poverty contributes to poor maternal and infant health outcomes; medical personnel are both scarce and underresourced; and the difference between a homebirth and a clinical birth, in certain places in Madagascar, is sometimes relatively small. The reality in Madagascar is that midwives shoulder a lot to deliver the kind of care that women need, especially given the structural inadequacies of the current healthcare system. They must be well versed in medical technologies and in culturally appropriate care in order to ensure the health and safety of their clients. Sometimes, too, they act as informal social workers, selling phone credits and helping their clients secure access to food, clothing, and family planning. In short, midwives, like other kinds of medical and religious specialists, must wear many hats, in line with what Tracy Luedke and Harry West describe as the kind of job-related border crossing that religious and medical specialists must do in East Africa and in other environments of medical scarcity and pluralism.[26]

In communities with inadequate healthcare systems, culturally appropriate care ensures that women can create networks of spiritual and social support critical to their survival and well-being. When women engage in traditional customs, they strengthen bonds with members of their community (kin and nonkin alike) in ways that increase belonging and access to the kinds of human and spiritual resources needed to "make people living"—to ensure that children are marked as worthy, that they belong, and that they have access to the provisions they need to acquire bones (i.e., their sturdiness within their communities). In Madagascar, as is true everywhere, childbirth is not just a medical event but also a social and spiritual event. In northern Madagascar, Malagasy describe birth as a "spear battle," rife with risk and with meaning. The rituals that women employ to navigate this journey ensure that women have what they need to both face these risks and glean meaning from an experience as harrowing as exiting a child from one's body.

Birth as a Spear Battle

According to Robbie Davis-Floyd, even in the highly medicalized birth culture of the United States, birth is ritualized and as much according to cultural norms as medical ones. In describing the rituals of the American hospital system, she writes, "Cumulatively, routine obstetrical procedures such as intravenous feeding, electronic monitoring, and episiotomy are felt by those who perform them to transform the unpredictable and uncontrollable natural process of birth into a relatively predictable and controllable technological phenomenon that reinforces American society's most fundamental belief about the superiority of technology over nature. [She goes on to say] these rituals, also known as 'standard procedures for normal birth,' work to effectively convey the core values of American society to birthing women."[27] In other words, these American ways of managing childbirth, which often appear as standard procedure, may not actually be the standard, or the norm, elsewhere, even in places that position medical technologies as central to the process. All that is to say, there is not *one* medical or cultural way of handling childbirth. There are many models, all of which draw from medical, cultural, and spiritual knowledge systems, to help ensure a smooth transition for women, and their babies, through the process.

Moreover, according to Davis-Floyd, all models of childbirth convey messages to women. For example, due in part to the particular experiences that women endure, but also in part to the rituals through which they are led, women might come to believe childbirth to be a natural process, a medical emergency, an empowering event, a traumatic event, or some combination of all of these. At the same time, women are active participants, arguably the *most* active of participants in childbirth, and therefore are also conceiving their own meanings from their experiences of giving birth, a point made by Pamela Klassen. According to Klassen, who writes about childbirth in the American context, women find significance in their birth experiences not solely in the ways given to them by their faith communities, midwives, or by the medical establishment. Rather, they also "procreate religion." They "[make] religious meaning out of the embodied memories and human connections forged in the process of childbirth."[28]

In Madagascar, this procreation of meaning from the birth experience shines through in Malagasy descriptions of childbirth as a spear battle (*ady antsaboa*) for women, similar to circumcision for men.[29] Pregnancy (*mavesatra*) is a serious affair. The word for pregnancy in Malagasy is the same word used to denote something heavy. Women must endure not only the physical weight of carrying a child but also some of the medical risks associated with pregnancy and the heaviness of the various ancestral taboos (fady) and postpartum practices they are expected to follow—both those imposed by their own family and those urged by the child's father's family, as the child in utero is a product of both lineages and may decide to abort his or her journey should the mother fail to respect both ancestral lines. Women recount narratives of being ushered through this battle with the assistance of doctors, midwives, and healer-diviners, some of whom channel spirits from the past to assist them on their journeys. At one point in Madagascar's history, babies were named for the passages they endured—names like "crossed over," "not struck by danger," and "good to see."[30] Women, too, are congratulated for "crossing over." As one woman explained to me, "we say, *ady saboantsika magnangy ny fitirahana,*" meaning "the spear battle for women is childbirth" or "birth is our spear battle." She went on to say,

> When you go to visit a woman after she has given birth, the first thing you say to her is "birth is our spear battle" [*ady saboantsika magnangy ny fitirahana*], and then you say, "Congratulations for you have made it over to the other side" [*arabaigny fa tody aroe soamantsara*]. You also bring the woman a gift; this gift is called *rôm-patsa* (which is small white dried crawfish). This is the traditional gift, and it is supposed to help a woman produce breast milk, but you can bring any gift, a bit of money or soap, and all of these things can be called rôm-patsa.[31]

This notion of childbirth as a spear battle, together with all the rituals that accompany it, provides rich insights into how Malagasy view the birthing process. Within Malagasy religions in particular, and within African religions more broadly, spears, as well as knives and scissors, are ritual objects that both literally and symbolically shape initiates into new kinds of people. During circumcision and haircutting ceremonies, spears and other kinds of sharp blades have the capacity to mark important moments and to mark and shape people passing through those important moments.[32] In the context of rites of passage, this is done by cutting away folds of skin or hair in order to provide a kind of spiritual earmarking as well as to shape initiates physically as they transition spiritually from one state to another. Likening birth to a spear battle, even though no actual spears are involved, suggests that childbirth is the defining process that transforms girls into women and mothers, just as boys, who undergo the knife during their circumcision ceremonies in Madagascar, find this rather grave experience to be the process by which they are made into men or, at least, made into boys who will one day belong as men within their communities.[33]

That said, in the context of childbirth, the metaphor of the spear battle also references the intense work of childbirth that can and sometimes does bring women and babies close to death. According to Bodo Ravalolomanga, Tañala of southeastern Madagascar think of birth in similar terms frequently employing the phrase *miadry tafika*, which means to "watch over the warrior," for they understand women to be engaged in a battle that could be deadly and to be in a liminal space that requires protection.[34] This conceptualization of childbirth as women's battle, comparable to the battles with the sword that men face, is not unique to Madagascar. Citing the autobiographical account of African midwife Auoa Kéita, Jane Turrittin remarks that "Sonrai, Bambara, Wolof, Malinke, Kassonke, Sere, Samo, Peul, Diola, Sarakole, and Bobo women" all conceptualize childbirth in this way.[35] According to Aoua Kéita, "The eternal refrain is the following: women do not participate in battle, nor in hunting parties, nor do they fish. . . . The field of battle is childbirth, whose pain they must support with courage and dignity."[36] Thus, in addition to referencing the transformation that occurs when a woman completes the journey of childbirth, the notion of spear battle also speaks to the kinds of work that women engage in to become mothers as well the risks and pain they assume in bearing children.

Thus, childbirth, despite or perhaps because of its associated risks, can provide Malagasy women with a sense of newfound strength, triumph, and companionship with other women who have endured the journey. This sense of having crossed over is why rituals of gift giving (rôm-patsa) and of speaking congratulatory words to women are so powerful. In a real material way, these gifts and words honor both the transformation that has occurred and the risk that was shouldered. The sense of childbirth as a transformative battle is why Malagasy women often rely on being guided through the process not only by medical attendants but also by elder women, healer-diviners, and spiritually attentive midwives, like Alicia and also Bernadette.

Likening birth to a spear battle also highlights the kinds of struggles that can unfold as families disagree over parenting decisions and matters of spiritual upbringing. Mothers, perhaps more than anyone, often find themselves in the middle of these disputes, something that will be discussed in subsequent chapters throughout this book. And in addition to the highly charged, real-life divisions such disagreements can cause, Malagasy also perform symbolic fights over children at religious ceremonies as a way to give voice to the conflicting interests of multiple family members. Maurice Bloch describes these as "mock" battles.[37] These playful scenes where relatives pretend to fight over and/or steal the child from one another occur both at haircutting ceremonies for young babies and at ceremonies of circumcision for toddler boys.[38] Each highlights the kind of mutual investment that paternal and maternal relatives have in their progeny.

In more recent decades, to the extent that mock battles still occur, actual spears are largely absent, due in part to the fact that weapons (including those used in religious ceremonies) were outlawed during the French occupation of Madagascar. Thus, during the colonial period, sticks came to replace spears as the instruments used in ceremonies.[39] In the context of my own research, no instances of violence or mock violence were observed. And spades, rather than spears, were used in ceremonies of blessing for the newly born. As one woman explained, when a newly born baby is brought out of the house for the first time, at two weeks postpartum, a maternal uncle takes a shovel or a spade (*angady*) and walks around the perimeter of the house, singing a blessing and invoking his ancestors while tapping each corner of the compound with his spade. He wears a lamba (traditional cloth) around his waist and encircles the house six times.

Though blunt objects have come to replace spears at ceremonies of blessing for the newly born, the notion of birth as a spear battle remained a provocative description for many Malagasy women with whom I spoke in the early 2010s. Likewise, certain forms of symbolic contestation over children's affiliation prevailed. During haircutting ceremonies, babies were sometimes made to be held by a paternal relative for fear that they would grow too close in affinity to their maternal relatives.[40] By contrast, one mother I knew insisted that all of her children's hair be cut by her sister in order that their hair might come to more closely resemble that of her sister's. Her sister's hair was thick and straight rather than curly, a physical characteristic of which many Merina families were proud. Thus, contestations over children occur with regard to not just maternal and paternal affiliations but also notions of beauty and racial hierarchies.

In recent years, as more Malagasy have moved from the countryside into larger cities, like Diégo Suarez, with hospitals and medical clinics, birthing options have rapidly increased. In these new urban contexts, childbirth, as rite of passage, has taken on new meaning. Women and the babies are now being ushered through the birth process by formally trained doctors and nurse-midwives. These practitioners address biomedical threats in addition to spiritual threats, which further dramatize the risks involved and serve to heighten people's sense of childbirth as a battle in new ways.

In sum, framing childbirth as a spear battle has many meanings and references many kinds of important cultural transformations. It also seems to corroborate Pamela Klassen's point that women, Malagasy or otherwise, often derive—even procreate—religious meaning from their birth experiences. When we rightly look beyond the physiological aspects of childbirth to see the rituals that help frame it, we are able to see more clearly the meanings that women ascribe to the birthing experience, the risks they shoulder, and the obstacles they face to bring their children into the world in safe and dignified ways.

Moreover, childbirth is one of the pivotal experiences through which women forge new meanings and identities, for themselves and their children. They do so by choosing support personnel who are knowledgeable about and sensitive to the customs they choose to observe as members of one ancestral community versus another. They do so by engaging in rites of blessing and initiation for children post-childbirth—bathing rituals, infant outing ceremonies, and ritualized haircuttings—that mark children with particular identities, identities that grant them belonging, or, to use the metaphor of my informants, identities, that grant them bones. All of these post-childbirth rituals are discussed in greater details in the chapters that follow this one, but suffice it to say, childbirth enables women to reimagine themselves as mothers and to celebrate the ways in which they have been transformed and crossed over. And childbirth also illuminates the socioeconomic, political, and infrastructural obstacles twenty-first-century Malagasy mothers face in their efforts to produce descendants and grow children who will be sufficiently anchored in the ancestral and religious communities that will sustain them. Midwives like Alicia and Bernadette are critical to this process.

Bernadette

When I first met Joffreville's traditional midwife (renin-jaza) Bernadette, she invited me into her modestly constructed wood-frame house, a house that served simultaneously as her home and as a birthing space for the dozens of women who gave birth under her care. She proudly declared that she had attended 147 births and never encountered a serious problem. In fact, her reputation within her community was such that when complications arose at the medical dispensary just up the dirt road from where she lived, the medically trained nurse-midwife (sage-femme) who worked at that clinic would sometimes send for Bernadette's help.

Unlike the sage-femme who worked at that clinic, Bernadette did not learn her work through any kind of formal training; rather, she described her work as a "a gift" (*un don*) bestowed on her by her ancestors.[41] She describes the story as follows:

> One day a man alone with his laboring daughter came searching for someone to wait with his daughter while he went to look for help. I had never seen a woman give birth but agreed to stay with the woman anyway. While the father was away looking for someone to assist his daughter, the baby started to descend. I caught the baby's bottom, and then legs, but as sometimes happens with breach births, the baby's head then became stuck. Fear swept over me, and sweat poured from my forehead, when suddenly, I turned around to discover, in a dark corner of her house, the hovering spirit of my grandmother. In an instant, a calmness replaced my fears, and my shaking hands steadied as the spirit showed me how to place my fingers inside the woman to make a space wide enough for the baby's head to descend. I did as the spirit showed me and the baby emerged screaming and full of life. When I turned around again, my grandmother's spirit was gone. Soon after helping the woman, I began having vivid dreams in which my grandmother would visit and show me the techniques of midwifery.[42] Word quickly began to spread, and people started coming to me to give birth. Over time, I became Joffreville's midwife [renin-jaza].[43]

As previously noted, Malagasy have a lot of different words for midwives, including *matrons*, *sages-femmes*, *renin-jaza*, and *mpampivelona*. Though all these names describe midwives, all but the term *sage-femme* are used more frequently in reference to "traditional" midwives, those who enter the profession by way of an informal apprenticeship or by way of a spiritual "calling." Residents of Joffreville referred to Bernadette as a renin-jaza (mother of children). When I would take a taxi-brousse from Diégo Suarez to Joffreville to visit her, townspeople greeted me on the road to ask where I was going. "Za mitady renin-jaza" (I am searching for the midwife), I would say. "You mean the sage-femme, at the clinic?" two women asked on one such occasion. "No, I mean the renin-jaza," I replied. "The Malagasy one?" they inquired incredulously. "Yes," I confirmed. Satisfied by my response, the women smiled and accompanied me to her yard, which was about a ten-minute walk from the town's main road. Of course, both of Joffreville's midwives are Malagasy in the sense that both are native to the island, but the women's description of

Bernadette as "the Malagasy one" provided some insight into the various kinds of midwifery options available to women in Madagascar as well as to people's thinking regarding the Indigenousness (or conversely foreignness) of certain birthing personnel.

Joffreville (Ambohitra), where Bernadette lives, is a small, forested town to the south of Diégo Suarez bordering Montagne D'Ambre Parc National. It has approximately five thousand inhabitants, most of whom farm or raise livestock and a small percentage of whom work in the tourism industry in the many guest houses where tourists come to stay to tour the national park. During the French colonial period, the town served as a retreat for French settlers and officials who spent most of the year in Diégo Suarez but occasionally escaped to Joffreville to enjoy the cooler weather that exists in the town due to its higher elevation and proximity to the rain forest. The father of the laboring woman who sought Bernadette's help in this small, forested town some decades ago had been looking for someone to assist his daughter in the birth of her child—help he presumably did not find, at least not in time for the birth. In crafting her story in this way, Bernadette lent legitimacy to her decision to become a midwife, by highlighting both the need within her community for more midwifery support and the spiritual endorsement received by one "called" into the vocation by an ancestral spirit.

While Bernadette narrated her story to me and to my research assistant Édith one afternoon in the dark den of her home, two different families with babies came to see her. The first family arrived at her door, entered her house, and sat down on the floor before her. The mother handed her baby over to Bernadette, who placed the baby on the ground, giving her a gentle examination, feeling the baby's stomach, checking her awareness and reflexes. Bernadette advised the mother to take the baby, who was experiencing some stomach pain (*marary kibo*), to a Lutheran-funded SALFA (Sampan'asa Loterana Momba ny Fahasalamana) clinic on the road between Joffreville and Diégo Suarez. The journey, when taken by bus, would likely consume much of the family's waking daylight hours.[44] When the next family arrived for a consultation with Bernadette, Édith and I left, fearing our presence might have altered the advice Bernadette had provided the previous family. Given our statuses, both of us students and one of us American, Bernadette sometimes gave us the impression that she needed to present herself in a certain way while in our company. She wanted us to know that she was knowledgeable about biomedicine, that she was on good terms with the personnel at the local medical dispensary, and that her clients sometimes included educated professionals. Earning the trust of the midwives like Bernadette was a delicate endeavor given my social status as an American and the assumptions that come with that, but the hours I spent with her nevertheless nurtured in me an understanding of the special, and comprehensive, relationship midwives forge with their clients.

Midwives in Madagascar, like midwives the world over, are charged with more than simply catching babies. Historically, the practice of midwifery has fostered more intimate relationships with clients than is typical of those between medical doctors and their patients. Midwives provide advice to families and not just about matters of health but also with regard to things like breastfeeding and emotional and spiritual support postbirth. Midwife-client consultations often take place in homes, or in homelike settings, and can sometimes last an hour or longer, which affords midwives an opportunity to be more thorough and holistic in the care they provide. Moreover, in the context of Madagascar, because of their special intimacy with ancestral spirits, renin-jaza pay attention to causes and treatments that might be overlooked by their more biomedically oriented peers. As mediums of ancestral power, they deliver mothers of some of the spiritual, in addition to the material, weightiness of their pregnancies. They do so by shouldering some of the knowledge pregnant women must acquire with regard to food taboos, birthing customs, and postpartum practices and by creating a space where women can attend to both matters of safety and spirituality in the birthing process.

Bernadette evidenced this kind of wisdom and spiritual attentiveness in her work. She spoke confidently yet cautiously about her practice, as if guarding what she deemed a sacred knowledge. She showed us what she does to help premature babies grow strong, an ethnographic observation I describe at the opening of this book, whereby Bernadette used ancestral coins and clay medicines (fameno) to envelop blessings around the bodies of the newly born. In Madagascar, ritual medicines (aody) contain a power that pharmaceutical medicines do not. Thus, ritual medicines can complement pharmaceutical medicines by invoking ancestral blessings on the sick, the dying, or the newly born and thus materialize a prayer for their survival. The transfer of sacred power (hasina) on them through the materials of fresh water, sacred clays, coins, and protective charms is prevalent throughout Madagascar and representative of the pervasive belief in the reciprocity of the ancestor-human relationship, whereby Malagasy viscerally care for and remember their ancestors in the hopes that their ancestors might in turn bless them with gifts of fertile land and wombs.[45]

Bernadette's modest housing where such esteemed spiritual practices take place is characteristic of most such spiritual specialists in Madagascar, whose wealth, or lack thereof, is carefully guarded in ways that speak to a spirit of servitude that healers are encouraged to exhibit. In the den in which we sat, Bernadette had very little furniture, save a few handwoven sitting mats (lamaka), some wooden stools, and mattresses and sheets leaning against the walls, which she used for clients' exams and, when necessary, as a birthing space. On most of our visits, Bernadette's toddler granddaughter ran around her dirt courtyard, wearing tattered clothes as she happily played outside sporting the same closely shaven hairstyle as Bernadette.

Bernadette's work falls within the domain of domestic ancestral observances, but Bernadette serves the public as well. As one charged with helping her clients mediate their relationship to their ancestors, she is all too aware of the kinds of political and authoritarian gazes that threaten to undermine her legitimacy. She is aware of her government's efforts to medicalize childbirth more thoroughly and knows she and other renin-jaza will not likely be involved in that transition.[46] Thus, the guarded nature with which Bernadette talks about her work can be attributed to many things—the inherently private nature of her work, the current move on the part of the government to eliminate traditional midwives, and the collective memory northerners have of the imperialistic policing of their customs by Merina and French incursions.[47]

Speaking to some of these issues, Bernadette wanted me to understand that she at times knew more than her medically trained peers and reminded me that the staff at the medical dispensary in Joffreville often consulted her and not the other way around. She also said that the sage-femme trusts her and that they sometimes work together, but implied that a kind of tension exists as well that further illuminated the different kinds of reputations that traditional and medical midwives have and the ways in which these reputations impact both their work and their ability to serve mothers who seek their care. At the close of one of my interviews with Bernadette, I asked if she had any questions for me. She asked if I could bring her some medical supplies, some materials for birthing. She wanted some things from "the United States government" to help her with births. She said the US government gives boxes of gloves and medicines to the midwives who work in the medical dispensaries and provincial teaching hospitals but not to her. "I too have need of these things," she pleaded. I explained to Bernadette that I had no control over how or to whom the United States government distributed aid to midwives in Madagascar but offered to have my father-in-law, a physician's assistant, bring her a fetoscope when he and his family came to visit my husband and me in Madagascar. Bernadette was pleased with this gift.

While it was not at first clear to me why Bernadette wanted gloves and other medical equipment from me, a person with virtually no medical expertise, I came to more fully understand what I represented to her as a vazaha. To Bernadette, I seemed like a person with ready access to resources. I was also associated with a very particular style of medicine from which she wanted to borrow and from which she understood her clients to be in need. And last, owning and using medical materials that came from the United States, rather than from her own home country, could increase her status in the eyes of her clients and the other medical professionals with whom she competed and collaborated. Harry West came to similar conclusions with regard to the request for razors he received from a healer in northern Mozambique. He wrote, "In time, however, it became apparent to me that Kipande wanted 'better-quality' razor blades than could be found in the local market. Such quality 'instruments' would set him apart from his *vakulaula* competitors. Similarly, latex gloves constituted a component of a more official 'uniform' that would enhance Kipande's credibility with potential clients."[48] Medical aid from wealthier countries to relatively more impoverished ones introduces materials and techniques that are creatively appropriated by medically and traditionally trained specialists alike, and not solely in the ways that donor countries and organizations intend. Practitioners use medical materials as part of the creative borrowing that comes with marketing oneself in an environment of simultaneous medical pluralism and scarcity. Of course, Bernadette would not necessarily have wished any kind of technical training to replace her spiritual ordination into the practice of midwifery, but she was nevertheless unopposed to medical technologies or more medical training and to the kinds of modern clinical materials that would give her work more legitimacy and clout.

As a white American, I became entangled in Malagasy perceptions about American wealth and foreign aid, regardless of my lack of relationship to the medical community, while spending time in doctors' offices, in sages-femmes' clinics, and in the living rooms of parents, grandparents, and midwives like Bernadette. I represented a particular image of healthcare to most Malagasy.

Because of this, Bernadette likely narrated her story to me in a distinct way. She wove into her narrative seeds of legitimacy, mentioning that one of the doctors in Joffreville brings his son to her for traditional medicines. Perhaps she assumed that as a white American I would be impressed by such a statement, or perhaps she simply wanted me to know the extent to which she was respected by a diverse clientele within her community.

Bernadette placed on proud display her knowledge of childbirth, herbal medicines, and certain traditional practices, like the use of fameno on premature babies, but also claimed to know nothing of other practices, such as the black cotton fabric tied around one of her clients' wrists. "It was probably given to the baby by a *moasy*," she declared, thereby positioning herself as distinct from other spiritual experts like moasy, who specialize in Islamic divination practices and ritual medicines. Traditional religious specialists share many common characteristics, but they also have particular areas of expertise and market themselves differently, borrowing from some practices, distancing themselves from others, and always presenting themselves in a light palatable to the persuasion of the person seeking their care.[49]

I had a limited window into Bernadette's life and work as a midwife, but even a partial view afforded me insight into just how integral midwives are to the process of guiding women and babies across the sacred threshold of childbirth. Midwives are instrumental in helping women navigate ancestral commitments like pregnancy fady, access the kinds of spiritual and emotional resources needed to endure the pains of childbirth, and engage in the kinds of rituals postpartum that will ensure ancestral blessings. Bernadette understands her work to be a calling, a gift bestowed on her by her ancestors, which meant that instead of charging her clients, she served them, receiving gifts of payment over time and trusting that they would support her when she needed it.

Moreover, midwives do all of this in the context of a reciprocal relationship that ensures that both parties are indebted to one another and thus held in the safety of an ongoing relationship. This kind of indebtedness and reciprocity is not just customary, as I have already articulated; it is also critical to children's survival, for it enables mothers to build spiritual and social safety nets that enable them to meet their children's needs in moments of insecurity. Bernadette was extremely knowledgeable and experienced—regarding the physiological and the spiritual aspects of birth—and had an excellent rapport with her clients, but she also sometimes struggled to find legitimacy in a country that is moving further toward a medicalized model of childbirth. However, it was also clear to me from our conversations, and from conversations with countless others, that her holistic and spiritually attentive model of midwifery support is not likely to fall fully out of favor any time soon. Mothers, like Françoise, whose story is told in the following section, were as committed as midwives to maintaining this model of spiritually attentive care.

Françoise

I met Françoise during one of my many walks from the neighborhood in which I lived to Diégo Suarez's main street, where one finds the specialty shops, restaurants, the shipyard, and the city's largest outdoor food market (*bazaar kely*). Françoise is a grandmother, though it should be noted that many grandmothers in Madagascar are in their forties and fifties and some are still having children even as their eldest children are providing them with their first grandchildren. Françoise was born in 1965 and was forty-six when I first interviewed her. Of all the women I interviewed, she was among the few who wholeheartedly insisted on the superiority of renin-jaza. She was concerned not only that children survived their births but also about the disappearance of traditions, or what she described as "Malagasy ways of doing things," which she deemed an important strategy for keeping children alive.

Françoise sat crouched in the doorway that led from her room into the courtyard when my research assistant Édith and I arrived to interview her.[50] Some of her children were with her, including one daughter who was twenty-nine. Françoise's daughter very much resembled her and sat quietly listening to her mother as we spoke. Françoise was making a ramen-style noodle soup on a charcoal cooker and feeding a little girl some bread dipped in concentrated milk. My research assistant Édith and I sat on a woven mat beside her. It was hot, and I covered my head with a long-sleeved shirt I had brought for that purpose. I started the conversation slowly, but soon Françoise began talking to me about many matters.

She told me that if I really wanted to know about *fomba fiterana* (birthing customs), I should go out to Ambobatany, which is sixteen kilometers from Ambilobe in northern Madagascar. "You can take a taxi-brousse," she explained. There were two renin-jaza who lived there, both of whom were in their sixties and whose names were Henriette and Marovavy. Françoise explained that neither of the midwives "needed injections" (*tsy mila piqure*).[51]

For Françoise, it was not a question of these renin-jaza not using injections as much as it was a statement that they, unlike the hospital-trained sages-femmes, do not have to rely on pharmaceutical drugs in order to help women deliver babies safely.

Attributing the source of these traditional renin-jaza's power to spirits, as opposed to synthetic drugs, Françoise clarified, "It's like there's something on them [*kara misy raha abony izy*]. It's like they have someone with them [*kara misy olo miaraka izy*]." Françoise gave birth to nine children in all. She had all of them in a hospital except for one, a girl who was one of her youngest but not the last to be born. Of the nine children, one died, though she did not say how, and I did not feel it appropriate to ask. "The girl, born at home, was the easiest birth," she declared. She described the other births as hard and complained that the medical staff gave her a lot of injections. But with the girl born at home, it was easy and fast, which Françoise attributed to the baby having been born at home with the help of a traditional midwife who appeared to be working with a spirit. She explained, "When my labor began, I called the renin-jaza (midwife). During the birth, the renin-jaza asked for her own grandmother's help. She laid her hands upon my stomach and called upon her grandmother saying, 'Eh mama, help me help to birth this person. Do not leave me without your blessings' [*Eh reniko, anao magnampy za hampi-teraka olo. Aza alagna Baraka*]. You could see that the renin-jaza was with her grandmother's spirit. You could see that she was possessed by something [*nisabohandroha*]." Françoise seemed to appreciate her midwife's spiritual inclinations, her acknowledgment of, and reliance on, the spirit of her grandmother, who was still granting her wisdom and blessings. This, she explained, is partly why people like her prefer renin-jaza and also why Malagasy as a whole continue to rely on traditional specialists even if they also consult with other kinds of specialists.

"They are starting to go back to *fombagasy* [Malagasy customs] for a lot of reasons," she explained. First, many women believe the renin-jaza are more knowledgeable. "If you talk to the renin-jaza in Ambilobe," Françoise commented, pointing to the notebook I was writing in, "you will fill a whole copy book." "I don't know much compared to them," she insisted. Françoise added that there are a lot of good birthing customs and the women who take you to the hospital do not always know these customs. "I went to the hospital with my aunt, and she used cold water to bathe me while I was in labor, and I was in labor for three days!" Françoise exclaimed. "My aunt did not know that warm water on the front and back of the mother is what helps the baby come out.[52] Once we tried warm water, the baby came out almost immediately."

Françoise's sentiment that renin-jaza possess a knowledge that doctors and sages-femmes are ill-equipped to provide resonated with other women I spoke with as well. That said, despite her praise of traditional midwifery, Françoise gave birth to only one of her nine children at home, which suggests that one's preferences is not always the greatest determining factor in one's birthing decisions. The majority of the women I interviewed gave birth under the care of midwives, but few insisted on the superiority of traditional midwives as opposed to medically trained midwives as fiercely as did Françoise. Many of the women I interviewed gave birth with retired nurse-midwives in their homes. And almost everyone with whom I spoke had consulted with multiple caregivers and specialists, piecing together the creative confluences of care that would best ensure their children's surviving and thriving. Some preferred to consult with midwives only during their pregnancy, relegating the actual birth to medically trained hospital staff. Alternatively, others decided to give birth with a traditional midwife while receiving prenatal care and postnatal checkups from government clinics.

Some preferred to see midwives for spiritual advice alone, and doctors for illnesses that appeared to have no spiritual causation. As becomes clear in women's stories in the chapters following this one, sometimes what might look to an outsider like an ideological preference is more a matter of mothers navigating the multiple social and economic factors influencing their decisions, including cultural customs, family traditions and obligations, financial considerations, and a lack of good options. As for women the world over, the childbirth decisions that Malagasy women make are layered and complex and intricately interwoven with personal beliefs, politics, and racial and economic circumstances. Investing in multiple options increases the chance that children will have the social, medical, and spiritual resources they need to acquire bones. The medicines, blessings, and rituals not only keep them safe but also confer on them particular identities that grant belonging and social status critical to babies' abilities to settle within their social milieu.

The New Hospital

Most of the women and men I interviewed for this book struggled to access the resources they needed to navigate pregnancy, childbirth, or the transition to parenthood. More often, for biological and social reasons, women bore the bulk of these challenges. As is true for women everywhere, the spear battle that is childbirth extends long before and after the momentous event of a baby's emergence from their mother's womb. And as becomes clear in the chapters that follow this one, among the women I interviewed in northwestern Madagascar, some women's struggles stemmed from the fact that they became pregnant long before they were ready. These women, who had become pregnant unexpectedly and decided to carry their pregnancies to term, had wrestled with both the joys of motherhood and a kind of sadness for the ways in which the birth had cut short their plans, most of which were educational in nature.

And still for other young women, their pregnancies came as a surprise but in ways they later interpreted as fortuitous. The women I interviewed experienced many obstacles—infertility, miscarriages, abortions, unintended pregnancies, financial and social insecurities, and so on. One woman, a longtime friend of mine, gave birth to a healthy baby boy only later to discover that he would need two surgeries, one for a hernia and another for a congenital heart condition, the latter of which could not be performed in Madagascar. She was forced to wean him before he was a year old so that he could be flown for the surgery to France, where he stayed with a French host family. Her family managed to come up with the expenses for his flight to France, but they did not have enough money to accompany him on his medical stay in France. Thus, she made the difficult decision to send her infant son away for two months knowing it to be his best chance at leading a long and healthy life. Another friend often complained that her cesarean surgery still caused her pain several years after her child's birth and feared having another child because "her uterus may have been damaged by the surgery."

Moreover, as Alicia's and Bernadette's stories convey, Diégo's healthcare workers also faced many obstacles in their efforts to provide medical and spiritual resources to meet the whole of their clients' needs around the welcoming of a new child. Not every midwife struggled to access running water and electricity as frequently as did Alicia, but given that power outages were frequent throughout the city and that not all medical facilities were equipped with generators, it is safe to say that all of Diégo's midwives and doctors worked under less than ideal conditions. And their work is made even more complicated by the fact that not all were sufficiently compensated. That said, most were highly knowledgeable and highly considerate of the various medical and cultural needs of their clients and worked tire-lessly to provide the kinds of holistic care that women in their communities needed.

In some ways, women in Madagascar encounter the kinds of struggles that women all around the world encounter during pregnancy. Many experi-ence their pregnancies as normal life events, but when complications arose, even the kinds of complications that are typical for women everywhere, the severity is heightened in places like Madagascar where women are living in poverty and there is insufficient healthcare infrastructure. Unfortunately, not all women perceived their situations of poverty to be improving, either for themselves or for their children. One older woman, Hélène, lamented, "Childbirth is more difficult for my daughter than it was for me. Things are different for my daughter. It's not like it was for me," she explained. "My daughter is a bit faint [torana] because she works all day in a factory. She sews from seven in the morning to ten at night. They make European clothing," Hélène remarked.[53] She went on to explain that under those kinds of condi-tions, "the baby does not get to move around as much because of her work. And then the baby cannot get into the right position before it comes out." For Hélène, her daughter's poverty and the long hours and conditions under which she works in a clothing factory have had a direct impact on her overall health and pregnancy outcomes.

That said, and as I have already intimated, not all of women's struggles dur-ing pregnancy and childbirth are medical, nor are they all related to poverty. One woman I interviewed, and whose story is highlighted at the end of the book, found it nearly impossible to merge her family's customs with those of the baby's father's family, because the two families had a hard time compro-mising on the traditions that were important to each of them. Though babies are meant to join families together, they can sometimes create an impassible divide between parents, underscoring disagreements, cultural differences, and social inequities. Some women experienced ancestral fady as burden-some, others as a more neutral matter or fact of obligation required of them during pregnancy. Still others embraced pregnancy-related prohibitions as an important part of their identities. As becomes clear in the stories in this book, the birth and postpartum rituals mothers performed (or did not per-form) carried many meanings for them and their families. The decisions that mothers made to keep their children healthy as well as spiritually supported were neither easy nor clear, given people's sometimes multiple religious and familial affiliations. Many mothers nevertheless found joy, and sometimes a sense of newfound belonging, in observing them.

Fortunately for residents of Diégo Suarez, approximately seven months after I completed research for this book, the "new" hospital, named Centre Hospitalier Universitaire Tanambao I Antsiranana, or Hopitaly Manarapeni-tra, of which my students at the University of Antsiranana had spoken about, opened its doors.[54] Yet the fact that the hospital, the project of then president Andry Rajoelina, might have met another fate was not just a baseless concern. Tangible evidence of abandoned projects decorated the city of Diégo Suarez then and now. To the southwest of Diégo Suarez, a $22 million hospital proj-ect in Menabe that was first initiated by Rajoelina's predecessor, Marc Rav-alomanana—though not continued under either of his successors—remains abandoned. In 2016, one journalist described,

> Inside the glass-fronted reception of the state-of-the-art hospital are rows of upholstered chairs. Not one has yet been sat on. Also unused are the x-ray area, surgical unit, dentistry and child health units, and an array of medical equipment.
>
> The hospital was almost complete, with just the morgue unfinished, when work suddenly stopped in 2012. A large metal fence was erected around the perimeter and a security guard installed to keep the public out.[55]

Thus, fears back in 2011 that the new hospital in Diégo might not be completed were well founded, even if the project did not meet that fate. It remains to be seen how adequately staffed the new hospital will be or if it will one day fall into disrepair much like the hospital it was meant to replace. When I returned to Madagascar in the spring of 2024, the building appeared kept up and in good use, but informants shared with me that the new hospital was not as well resourced as they had hoped it would be and that some of the more experi-enced medical personnel chose to remain at the older Hôpital Be.

During both the colonial period and later, during the late twentieth cen-tury and early twenty-first century, Malagasy have endured considerable po-litical instability. This political instability has been caused by corruption and a switch to a neoliberal economy that has bankrupted the island nation of its healthcare and education funding. As a result, projects initiated by presiden-tial administrations are not always guaranteed. Sometimes hospital projects like the one in Diégo Suarez bring much-needed infrastructure and resources,

Scenes of Diégo Suarez in 2011/2012. *Photos by author.*

Scenes of Diégo Suarez in 2011/2012. *Photos by author. (continued)*

and sometimes they *are* mere publicity stunts or at least not prioritized or finished by later administrations. Hopitaly Manarapenitra offers Malagasy women a newer, more resourced venue for bringing their children into the world, but many are still experiencing reproductive insecurities.[56] Colonial medicine, neoliberalism, and ongoing political corruption cast a shadow on Malagasy mothers' ability to bring their children into the world in safe and meaningful ways, underscoring the notion that childbirth is women's spear battle in more ways than one. The stories of mothers trying to access these resources, told in the next chapter, reveal that the resiliency of Malagasy families, and of mothers in particular, are often one step ahead of these shadows.

Scenes of Diégo Suarez in 2011/2012. *Photos by author. (continued)*

TWO

MOTHERHOOD AND CREATIVE
CONFLUENCES OF CARE

As the previous chapter makes clear, midwives and other kinds of medical and religious specialists do a lot of vocational border crossing in order to meet the diverse, complex needs of their clients, especially in contexts like Diégo, where cultural and religious diversity is the norm and where the medical infrastructure is wanting. Parents, and mothers in particular, must cross borders as well, dipping into a variety of spiritual- and health-based therapies in order to meet the whole of their children's needs. In an environment of poverty, where healthcare resources are scarce, parents are desperate to try any and all means necessary to ensure that they and their children are well incorporated into the kinds of social and spiritual communities that enable them to flourish.[1]

In 2011, in the city of Diégo Suarez, there were many infrastructural obstacles in the way of women's ability to give birth to their children in safe, medically supportive settings. That said, as chapter 1 lays out, birth is not merely, or even mainly, a medical event. Birth is biological, cultural, and, for many, a sacred spiritual journey that invites reflection on family traditions and legacies, on motherhood, and on one's place and purpose in the world. Thus, in the midst of the medical and infrastructural changes and insufficiencies women faced, or perhaps because of them, families in Diégo Suarez have created many rituals around birth that both speak to and enhance the sense that childbirth is an experience of rich spiritual meaning and a ripe opportunity to contemplate both the religious and ancestral identities vital to children's inclusion into the kinds of communities critical to their well-being.

68

This chapter demonstrates that the process of instilling bones in the newly born, of granting them their stronghold in this world, requires pulling together creative confluences of care. Much of this work is about belonging—about immersing children in the kinds of rituals that bless and protect and also mark them with the kinds of identities that grant inclusion within and across multiple different kinds of communities. By strengthening children's belonging within particular religious and ancestral communities, parents, in turn, strengthen and reinforce their own belonging within these same communities, ensuring they have the social, financial, cultural, and medical resources they need to raise children through the fragility of their early years. Sometimes, as the first story reveals, engaging in postpartum rituals can be a chance for mothers to reexamine their own commitments and belongings and to create new networks of critical support. For others, engaging in postpartum rituals enables mothers to continue, perpetuate, and deepen the kinds of belongings that sustained their ancestors and will continue to sustain and bless the newest generation.

Moreover, what the following stories demonstrate is that people's decisions to perform, or not perform, various ancestral and religious ceremonies have less to do with strongly held beliefs about their efficacy and more to do with negotiating commitments and strengthening relationships. For example, the choice to avoid ancestrally inherited taboo foods during pregnancy, or any kind of activity that honors one's ancestors for that matter, enables mothers to act out the kinds of kin-based obligations that ensure that others are in turn obligated to them and invested in their children's futures. While many of these efforts to bless, protect, and integrate children into relationships of reciprocity are fruitful, it is also true that occasionally, some of these efforts fail, despite mothers' best efforts, emphasizing why the stakes are so high. Nasreen, a young mother and university student in her twenties, shared how her own journey of motherhood invited reflection, a reexamination of her purpose, and a recommitment to the communities to which she belongs.

Nasreen

"I was not lucky enough to have a father," began Nasreen as she shared her story of motherhood with me.[2] She went on to say,

> OK, he exists but he lives very far away. My mother had me when she
> was still in school. My parents decided to continue their studies, so they

eventually separated, and my father left for Yemen when I was still small.
He lives in Saudi Arabia now. And then my mother left for Russia and left
me with my grandmother. I was raised by my grandmother. So, I had a lot
of difficulties. It was a very difficult experience. Then when I was ten years
old, my mother returned and took me, and she remarried someone else.
My stepfather loved his children but wasn't able to love us. Thus, that was
an equally difficult experience for me. I had a lot of problems with affection growing up. My mother is Malagasy. She was born here, but my father
is mixed. He is Arab and Malagasy, which is why he returned to Yemen.
Perhaps he may be remorseful about what happened, perhaps, but there's
no way of knowing.

As the child of a union between a Malagasy mother and an Arab Malagasy
father who returned to Yemen shortly after she was born, Nasreen did not
receive the affection and stability she felt she needed as a child. At best, her
experience of childhood was lonely; at worst, these early years were traumatic as she felt abandoned and unloved by her father, mother, and, later,
stepfather. But, as someone who felt abandoned by both parents, especially
by a father who remained lost to her by an impassable oceanic distance,
Nasreen was nevertheless able to build a meaningful network of spiritual
and social support for herself and her children. Falling in love and becoming
a mother, despite its challenges, opened a doorway into a newfound interest in, and engagement with, the religion of her childhood. This engagement with religion, especially through the rituals that marked her children
as Muslims, enabled Nasreen to experience, by virtue of them, a sense of
belonging critical to her healing. Nasreen's story, alongside other stories
told in this book, demonstrates the creative ways parents, and mothers in
particular, engage with religious and ancestral customs in order to secure
for themselves and their children the social and spiritual resources they
need to thrive.

In addition to her story of parental abandonment, Nasreen also narrated to
me other aspects of her life story, including the early years of navigating her
relationship with her now husband and their experience of becoming parents
while they were still in school.

When I was in my second-to-last year of high school, I met my husband.
And right away . . . well, we were friends for one year, but after that, we fell
in love. I was nineteen when I fell in love, and until today, we have never
separated. He has fulfilled everything in my life, especially everything

that happened with my father. I was really lucky to have met him. We had our first child in our second-to-last year of high school. I had a difficult pregnancy, so I decided to abandon my studies temporarily with the intention of returning to school right afterward. But as soon as I returned, I got pregnant with my second child. I was embarrassed about this and didn't go back right away, but my teacher encouraged and even insisted that I return and so I did. So, after four years of not going to school, I returned. And then I met my friends and that's that. That's how I had my children successively like that.

The early years of Nasreen's relationship with her boyfriend were hard, especially given that they became parents while still in school, but she remembers fondly the love they shared, the sense of trust and attachment that characterized their relationship, and the encouragement she received from her teachers to continue her schooling.

Her faith in Allah, though wavering through the years, is also something she remembered as significant.

My faith in God is really important to me because it has helped me to surmount so many problems. Without God I wouldn't have had the chance to do anything in my life. So, I took God as my parent. I talked to God by myself. And as I got older and grew deeper in my faith, I started to wonder why I believed in the God that I imagined and started to ask questions. Then I did some research on Islam, and I was convinced that it was the best religion for me.

During high school, I was sent to study in Ambanja for a year because my mother didn't like it that I was in a relationship with another boy, my now husband. I was not very devoted to Islam at the time. I was not deep in my faith as I am now. So, my mother sent me to Ambanja to keep me from my boyfriend and to encourage me to return to my faith. But I refused to end the relationship. Later my husband, who was Christian at the time, decided to adopt the Muslim faith. He liked Islam. He liked that there were intergenerational relationships within the community.

Though the relationship Nasreen had with her mother felt strained, by contrast she remembers her relationship with her boyfriend as more sincere. His willingness to adopt the Muslim faith even helped facilitate for her a return to Islam, which provided her with great consolation as she learned to take God as her parent. And as would become clear to me, in subsequent interviews and in the further unfolding of her story, having children enabled her to deepen her commitment to Islam, as integrating her children into Islam added layers of belonging both for her and for them.

Nasreen's choice of names for her children as well as her choice to observe haircutting ceremonies and a style of postpartum bathing called ranginaly enabled her to set her children on a path toward virtuousness; mark them as ranginaly, or as members of a particular descent group; and anchor them, and she and her husband, within the *ummah* (Muslim community). She described,

> The Prophet instructed us to choose the best names for our children, to never reference anything harmful, but to choose the best. You can choose the name of a virtuous person like Ibrahim for example. [*She patted her son Ibrahim on the head as she spoke.*] And when the child is born, the father must speak the call to prayer in the child's ear because the child's mission on earth is to obey God, and so it's the first thing the baby should hear when he is born.
>
> In Islam when the baby is born, after seven days if you have the means, you must have a ceremony. If it is a girl, you have to kill a goat, and if it is a boy, you have to kill two goats or sheep. It's a ceremony the Prophet used to protect children from all sorts of diseases. Because children do lots of things that could make them sick and that ceremony protects them. During that ceremony, you cut the baby's hair. Everything happens on that day. And you also give to the poor a gram of gold. For example, if the baby's hair weighs a gram, you give a gram of gold. The ceremony is especially important for poor people. I mean, you should especially share the meal with poor people. We call it *aqiqa*. If you can't do it seven days after the birth, you can do it after twenty-one days or another time related to seven. I did this with all of my children.
>
> I also did ranginaly [cold-water postpartum bathing]. I took cold baths every day. And then, after one week, I bathed with hot water and I used *ravintsôha* (lemon leaves). For this, you can bathe with either rômba (basil leaves) or ravintsôha.³ My religious community helped me with this. They gave me the bath, because it's too hot! You can't do it yourself. You have to have someone do it for you. And sometimes you even cry when they do it because it's simply too hot. And according to Malagasy customs, all women must do this (bathe with basil leaves or lemon leaves). If you don't, you won't heal. That's what we say, but I've never met someone who hasn't done it. Usually, it takes forty days to heal. That's how long it takes in Islam, but for the Comorians or the Arabs, it's just two weeks or maybe even one week and you can be healed. I really like to learn about the

culture of others, how they heal, because for them they heal very quickly. I'm not sure how they are capable of this.

Nasreen's story bears witness to the struggles she faced as a child but also to the creative resilience she exhibited as a mother, engaging with both ancestral (e.g., ranginaly) and religious rituals that marked her children in particular ways and granted them the kind of belonging she felt had been missing from her own childhood.

Nasreen's story is very much one of triumph, but her entrance into motherhood was not without its struggles. As she described,

> When I went into labor with my first baby, it was very difficult; he wouldn't come out. We had to force him out and when he came out, he was already blue. But the midwife brought him back to life. He was almost dead. He was too blue because for one hour he was in the birth canal, so it was too long that he was in there. But eventually he came out. I was a bit discouraged afterward because the birth had been so difficult. But then I had my baby, and it was fine. Right now, he is a little slow. He's not very slow, but he has trouble understanding things quickly. He's got a lot of strength and energy though. He's robust but also a little fragile.

Despite the stress of becoming a parent at such a young age and the medical struggles Nasreen faced giving birth to her firstborn, motherhood nevertheless offered her the chance to reexamine her faith and her relationships. Given the fragility of her relationship with her mother, Nasreen chose to invest instead in her relationship with her husband, in the larger community of Islam, and in the larger collective of those who observe the ancestrally inherited practice of ranginaly. She did so by punctuating her birth experiences with moments of dignity, with rituals that granted her, by virtue of her children, a deepened sense of purpose and inclusion. In the first moments of her children's emergence from her womb, for example, she instructed her newly converted husband to whisper the call to prayer in their newborn babies' ears, orienting them to the worship of Allah. She also chose names for them that she hoped would enable them to carry forward the good character of the prophets within Islam. She performed ranginaly, an ancestrally inherited postpartum bathing ritual that links her (and now her children as well) with their ascendants. And she performed haircutting ceremonies for them, marking them as wanted and blessed, immersing them in the Arab Malagasy traditions (culinary and religious) that lend their lives meaning.

Though abandoned by her parents, left alone for many years on the land mass that drew her parents together for only a brief foray of love, Nasreen used the religion of both her father and mother and ancestral customs of her mother to craft a sense of self and place in the world. Nasreen's ancestries are multiple and ocean spanning, but she has nevertheless managed to pull from the various streams of influence something particular, something bone filled and coherent for her children, through these rituals of initiation performed for them and for herself. In this way, Nasreen's sense of self as a Malagasy Arab is not dissimilar to what Ananda Devi described of her own hybridized identity as a Mauritian belonging to multiple worlds and also striving to "extract something new and authentic" from the relationships and experiences that come together in her.[4]

Several months after my initial interview with Nasreen, I returned to her house to bring her a gift and some pictures. When I arrived, she was wearing a beautiful blue dress and headscarf (hijab). Her children ran around the dirt courtyard in front of her house. They were eating candy that Nasreen's husband had brought back from a recent trip to Paris for a tourism conference he attended earlier in the month. In the pavilion area where we conversed, there was a chalkboard with the Arabic alphabet on it that Nasreen explained was from an Arabic lesson her husband was teaching their children. Then Nasreen promptly placed her hand on her belly and excitedly shared the news that she was expecting another baby in July, which she explained would work well for her school schedule at the university. At that point in her life, Nasreen had reached a sense of peace about who she was. For her, the entrance into motherhood was not just a physiological stage, though it certainly was that as well; rather, it was primarily a chance to reconsider her worth and her place within her family and community as well as an opportunity to draw from the multiple streams of religious and ancestral influences in her life to instill in her children a similar sense of assurance about their place within their family and community.

Céline and Roland

Céline's and Roland's stories are different from Nasreen's in that neither spoke of overcoming a painful childhood. Both grew up in families where they were loved and supported. Moreover, that familial support continued as they navigated their own transition to parenthood. Thus, while their motivations for doing so were different from Nasreen's, they, too, engaged with ancestral and religious customs upon the birth of their son, that he might be protected, blessed, and granted inclusion into the communities—religious and ancestral—that enabled their flourishing and will similarly enable his. In other words, for these young parents, immersing their son in the traditions of their respective families was not about granting him a belonging for which they had not been privy; it was about continuing and updating a set of trusted practices that had sustained their families for many generations.

I met Céline and Roland through one of my research assistants. Both were born in Diégo, though Roland's family was newer to the city than Céline's. They met one another at a postsecondary school graduation party. Roland described, "I was in my first year and Céline was ahead of me, but I didn't know that when I first met her. We met when we went to Boom, a dance held at the Hôtel de la Poste for students who completed 'le bac' [secondary degree]. I went to the party early because I thought my friends would already be there, but they weren't there and then I saw this beautiful girl. And that's how our relationship began. We've been together for eight years now." Of all the couples I interviewed, Céline and Roland were the most candid about their love for one another, exhibiting both a playfulness with one another and a genuine concern for each other in ways that made them particularly endearing.

When Céline became pregnant, it came as no surprise, for the couple had already been together and felt ready for such an event. As Roland described,

> I was not astonished [tsy manaitry] when Céline became pregnant because we were already together and ready to have a baby. If two people are together as a couple, then they should be ready for a child. I remember that I could not believe it when she told me, but I was happy. And from then on, I realized that I had to work hard because I did not yet have a fixed job. When a woman is pregnant, the man has a strange strength to work hard in order to have everything that the baby needs. Even if I am skinny, I still work hard, and sometimes I am sick or I feel pain, but I still work hard.

Despite the initial excitement, the transition to parenthood was difficult as Roland had to work longer hours in order for them to have enough money to eat and pay their rent, leaving Céline feeling lonely.

Céline remembered the pregnancy fondly but also remembered it as a time of hardship, as they struggled to acquire the resources they needed to enter this next phase of their lives.

CÈLINE: Really our lives changed even before the baby because we had started to prepare. Roland started working more, and I began to take care of myself during the pregnancy. I didn't follow very many fady when I was pregnant, nothing complicated. I followed the fady of not eating *sabeda*, *sakay tany*, and *bengy* [sweet rice porridge, ginger, and goat meat]. These are the only things that are fady for me.

ROLAND: Céline said she didn't need special food when she was pregnant, but that is not true. She liked sour cherries. She loved sour foods [*matsiko*] too much! When she was pregnant, she was brave [*mahasaky*]. She wasn't afraid to climb trees to get fruit. And the cherry tree is very soft; it is easy to cuwt up. I did not know its limbs could support a pregnant woman!

CÈLINE: When Roland was gone, I was always looking for him. I preferred him to stay with me, but he had to work in the countryside often and sometimes we argued because of it. But if he didn't go to work, we wouldn't have had anything to eat, so I talked to everyone while he was away—older people to keep from being bored and even little children.
I also spent a lot of time talking to Giovanni [the baby in her womb]. I think it's habit for all women to talk to their children. I spent a lot of time with him, even when he was in my stomach. I read books to him, and I talked to him a lot, especially at the end of my pregnancy, when I was in bed, because I could not go out of the house due to the problems I was having. I just caressed my stomach. And then Roland would come home at 7:30 or sometimes 8:00, and I would talk to him. Sometimes it was very hard. It is difficult to carry a baby, give birth, and raise him.

The couple's recounting of their pregnancy journey was charming as they took turns sharing details and occasionally finishing each other's sentences, but their story also evidenced the kinds of economic difficulties many young couples in Diégo face. Time and time again I was told by young people, even if you have a college degree, there are simply not enough jobs. Céline and Roland were slightly better off, as both of their parents lived nearby and offered support when they could. Still, the pregnancy required a resourcefulness from each of them that up until then they had not had to cultivate.

When it came to talking about their son's birth, Céline struggled. She had experienced complications toward the end of her pregnancy and was still visibly shaken by the experience, her lips quivering as she shared,

I had a cesarean section. Is it OK to talk about that? It was very difficult to carry the baby [*mitondra kibo*]. At seven months, the baby turned down and tried to come out, and it felt really painful [*tegna narary*]. I had to go to the hospital. They said the baby was not in a good position because I had a uterine cyst [*fibrome*]. They said the baby was coming out, but he didn't come all the way out. And then the doctor told me I needed to stay in bed until nine months. I couldn't move. I couldn't do anything. I just had to stay in bed, and at that time, Roland was working away from home all day and well into the evening. So, it was very hard. I couldn't even sit on the floor. I just had to stay in bed. The doctor let me wait until after Christmas, and I had the baby on the twenty-eighth day of December. I didn't hemorrhage, and they did not have any trouble with the surgery. The cause of my pregnancy complications were all because of the uterine fibrome.

They did the surgery at Hôpital Be and the *sage-femmes élèves* [student midwives] were very happy because they were able to learn from my case because they had never seen a woman with a baby and a fibrome. Normally a woman who has a fibrome cannot have a baby because the fibrome can disturb the placenta and cause the baby to die, but I was able to have a baby and the baby came out with no problems, no fever, and the weight of the baby was normal. The doctor said the baby was a precious baby because it was a special case.

Céline and Roland were lucky, for even though they struggled financially during the pregnancy, relatively speaking, they were still well resourced compared to most. They lived in their own home (which they rented) and had family nearby. Both also had completed high school, which meant that they were able to afford the medical care Céline needed and received toward the end of their pregnancy. It's not clear what would have happened had they not been able to receive this care or had the doctor they needed not been available at the time of the birth. What is clear is that many in Diégo struggle to both access and afford the medical technologies they need to ensure the safe delivery of their children.

For Céline and Roland, parenthood presented struggles they had not anticipated but were nevertheless able to overcome. As Roland described, Céline's pregnancy inspired a kind of strength in him to work hard so his wife and family would have enough money to eat, to afford rent, and to have access to medical care for the baby. Céline had a difficult pregnancy and felt lonely for much of the nine months, but the outcome of the pregnancy was a beautiful child deemed a miracle for the difficulties the mother and baby pair endured. And Céline and Roland had the support of their parents both during the pregnancy and after their son, Giovanni, was born, something not all youth in Diégo have, given that some young people have to travel to the city alone in search of work or school and are then far from the support of their families. As Céline remembered,

> My mother and father were there and also Roland's mother and father. Everyone was there for the occasion. I was very spoiled because everyone was there, and everyone was taking care of me. I don't know if it will also be like that the next time. After he was born, I bathed with ravintsôha. And I am also ranginaly so I did cold-water bathing as well. After one week of me and the baby bathing this way,[5] we took him out [*mampiboaka tsaiky*] to see the sunrise and gave him a blessing. For women here in Madagascar, when we give birth, we must go back to our mother, especially for the first baby. And if we cannot go to them, we ask them to come to us. So, I stayed with my mother in Diégo after the birth, and it was she who taught me what to do.

Living in proximity to her mother, with whom she had a good relationship, enabled Céline to draw on her mother's wisdom and receive the transmitted knowledge her family wished to pass on to her. Some of the mothers in this book, whose stories are told in subsequent chapters, were living much farther from family and were unable to return home for birth. Thus, they relied on whoever was proximate to help them navigate childbirth and the postpartum blessings they imparted on their children, which offered different possibilities for belonging.

The rituals of care Céline and Roland used to bless, protect, and integrate Giovanni into their families included following certain fady, ancestrally inherited food restriction during the pregnancy; naming him after multiple personalities within the family; adorning him with protective amulets and bracelets to keep him safe from roaming spirits; observing ranginaly to link him to his ascendants; giving him a chicken leg, which is part of the haircutting ceremony observed by some Malagasy, to symbolically feed him particular attributes; and baptizing him as a Christian.

> ROLAND: We named him Giovanni. His maternal grandfather gave him the name Giovanni. His full name is Andrianasolo Marc Alexandre Giovanni. It's a little bit of a long name. Marc was a name we imagined.

M stands for Manitra, which is the family name of Céline. A is for Andrianasolo, which is my family name, R is for Roland, and C for Céline. Thus, he is the fruit of our love. That is why we also sometimes call him Marc.

When he was first born, we used a black bracelet called *vonjy* to protect him. But we eventually took if off because there are many Christians who come to pray in our house, and they told us it is not good to have something like that. They told us we just needed to believe in God. So, we took off the black bracelet and replaced it with a silver one.[6] People told us the silver one would help him to "grow up" [*mampitombo izy*]. The black bracelet was supposed to protect him from devils. [My research assistant Zafisoa, who is Muslim, interjected by saying that it's Muslims who wear black bracelets.] They need something. It is not good for a baby to go out at night even if you are just taking him out to go and get something to eat. It is dangerous for the baby, which is why we wanted to protect him. [My other research assistant Édith agreed adding that if you take the baby outside at night, the baby can get *arakaraka*.][7]

CÈLINE: Yes, our baby had arakaraka, and he was really sick and had to be hospitalized. When a baby gets arakaraka, there are things you can do in addition to going to the hospital. You can burn newspaper and put it in water and have the person who is sick drink it.[8] Or to prevent the arakaraka, when you are coming in the house, you can burn a piece of lamba [cloth] and encircle the smoke around the baby or put the piece of burned fabric under the bed. The smoke smells and will scare the spirits away.

ROLAND: When his teeth came in, we gave him *fen'akôho* (a chicken leg), but we did not have a special ceremony. Life is changing [*evolué*], and we're not the kind of people who complicate customs [*zahay tsy mankasa-rotra raha*] because a joro [speech-prayer, invocation, or ritualized bless-ing] needs many things [*satria joro mila raha maro*], and we do not know how to do all that. [Céline interjected that joro is normally transmitted from parents to children and that they had not been taught how to do it.] Yes, and we don't know how. We baptized him, but we did not have a big party for him as some parents do. But baptism is important because baptism for us Christians is like our *fahasoavana* [traditional blessing]. [Reacting to the use of the phrase "us Christians," Zafisoa interjected that she is Muslim though she was raised Christian.] I am sorry then for the way I said "us Christians" [replied Roland]. Well, we all pray to one God. For Christian culture [*fomba Chrétien*], baptism is a very good thing [*raha tsara*].

Céline and Roland borrowed from a multitude of religious and family-specific traditions to bless and welcome their son into their families and into the larger communities of which they were a part, receiving advice from friends, family, and neighbors—all of whom had different opinions about which blessings and protective materials were "of God" and which were not, which rituals were necessary, and which were superfluous. Through the naming of Giovanni, the observance of food taboos and ranginaly, and the blessing of baptism, Céline and Roland have marked Giovanni as a particular kind of descendant with a particular way of eating and bathing and a particular kind of religious identity, all of which give him bones—a coherent yet hybridized sense of identity that grows out of his parents' diverse relational encounters and experiences.

At the time of the interview, Céline and Roland rented a relatively comfortable house by most Malagasy standards, but they also lived in a country where even among the educated and those with jobs, "it is often difficult just to eat."[9] Their story was heartwarming for the love and support they demonstrated toward one another during the difficult but joyous event of bringing their first child into the world and for the discerning ways in which they created rituals of care around his birth. Their collective account of the ritual practices they engaged with around the birth of their son sheds light on the many relational influences that can feed into parents' decision-making as friends, neighbors, fellow congregants, and relatives weighed in on Giovanni's care. It was also clear from Roland's apologies to my research assistant Zafisoa for saying "us Christians" that he is accustomed to framing his conversations mindfully given the religious and cultural diversity of Diégo Suarez. These are the kinds of pluralistic environments in which parents are making decisions about their children's care—their births and the rituals they use postpartum to bless, protect, and welcome them into their communities.

Amélie's story is similar to Céline and Roland's. Like the previous couple, she and her partner also chose to immerse their firstborn son in rituals that held importance in their respective families in ways that kept alive the traditions that had served and sustained them. Her story also highlights the point that beliefs are often overemphasized as determining factors in parents' decision-making around the childbirth and rites of incorporation for children. Rather than being especially motivated by beliefs alone, mothers like Amélie often feel compelled, or obliged, to observe traditional birthing rituals, not because they always believe them to be necessary, but because they understand the importance of linking babies to their ancestral roots, to connecting babies to both matri- and patrilineages in generative ways. Amélie's story challenges the assumptions Westerners often make about women in third-world countries, who are sometimes presumed to be more superstitious than rational. The reality is that mothers like Amélie are deeply rational, but they are also communally oriented in ways that enable them to pull together the confluences of care they and their children need.

Amélie

Amélie was living in the university dormitories when she discovered that she was pregnant.[10] At that point, she promptly asked to be moved to larger university housing to help accommodate her expanding family. Her new home within university housing was indeed large by Malagasy standards with a much-coveted concrete foundation, metal siding, and a metal roof.[11] At the time, Amélie was a master's student and the appointed secretary in the French Department at the University of Antsiranana. She was intelligent and had a friendly yet striking appearance, an independent spirit, and an effervescent and generous personality.

When she and I arrived at her house after a walk from the university library, she immediately grabbed her one-and-a-half-year-old son, Lawrence, from his nanny. I sat down on her sofa, and she and Lawrence sat together in an armchair. Then she offered Lawrence her breast. He nursed for a minute and then resumed eating the eggroll he held in his hand. Amélie explained to me that her husband, Laurent, had wanted to have a baby before she had. As Lawrence got down from her lap and stood in front of a full-length mirror smiling at his own reflection, Amélie described the difficulty involved in deciding when to have a child. Her sister-in-law had had a baby a few years prior, and Laurent had been eager for one ever since. Amélie had wanted to wait until she finished her master's degree and until they had more money, but her husband assured her that she could breastfeed the baby, that they did not need money for that, and argued that people poorer than them have babies all the time, reassuring her that she could continue writing her master's thesis. Amélie laughed and said, "My husband and my sister were co-conspirators in encouraging me to have a child now. And I guess they won out, because he [Lawrence] is here!"

Given her educational pursuits, Amélie wrestled with the question of right timing more than some of the women I interviewed. That said, most of the women I interviewed experienced motherhood as an event for which they were relatively unprepared. As Amélie described, she was not at first aware of, or very attentive to, all of the spiritual aspects of childbirth when making decisions about who her provider would be for her first child's birth. Instead, she, like many young people, pieced together bits of information from family, friends, and neighbors and made the decision she felt most comfortable with given the resources available to her at the time.

Amélie describes herself as "not very traditional" but indicated that she became more acquainted with traditional birthing practices (fomba fit-erana) when she became pregnant with Lawrence. She visited a massage healer, who, like the midwives we met earlier, came to his work by way of a calling and was thus equipped at not only providing therapeutic prenatal massage but also attending to spiritual matters. In addition, Lawrence's paternal relatives held two ceremonial haircuttings for him, one soon after his birth and the second when he cut his first teeth.[12] And, per custom, Amélie bathed with rômba after the birth. "I wouldn't have known to bathe this way, except that my mother-in-law instructed me to do so," she admitted. "What's more," she added, "we happened to have a rômba plant growing behind our house." She and her husband had cut down a lot of grass and weeds when they moved into their new house but left the rômba plant, even though they did not know what it was at the time, an event she later interpreted as fortuitous.

Customarily, women in Madagascar return to their natal homes to be with their mothers for the birth of their first child. However, Amélie's own mother had passed away and thus could not be with her for Lawrence's arrival. Increasingly though, even for women whose mothers have not died, returning home to give birth is proving more difficult than advantageous, especially among women who have moved into cities far away from the communities in which they were raised for better work and educational opportunities. Increasingly, these women are relying on various other kinds of social support during childbirth. In Amélie's case, her mother-in-law fulfilled this role and introduced Amélie to the traditional customs she might not have otherwise observed during the pregnancy, birth, and postpartum period.

Amélie explained that she feels she must (tokony) observe these birthing customs, even when she does not always believe in their necessity, because she has to respect her husband's family. She also confessed, "I'm not sure. They might help." But she indicated that she also knows that non-Malagasy people do not always bathe in the same manner after giving birth and under-stood that these people heal just fine. In conversations with other informants about the necessity of observing Malagasy customs (fombagasy), such as the hot and cold postpartum bathing, most indicate that the "need to do this" stems from the fact that their ancestors also did so. Unlike Amélie, many of the other women with whom I spoke did not wonder why vazaha have differ-ent practices. Vazaha have different ancestors, so they would have their own postpartum rituals. Even among various Malagasy groups, people are born into different ancestral lineages, and ancestors require of their descendants things they do not necessarily require of everyone. In other words, according to some, the danger involved in not observing the prescribed postpartum bathing customs is not simply that a person will not heal properly but also that one will anger one's ancestors or that one will abandon something that has become sacred in one's family or religious culture, and doing so is enough to make a person deathly ill.

Amélie's family, like that of her husband's, is Catholic. According to Amé-lie, her maternal grandmother was a fervent Catholic. Her grandparents on the paternal side, however, "were not very religious." Her father, born in the 1940s, was the first among them to have what Amélie described as a "devel-oped religion." He was the president of the church he attended, participated in church trainings, and often traveled for the church. Amélie did not use the word *missionary* to describe him but implied that his work for the church was of an evangelical nature. When Amélie's father asked to marry her mother, her maternal grandmother was the first to accept, but the rest of the family remained reluctant, complaining that her father was "too religious" and would not be able to make money that way. But Amélie, as if countering her maternal relatives' long-ago arguments, defended her father's position, arguing that "he thought that church was good for children—that it provided them with a good education. He really valued education."

Despite her family's deep roots in Catholicism, Amélie did not immedi-ately think to baptize her son. Instead, she was encouraged to do so by a family friend. "After his birth," Amélie recalled, "one of my husband's father's friends came to us asking about when we wanted to baptize him." She clarified, "Prior to this, we hadn't really given it much thought, and we didn't go to church that often." But when she and Laurent heard that the Catholic church at the university was going to have a baptism service for babies, they decided to take advantage of this opportunity and baptize Lawrence.

Midway through my interview with Amélie, we moved our conversation outside, as Lawrence was getting antsy. "He likes to walk outside," she said. As Lawrence cheerily made his way across the arid and uneven terrain of the university grounds, Amélie cautiously guarded her novice walker. We talked outside about "growth medicines" (*aody be*), in-laws and childbirth, and how people around you have so many opinions. "People in Diégo Suarez are very traditional," Amélie explained, and "if you pay attention, you'll see that many of the babies wear necklaces with things tied to them." She referred to these as *aody be*, or "growth medicines," which is a cultural, rather than ancestral, practice that is believed to help babies grow faster. Some of her neighbors encouraged her to get some for Lawrence, advising that it would help him grow bigger and stronger. She worried that he was looking thin. "But he used to be plump," she complained, "and mothers who use growth medicines still have babies who look thin and mothers who don't eat eggs still have babies who get bumps on their heads so I don't see the point of all the customs, even though I still wonder sometimes whether I should do them." Amélie referred to mothers who aren't traditional as more "knowledgeable, educated, and civilized" and counted herself among this faction but also frequently felt pressure to use some of the growth medicines her friends and neighbors recommended.

Amélie then volunteered a story about a joro that her father-in-law gave her before giving birth to Lawrence. During the religious speech, he did not use her name and asked twice of those around him knew what her name was. She was very confused by this and asked her husband, Laurent, about it afterward. She implored incredulously, "How can he not know my name? It's not like we've been together for just a short time." Laurent reassured her that, of course, his father knew her name but that it was custom for fathers-in-law not to say the names of daughters-in-law during the ritual and custom for her not to use his name either. She had not known of this custom and did not understand the rationale either. "He's Tsimihety," a member of an ethnic group from the north-central coast of Madagascar, she explained to me, and that is their custom.[13] Amélie asked me if there was anything like this in the United States—if there was any kind of respect between me and my in-laws that manifested itself in an interesting way. I confessed I was not sure, explained that I had not been married very long, but affirmed her sentiment that when you have a child you become wedded to, and influenced by, the child's father's family in complex and sometimes tenuous ways.

Amélie did not necessarily believe in, or feel compelled to follow, her or her husband's cultural and lineage-based customs, nor did she ascribe to some of the superstitious practices like not wearing scarves during pregnancy so the cord would not wrap around the baby's neck; however, neither was she sure she could entirely ignore them. In the end, her husband's family persuaded her and instructed her to abide by some of the customs they deemed important to Lawrence's upbringing. In discussions on religions and medicine, clients' beliefs are often emphasized over and above all other motivating factors that inspire people's decision-making for the spiritual upbringing of their children. But of course, more than matters of belief influence people to participate (or not participate) in various religious practices. And participation does not always serve as evidence of one's wholehearted endorsement of the practices in which one participates.

Sometimes mothers are compelled to observe postpartum bathing rituals. In other instances, parents perform blessing rituals for their children as acts of duty or respect for the family members who wish them to be performed. Alternately, some women observe pregnancy fady and adorn their children with ritual medicines because they wish to be linked or bound together with members of their family/community who abide by similar observances, akin to what Nancy Jay wrote when she said "the means are the ends. The ritual is done because it is important to do it. . . . There is no separate effect, it is all in the doing."[14]

This "all in the doing" is why some Malagasy explained to me that they observed their certain religious and/or ancestral practices. "It is simply what we do." For doing so was what was required of them and enabled them to remain connected to those within their community both living and dead. This sense of connectedness and belonging can have a significant impact on a person's spiritual and physical well-being not only by combating loneliness but also by granting people access to networks of spiritual and social support that in a landscape of poverty and medical scarcity is sometimes critical to a person's survival. Few of the people I interviewed found it necessary to contemplate the meanings behind the rituals they observed or to eloquently describe the beliefs behind or ritual logic of the blessing rites they observed. Instead, they understand the rituals, medicines (fanafody, aody), and taboos (fady) as what they as particular kinds of people simply must do, and the massage healers, diviners, and midwives they consulted helped ensure that the doing was done right.

Amélie and I found many points of common interest, particularly in discussions of the timing of a pregnancy, given we both were women/mothers pursuing careers in academia. However, a discussion of childbirth venues brought to the fore our diverging opinions about where the safest, most comfortable place was for us to give birth to our children. Amélie gave birth to her son, Lawrence, at the government hospital (Hôpital Be) in Diégo Suarez and paid extra to ensure that the single obstetrician in town attended her birth there. When I confessed to her that I planned to give birth to my children at home under the care of a midwife, she spent the next twenty minutes or so trying to convince me otherwise and jokingly referred to me as "the Malagasy one" and her as "the American one."

As an outsider conducting research on religious and cultural practices surrounding childbirth, I frequently encountered sober reminders of the distance between me and the women I interviewed both in terms of our access to high-quality healthcare and information and in terms of my ability to understand the cultural contexts in which women in Madagascar are birthing their babies. Amélie and her peers were not concerned about unnecessary medical interventions, as some of my peers were; she was worried about not having access to high-quality lifesaving technologies should an emergency arise.[15] Yet these points of divergence, or points of tension, between us represented for me the moments that best answered the question of why more research on the birthing practices in nonindustrialized countries is needed. Despite what is often said about mothers in the global south, that they prefer "tribal" medicine and are resistant to seek healthcare in clinics, many factors influence women's abilities to access quality healthcare during their pregnancies, a point I also illustrate in the preceding chapter. Many women, like Amélie, wanted more medicine, not less, but accessing that medicine is not always easy for a variety of social and economic circumstances, which is why women like Françoise, whom we met in the previous chapter, are also deeply concerned that traditional medicines and caregivers do not disappear.

While Amélie describes herself as "not very traditional," even she sought the help of what her peers might describe as a "traditional" specialist, a massage therapist (*mpanindry*) who proudly combined traditional Malagasy massage with knowledge of Chinese acupuncture, which further supports that women's decision-making often transcends the kinds of categories we try to label them with. Embedded in Amélie's story of motherhood, a journey into which she was only two years deep at the time, is yet another example of the kinds of complex decision-making mothers must make to create networks of support for their children. Amélie engaged with many different kinds of rituals and therapies over the course of her pregnancy, birth, and postpartum period, from the benediction she received from her father-in-law before giving birth to her decision to pay extra to have the one obstetrician in Diégo Suarez attend her birth and the postpartum blessing rites she and her family held for her son, including traditional haircutting ceremonies and a Catholic baptism. These meaning-laden actions, together with the decisions she makes on a daily basis to use or not use aody be, represent the many real-world decisions Malagasy regularly face. These women's decisions—rather than being time-less "tribal traditions," as one New York Times journalist once described—are among the timely strategies that women and their families employ to create a culture of infancy that connects babies to the social, spiritual, and medical resources available to them in the form of family members, faith communities, medical and religious leaders, and sacred ancestral wisdom.[16]

Ritual Bathing at Nosy Lonjo

In addition to consulting family members, midwives, and other kinds of reli-gious and medical specialists, women in northern Madagascar also sometimes frequent the site of Nosy Lonjo to make vows to their ancestors or vows to the royal ancestors that preside over that sacred site. Doing so ensures that they keep open communication and maintain right relationships with the spirits that sustain them. This conical island in the middle of Diégo's largest bay, also sometimes referred to as the Pain du Sucre because of the island's resemblance to other famous "sugar loaf mountains," is one of the more sacred sites in Antsiranana. The French name, originally invented by colonial resi-dents ignorant of the spiritual significance of the place, remains in use today, which speaks to the persistence of a distinctly colonial culture in Diégo, a city that continues to draw French tourists, expatriates, and Malagasy from other parts of the island. Aside from a very small number of religious experts, it is strictly forbidden for anyone to set foot on the island, but Malagasy from all over come to bathe along the shore in the sacred waters that surround this picturesque rock formation.

Located in the sandy beach where people enter the water is a stone on which people offer gifts of honey, tobacco, and rice to the ancestors to whom they make requests in the form of vows. Zebu (cattle) horns, remnants of sac-rificial offerings, adorn the trees that line the water's sacred shores, offering evidence of the ancestor's faithfulness to their descendants' prayerful pleas. One Saturday morning, I accompanied two women, Amélie and Camellia, on their bathing pilgrimage to this site. As Amélie and Camellia were leaving their homes to embark on a morning pilgrimage toward the waters near Nosy Lonjo, Camellia remarked that it was already getting very light out and she was not sure how many people would still be down by the water.[17] "These days some people are embarrassed of their traditions because of the European religions, which discourage people from praying to their ancestors," she said. As a Catholic, Camellia maintained that it was not necessary to give up her "culture," a position shared by many Catholics in Madagascar in keeping with the Second Vatican Council's encouragement of inculturation.

When we arrived, Amélie and Camellia knelt before a stone near the shore and across the water from the sacred mountain island of Nosy Lonjo.[18] They laid out their offerings of snuff, honey, rice, and coins and made their requests before their ancestors. Behind them, a line of people waited for their own chance to visit the stone, sitting in groups ascending the grassy hillside. One family gathered around a large plastic crate of beers, which they intended to offer to the ancestors as a way of upholding their end of a vow after a request they made earlier in the year had been granted. People of all ages, including several small children, congregated in clusters along the slope of the hill that descended into the bay. The group in front of us, with whom we casually spoke while waiting for our turn to lay down our offerings, indicated that they would not leave until the beer was finished. "Especially in the case of alcohol, nothing can be brought back," they explained to the three of us.

After making their requests, Camellia and Amélie removed their clothing and jewelry, and hung them in the tree. They donned lambas (traditional Malagasy wraps), which they had brought along for the occasion, and processed out into the water with other pilgrims who had come there to bathe. They walked up to their waists; bowed several times, immersing themselves in the salt water; and finished by circumambulating a tree and returning to the shore. Upon completing the ritual bath, they walked up the hill and stopped at the home of the sacred site's spiritual guardian, Hussein, who lived in a small metal-framed house just up the hill from Nosy Lonjo. Camellia had wanted to interview him for a project she was working on, as part of an effort to have Nosy Lonjo designated as a protected religious site. Hussein, of Anjoaty lineage, like his father before him, lived on site and served as the spiritual guardian of the place. He is charged with "opening the door," though

Ritual bathing at Nosy Lonjo. *Photos by author.*

Ritual bathing at Nosy Lonjo. *Photos by author. (continued)*

not in a physical sense as there is no material barrier that prohibits would-be bathers from kneeling at the stone, making offerings, or bathing in the waters that surround Nosy Lonjo. But in order for this rite to be effective, a medium is required to daily invoke the ancestors that their spiritual presence might be more readily available to those who come to the water in search of them.

When Camellia and Amélie approached the house, Hussein invited them in. He sat on the floor against the wall, his knees held loosely in between his arms, while Amélie and Camellia sat on traditional Malagasy wooden stools that hover only a few inches off the ground. Hussein spoke in a very relaxed and gracious manner and wore nothing in the way of clothing save a pair of old tattered shorts. His teeth, however, especially for a traditional specialist, appeared remarkably healthy, white and straight, a fact Amélie would later comment on.

Camellia and Amélie asked him questions not only about his life as Nosy Lonjo's spiritual guardian but also about the fady they are expected to observe around the area and the correct ways to perform a joro. Camellia informed Hussein that she was a student but also a practitioner of Malagasy Indigenous religions. He appeared comfortable and pleased with her inquiries and explained the various fady and fomba associated with the practice of bathing near Nosy Lonjo. He explained that sometimes people ask him to help them with their joro and he always agrees. Occasionally if their requests are fulfilled, they remember him and offer a gift. He made a point of telling Amélie and Camellia, however, that he never asks for recompense. After they said goodbye and began walking up the hill from Hussein's house and back onto the road, they saw some people escorting an older blind man down to the water. They also met some Malagasy missionaries, men and women in suits and dresses, together with their children, handing out religious tracts clearly meant to steer people away from Indigenous bathing rituals such as this one. Amélie received one of the tracts from a small little boy. She smiled at him and politely thanked him. "If we did not take their pamphlets," she said to me, "they would feel sad."

On the walk back to their respective homes, Amélie voiced concerns about Hussein's poverty, commenting on his tattered shorts and the small, impermanent nature of his house. "Someone as important as he should be taken care of!" Amélie insisted. Amélie's view was that if someone asked Hussein for help with a joro and then received an ancestral blessing as a result, they should in turn offer to build Hussein a nicer house. Camellia was taken aback by Amélie's concerns and was not at all bothered by his simple attire. "But he's not supposed to be rich," she countered. "Even if he has money, he should not spend it on a nice house. Making money is not a priority, and it can even detract from his power," she further explained. According to Camellia, poverty comes with the territory for spiritual leaders like Hussein. She was also under the impression that his living conditions only gave an appearance of modesty. In other words, he might not be as poor as he looks. She reminded Amélie that his children were after all living in the capital of Antananarivo, an opportunity available only to a minority of Malagasy. On this point, Amélie agreed, remembering his white teeth.

One of the purported reasons why religious specialists, like Hussein, remain poor is that they refuse payment for their services. People like Hussein, much like the midwife Bernadette whom we met in the previous chapter, view their work as "a gift" (un don) from the ancestors, an extension of the ancestors' power. They are the mediums through which ancestors continue to offer advice and healing, in the form of herbal and ritual medicines (fanafody), to the living. Such a relationship requires investment in mutual care both between ancestors and religious specialists and between religious specialists and their clients and is an important resource for mothers. Paying for services, as opposed to gift giving, can terminate (or close out) debts rather than further the mutual responsibility both parties seek to establish with one another. Gift giving helps mothers enter into relationships of reciprocity with midwives and other kinds of specialists, which increases women's connections within the larger community and ensures a larger social safety net critical to the work of raising children.

I have entered into several such relationships of mutual responsibility throughout my many travels to Madagascar, though it has taken me years to realize how best to honor these relationships. Initially, I did not understand that paying for a friend's hospitality toward me indicated an unwillingness on my part to engage in the kind of long-term relationship my Malagasy friends were seeking to invest in me. According to Oyvind Dahl,

> Malagasy society places a fundamental value on personal relationship. Different members are bound together through mutual rights and obligations, both horizontally and vertically. A person is forever indebted to others, who, in turn, are constrained by their own. Under this system of reciprocity, the individual does not calculate what he or she gives and receives. To calculate would be to think about immediate personal profits,

which is contrary to the principle of fihavanana. The practice of basing relationships on complementary bonds creates lasting human relationships.
Investment in ceremonies of "turning the dead," for instance, cannot only
be seen as a "hemorrage of the Malagasy economy," as it has been characterized (O. Dahl, 1976). It is also an investment in social relationships.
Mutual exchange of services and gifts is a way of expressing communal
identity and maintaining adherence to a greater social unit, which is also
the ultimate social warrant in case of personal or family crises.[19]

In other words, according to the Malagasy ethic of reciprocity known as fihavanana, people invest in one another by making exchanges that engender a
kind of indebtedness. By helping someone out in a time of need, the likelihood
increases that that person will in turn be there for you, months or perhaps even
years down the road. People engage in this kind of indebtedness across friendships, among relatives both living and dead, and with traditional healers.

I observed this tendency on the part of many people—on the part of mothers and others seeking care as well as those delivering care: midwives, spiritual
guardians like Hussein, and traditional healers like my research assistant Zafisoa's cousin Fred. Fred is a massage healer and bonesetter in Diégo whom I
met in the back of a small *épicerie* (small grocery store) where he worked. One
afternoon, when I arrived to consult with him, he was sitting on the floor of his
office, which was dressed with woven mats atop a dirt floor in the middle of a
room that could not have been much larger than ten feet by five feet. Zafisoa
and I entered the room and sat down on the ground before him. It was dark
until he reached his hand up to open a window. In the corner of the room was a
bowl with water and some leaves in it, some other bottles that appeared to contain various kinds of liquids, and a pack of cigarettes. Fred began massaging
my injured leg, pushing on it at certain points and also altering the orientation
of my foot, as a chiropractor might do. He cracked my toes and feet, applied
intense pressure in a couple of locations along my leg, where I had incurred a
running injury, and kneaded the surrounding muscles with a lubricating oil,
all the while holding a casual conversation with Zafisoa and me.

Fred did not learn massage formally; it was a gift passed down to him by
his parents. He showed me the inside of a basket where he had some sticks and
cloth that he used for fixing broken bones. Zafisoa indicated that he once fixed
a man's broken foot so the man could walk again. He purportedly performs
surgery sometimes as well, though not often. There were many miraculous
stories that circulated around his practice. As we were leaving, I asked him

how much I should pay him. He replied that I could pay whatever I liked, which prompted me to look to Zafisoa, who often advises me in these kinds of situations, but in this moment, she, too, refused to give me any kind of estimate. When we left, there were two women waiting on a bench outside of his consultation room waiting to see him. They were there with a sick toddler who appeared to have some kind of disability. Fred receives lines of clients daily. Later that day, I continued to wonder why Fred had not asked me for a set amount of money. Was he testing my generosity? Did he think that by not designating a set amount I might be inclined to give more? Was it something he did only with me, a vazaha, or with all his clients? And if the latter, how could he earn a living this way in a society that increasingly values capitalistic modes of exchange? Later, I would come to understand that Fred's reluctance to name a price for his services had little to do with me and much more to do with the customs around reciprocal gift giving that take place between religious specialists and their clients.

In Madagascar, gifts of payments to religious specialists are referred to as hasin-tanana and can come in the form of money or other material goods like chickens, rice, food, or soap. British missionary James Richardson translated *hasin-tanana* as "a present given to the *mpisikidy* [diviner], etc., after the cure of a disease, or to a midwife after the birth of a child."[20] Malagasy linguist Rakotosaona translated the phrase as "the customary money given to a massage-healer."[21] In Malagasy, *hasin* comes from the word *hasina*, signifying sacred power. And *tananana* means hands. Thus, *masin-tanana* refers to a healer or someone who possesses a healing touch. *Hasin-tanana*, which is different from the former only in that it is in future tense, refers to the customary gift given to such a healer, which suggests that gifts of money and foodstuff contribute to a healer's hasina in the future. As my research assistant Édith once explained,

> When you give someone hasin-tanana, it should not be a lot of money. Before it used to be coins, but now it is paper money. Now it is paper money because you can no longer buy anything from coins. *Hasin-tanana* literally means "holy hands," and it is a gift from the ancestors. It is power, and it is also what you ask in payment, because giving it to one of these specialists contributes to their power. If hasin-tanana is a large amount of money, then it's like the hospital payment at a hospital rather than true hasin-tanana. If people ask for a large amount of money, it is like their power may diminish. That is why when you ask a healer for the price of something they will say "Ameza zaho hasin-tanana." They should not

name a price, if they do, it may destroy their power, but if you give something to them, it is OK.

In other words, religious specialists gain credibility by offering advice and
medicines voluntarily, out of benevolence rather than for profit. If they ask for
payment, then the ancestors, from whom this specialized knowledge comes,
may decide to relinquish their powers.

Massage healers (mpanindry) like Fred, diviners (moasy), and traditional
midwives (renin-zaza) often describe their work as gifts, but these gifts are
best understood in the Maussian sense, where a gift is never freely given but
instead embedded with the expectation of reciprocity.[22] This notion of reciprocity is not dissimilar to the gift economies found in other kinds of Indigenous societies where one's relationship to land and ancestors is less taken for
granted. As Robin Kimmerer describes, "Gifts from the earth or from each
other establish a particular relationship, an obligation of sorts to give, to receive, and to reciprocate."[23] In the Malagasy context, healers' power belongs
not to themselves alone but to the ancestors from whom the gift is given.
Healers attest to this fact by emphasizing the great deal of tireless work and
responsibility their talent requires of them. Countless specialists described
their work as "difficult" (sarotro) and emphasized that they had been chosen
for this work rather than choosing the vocation themselves.

Clients' giving of gifts (hasin-tanana) to religious specialists can be understood within the broader context of Malagasy relationships of reciprocity,
which occur on the human-divine level, between royalty and their subjects,
and in a less hierarchical manner between family members and friends (fihavanana). Malagasy commonly provide conciliatory gifts of rice, tobacco, and
honey to their ancestors when asking for fertile harvests, just as royalty commonly request gifts of hasina from their subjects. During the reign of Merina
queen Ranavalona II (1868–1883), subjects provided hasin-tanana as tributes
during the royal bath (fandroana) at the annual New Year's celebration: "the
scene on the first day of the festival is most imposing. Representatives of all the
various tribes and families of the people, arrayed in holiday lambas, robes of
coloured stripes, and often of silk or other rich material, assemble and proceed
in procession to the rova, or palace, and present hasina, as a sign of subjection
and submission to the central authority."[24] Whether between royalty and
subjects, ancestors and the living, or healers and their clients, gifts of hasin-
tanana work to both acknowledge hierarchies of power and establish a kind
of mutual indebtedness and accountability that is fundamental to society.

Malagasy rules around payment of religious specialists can be theorized from a variety of different perspectives. Some have emphasized that restrictions around the use of money can serve as symbols of resistance, function in redistributive ways, and sometimes serve as a critique of capitalism.[25] In Madagascar, there is a long of history, and not only among religious specialists, of resisting labor that works toward the benefits of outsiders rather than in engaging in work that furthers the foundational efforts of one's ancestors and consequently works toward a better future for one's children. Gillian Feeley-Harnik and Christiane Rafidinarivo Rakotolahy both discuss the strategic ways in which various Malagasy groups have resisted efforts on the part of French administrators to draw them into the colonial labor force, insisting that engaging in such work is dirty and even tantamount to slavery.[26] By contrast, specialists who earn a living through honoraria rather than through salaried labor take pride in the fact that they work for themselves or for a higher calling, rather than as slaves to someone else's work.[27]

In sum, religious specialists like Hussein and Fred, and like the traditional midwife we met in chapter 1, Bernadette, refrain from asking for set amounts of money because they want to be seen by their clients as legitimate—as benevolent and concerned for the greater good rather than as simply out there to earn money. They do not flaunt their wealth, even if they are in fact wealthy, because such an attitude flies in the face of the belief that wealth should be shared by all rather than hoarded by a few, and no one wishes to appear as though they are violating such an ethic. Wealth belongs to all the benefactors of the ancestors' blessings. And health, rather than being a commodity, is about being firmly woven into relationships of reciprocity with friends, family, and medical specialists who can provide for you in times of need, a health that mothers begin to cultivate for their babies even before they exit the womb.

While most religious specialists abide by the principles of mutual care through gift giving rather than contractual payments, there are a growing number of specialists who are setting a price for their services. According to Josette, the mother of Alicia, the medically trained midwife we met in chapter 1, "it used to be that three cups of rice, a chicken, and a couple of bars of soap were the standard payment for a renin-zaza, but now they cost upward of 300,000 FMG [the equivalent of around twenty United States dollars at the time]."[28] This comes as a disappointment to those seeking their care, for such a price can make giving birth under the supervision of a midwife as cost prohibitive as giving birth in a hospital, government dispensary, or privately owned clinic.

There is a social cost to these changes as well. Josette's complaint that midwives can no longer be paid with chickens is indicative of her frustration that certain modes of exchange, and consequently certain forms of social assurance, are no longer available to her. In times of social crises and in a turbulent economy such as the one Malagasy are currently living in, such a social safety net is vital, for it may in fact be a greater predictor of a child's ability to survive and thrive than the frequency of time she or he visits a medical doctor. A mother who must choose between spending her money on pharmaceutical medicines or food is less equipped to produce a healthy child than one who can trade a chicken or soap for a prenatal checkup or who can pay for services or medicines over time. For these reasons, women like Amélie and Camellia were frequently engaged in discussions about the customary ways of relating to religious specialists and about changes within the gift economy. Commodification, or even the threat of commodification, of these traditional services compromises their ability to raise healthy children.

The women I met in Madagascar employed prudent strategies to ensure their children received the kinds of social, medical, and spiritual resources that enabled their flourishing, but as time passed, I also learned of some of the ways in which their efforts sometimes failed, not for lack of trying or resources spent, but because sometimes, tragically, babies die anyway. In the midst of my research, these lives lost were sobering reminders that while the efforts of Malagasy mothers are often creative and beautiful, such efforts do not always rescue every mother, every family, from the unimaginable pain that awaits a few of them. Sylvie was one such mother.

Sylvie

I met Sylvie during the earlier months of my field research as she was one of the women who cleaned the common areas of la Gite d'Etape, the university guest housing where my husband and I lived during our time in Diégo Suarez. Of the women who worked there, Sylvie was the youngest, a cheerful mother of four children, two of whom were twins. One morning, she brought a picture of her children to show to me, as well as a picture of herself while pregnant with the twins. I gestured to the picture with admiration pointing out that "these two were in your belly at the same time!" She laughed and said "yes." To which I replied, "Sarotro," meaning difficult, and Sylvie laughed again.[29]

Sylvie was almost always smiling, and we talked often; however, rarely did our exchanges include long, in-depth conversations.

Once, she brought two of her children to la Gite. They were the three-year-old twins, and they were dressed in their preschool uniforms, water bottles and backpacks in tow. I talked with them, and they shook my hand like little grown-ups. They ran around a little too but were mostly very well behaved and listened to their mother's instructions. I told Sylvie they were cute, and she responded playfully by saying, "Yes, but they're also *maditry* [naughty]."[30] Then she left to escort them to school. "Handeha l'école [off to school]," she said merrily as she scooted them along.

Sylvie knew nothing of the research I was conducting in her city, as I had not yet discussed this with her; she knew only that I was occasionally teaching English classes at the university and that I was from the United States. Thus, our conversations remained casual and occurred in the hallway and in the kitchen as I was cooking breakfast and she was checking the status of the gas tanks in the common area. She shared with me the aspirations she had for her children's schooling and playfully requested that I find her an American boyfriend who could finance all of these dreams.

Months into our relationship, Sylvie began asking me if she could wash my clothes. Normally, I handwashed my own clothes in the concrete basins behind the row of rooms in which we lived, but one week, she asked with enough persistence that I began to wonder if she needed the money. So, I gave her some of my clothes, and when she returned them all carefully folded, I gave her a 10,000 ariary bill, the equivalent of 50,000 FMG, which was roughly the equivalent of five dollars at the time. Since she was only charging 20,000 FMG for a small bag of clothes, and I did not have any smaller bills, I told her she could return the 30,000 FMG on Monday of next week.[31]

About a week later, on a Wednesday, Sylvie came to our door. It was cracked open, but rather than entering, she stood at the door and knocked softly. She had not been at la Gite on Monday or Tuesday of that week, and I remembered wondering if she had been sick. There was also a part of me that wondered if she had not come on Monday because she had spent the extra money I had given her. I was not concerned about getting my change back, but I was worried that if she had spent the money, she might be too embarrassed to come back to work until she had recovered it.

However, there she stood at my door on Wednesday with a big basket of another resident's clothing at her feet and the change she owed me in her hands, but she looked awful. Her eyes were red and swollen as she stood there rather stoically. I greeted her normally and then asked if she had been sick, both because of how she looked and because she had missed two days of work. As we stood there, face to face, she whispered softly, "Zanakanaka mort [my child died]." I know I must have had a look of shock on my face. I repeated aloud in disbelief, "Zanakanao naty (your child died)?" I had tears in my eyes and did not know what to do or say. I asked what the child's name was, and she whispered. I asked how old, and she whispered. I held her hand. She handed me the change, and I handed it back. She looked away and tears started running down her cheeks. She wiped them away and then, barely able to speak, asked me to take another resident's clothes, which she had placed at the door. I wanted to hug her, but in my observations, hugging does not seem as common in Malagasy culture as it is in my own. I stepped across the threshold and put my hand on her shoulder. I took the basket and put it in the room. Soon Valentine, another of the women who cleaned at la Gite, arrived with a woman who cleans the university's president's house across the road from la Gite. I was relieved that they had arrived because I thought Sylvie needed them. They talked with her, and then Sylvie left.

Sylvie's baby died of diarrhea. I had not even known she had a baby. I knew she had four children, but I hadn't known the youngest was a baby. She had taken this little one, her son, to the Hôpital FJKM (Fiangonan'i Jesoa Kristy eto Madagasikara, Church of Jesus Christ in Madagascar) and assumed he would recover.[32] Though I will never know for sure because I did not ask, I think my suspicions were right that Sylvie needed money in the weeks leading up to her baby's death, which is why she was so eager to wash all of our clothes. I stood in the bathroom paralyzed after she left, not knowing whether to cry or be strong. It changed the way I saw my research. I had seen dead babies hanging in baskets in the trees near the bay, at a special burial site for young babies, something I discuss in greater detail in chapter 4 of this book. I had smelled death, but still there had been distance between me and the realities people face every day. That week, death came just a little bit closer. It had shattered the life of a mother I saw on a near daily basis in ways I could not even imagine. Her everyday smiles were replaced by feelings of sorrow and regret and shame and loss, and I and my money had been involved.

The next day, I asked one of the other women who worked at la Gite if Sylvie was OK (karakory Sylvie?). She seemed annoyed by the question, insisting that Sylvie was fine (tsara fo). "It was her child who died," she explained to me. "Sylvie is fine. She was at work yesterday." When she said this, it occurred to me that she might have been worried that I would report her absence to someone in authority. I had failed to convey my concern for Sylvie and interest in how she was doing after losing a child.

Later that week, I asked my friend Amélie what I could do to give Sylvie my condolences. She said I could put money in an envelope and give it to her as we had done for Michel, a friend we had in common, when Michel lost his mother. Amélie said she gives one or two thousand ariary for an acquaintance and sometimes around ten thousand for a good friend but that I could give more if I wanted to because I am a vazaha. Later I told Amélie that the child who died had been a baby, a year and a half. "That's Lawrence's age," she said, and I watched it hit home. "This is why I worry when he gets sick. They're so little," Amélie said. After we went to the bank together, we were walking down a sidewalk and saw a little boy who sat on a wooden stool eating an ice cream cone. He looked to be around five or six. Amélie remarked, "I can't wait until Lawrence is that age," to which I replied, "It won't be long." But Amélie seemed to think it would be long. And then I realized that for her, getting through this period of fragility meant something. She was not worried about her son growing up too fast. She was worried of the small but terrifying risk that he might not grow up at all.

Sylvie was not the only woman I knew who lost a baby during my nine months of research in Diégo. I knew of one other mother who lost her young baby, and many others shared stories of losses that had occurred in previous months and years—miscarriages as well as stories of babies who died in their first few months of their life. Mothers processed these losses differently, attributing their young babies' deaths to a multitude of factors including illness, poverty, and lack of access to good medical care. Mothers also attributed infant death to spiritual causes that are sometimes intertwined with biomedical causes, asking questions like: "Perhaps the conditions were not right for that baby's arrival in the world? Or perhaps God or the ancestors are angry with me or have a different timing in mind?"

In other words, according to this thinking, if ancestors confer blessings on people who remember them, in the form of fertile landscapes and wombs, when their descendants remember them well by carrying on the fomba and fady of their lineages, then ancestors might also decide to withhold or interrupt these blessings from time to time as well. To some, these painful interruptions are a reminder of the fragility of life and the fragility that is the relationship between humans and ancestors, the roots from which children grow. Loss invites reflection on these relationships, on how they might be better maintained or perhaps dissolved so that children might enter the world with the social and spiritual resources they need to survive and thrive.

Mothers Meeting the Whole of Their Children's Needs

In countries plagued by poverty, with meager healthcare systems, mothers must borrow from many confluences of care in order to meet the whole of their children's spiritual and health-related needs especially when an episode of a child's cough, fever, or diarrhea could mean loss of life. And even then, sometimes these therapies fail, leaving them with unfinished stories, with children who never had the chance to become the bone-filled ancestors that their children and grandchildren might one day remember. As we learn in the previous chapter, for their part midwives—those traditionally trained and those with medical training alike—must offer therapies that reach slightly beyond the scope of their practice in order to meet the whole of their clients' needs without violating the integrity of the professional boundaries that give them legitimacy. This chapter demonstrates that mothers must pull together multiple therapies and resources as well.

In societies that value holistic healthcare approaches, health is understood to be more than the absence of disease. As Lesley Sharp notes, "well-being [in Ambanja, a northern Malagasy town] is defined in broad terms and extends into the social and economic realms of human experience."[33] In time, I learned that in Diégo Suarez, a child is considered healthy (*salama tsara tsaiky io*) when they are free of sickness, when they are moving toward a "bone-filled" (read, solidified) status within the ancestral lineage(s) and social circle(s) of which they are a part, and when they have a good rapport with the people and spirits that inhabit their universe.[34] The word for health in Malagasy, *fahasalamana*, comes from the Arabic word *salam*, meaning peace. The various contexts in which Malagasy use the word *salama*, in greetings and to describe a person's physical and emotional states, underscore the degree to which health is understood to comprise a variety of different facets of a person's overall well-being.

Midwifery biographies, together with the narratives of their clients, help us compose a more complete picture of the ways in which mothers begin to instill bones in their children from a very early age, setting up the conditions for their inclusion in the communities that will sustain them sometimes before they are even born. Parents visit diviners, massage healers, bonesetters, traditional midwives, and sacred ancestral sites like Nosy Lonjo not because they are wary of or resistant to modern medicine but because they know that health is not just the absence or presence of certain bacteria or viruses; it is also contingent on being grounded in the social and spiritual networks that give our lives worth and value. This means consulting specialists whose power is derived from degree-conferring institutions as well as specialists whose power (hasina) is derived from the acquisition of ancestral knowledge, like Fred and Hussein. In this healing marketplace of sorts, methods of healing are not entirely independent of one another but emerge in relation to one another and in both competitive and complementary manners. In other words, the decision to consult a traditional midwife or a traditional healer can supplement biomedical therapies by ensuring that mothers are invested in multiple healing therapies in order to spread out the risk that any one of these methods will fail while also increasing the likelihood that any one of them will succeed.[35]

For Nasreen, giving birth with the assistance of midwives enabled her to give birth to her children in ways that were both medically and culturally supportive. Whispering the call to prayer in her newborn children's ears and observing ancestrally inherited practices like ranginaly enabled her to mark her children with particular religious and ancestral identities from the moment of their emergence into the world, granting them belonging and also opening opportunities for her to reexamine and recommit to the religious and culture aspects of her faith that have become increasingly important to her in recent years. As becomes clear in another story about Nasreen told in chapter 4, investing in the ummah, her faith community, by not only immersing her children in religious rituals but also hosting rituals for others has become paramount, as it gives her and her children a sense of purpose and connection to the larger community, ensuring that many people are invested in their upbringing. Given that she was not always privy to these rituals of blessing herself as a young child, enacting them on behalf of her children carries added meaning and contributes to both her children's and her own sense of well-being and worth.

The birth of their son, Giovanni, was a welcome event for Céline and Roland, a welcome event that thrust them into the throes of parenthood. Though they experienced both financial and medical stresses, they were amply supported by their relatives and by their religious community through the process. Though they did not observe all the traditional customs important to their respective families, observing some of them empowered them to further the traditions that grant them, and their son, inclusion and connection to the communities that sustain them. By observing pregnancy fady, ranginaly, baptism, and ceremonial haircutting, Céline and Roland helped their young son embody the rituals of his communities, connecting him to many important resources. These resources, spiritual and social, bolstered the young couple through the insecurities of Céline's difficult pregnancy and through the financial struggles they faced, for it ensured that they, and their newborn son, shouldered these together with many others invested in their future.

For Amélie, having an obstetrician attend her birth was an option that made her feel safe. Some of her other decisions, a number of which she alone made and others of which were made for her—regarding pregnancy fady, burying her son's placenta near her home, the postpartum bathing rituals she practiced, her choice not to use growth medicines on her son, the haircutting and baptism ceremonies she and her family held for her son, and her consultations with doctors and massage healers—created a culture of infancy that marked her son as Catholic, as Tsimihety, and as a sacred member of her and her husband's ancestral lineages. The religious environment she and her family fashioned around Lawrence drew from many cultural and religious confluences and not only encouraged his survival but also helped shape his identity, together with hers and theirs, by awakening in him the legacies she and her family wished to preserve.

Last, none of the individual decisions of mothers can be understood outside of the larger religious context in which these particular healing and birth-related rituals have emerged. That larger religious context includes all of the Indigenous, Christian, and Muslim practices that help Malagasy create communities of belonging and forge relationships of reciprocity with one another and with the spiritual energies that sustain them. In this way, making requests of the ancestors at the sacred site of Nosy Lonjo should not necessarily be seen as entirely separate from the more obviously birth-related rituals and therapies with which mothers engage. Bathing at Nosy Lonjo and other practices of ancestral commemoration are traditions that emerged from, and evolved alongside, multiple streams of religious influences from East Africa, Asia, and the Middle East and form a rich hybridized religious culture that supports and informs the smaller decisions mothers make on a day-to-day basis regarding their children's birth, health, and spiritual upbringing.

Of course, Malagasy have differing relationships with the various religious and cultural traditions with which their island is associated. Some consider bathing at Nosy Lonjo a demonic practice; for others, it's a source of pride connected to their Malagasy heritage. The island traditions for which Malagasy are famous—ceremonies of invocation, exhumation, and spirit possession—serve as means by which to connect people to larger communities of people and spirits, those still living and those long gone. These traditions build on customs of reciprocity that require people to invest in their ancestors through vows and exchanges that engender indebtedness and a kind of mutual sustenance. This kind of reciprocal engagement offers people tangible and intangible social capital that gives mothers and children the kind of care and security integral to children's firm placement in society and ultimate success.

Bathing at Nosy Lonjo is but one example, one point on the mosaic that is the larger religious context that informs the actions and orientations of mothers, midwives, and healers in their efforts to tend to the spiritual and health-related needs of the newly born. There are many other points on the mosaic not highlighted here, but it is nevertheless important to remember that all of these birth-related blessings and practices are part of something larger—an ever-evolving culture of traditions that supports and informs Malagasy efforts to instill bones in the newly born, or to provide their children with a sense of identity and social and spiritual well-being and worth amid the plurality that surrounds them.

THREE

BATHING AND SECLUSION

Making Mothers Who Will Bless Their Babies

Societies around the world and for much of human history have commonly observed a period of postpartum rest/seclusion for mothers and infants.[1] In northern Madagascar, common characteristics of this period include providing women with special meals or restricting their consumption of taboo foods, abstinence from sexual activity, postpartum bathing, ritualized first outings for babies and mothers, joro (speech-prayer, invocation, or ritualized blessing), and, last, a suspension of the mother's normal daily household responsibilities. This chapter is an exploration of these rituals with special attention given to fady (taboos) and the practice of cold-water postpartum bathing, or ranginaly.

By designating a period of rest and seclusion and orchestrating a set of daily bathing rituals for new mothers to move through, the observance of postpartum rituals within the home creates a space where women can heal, recover, and enjoy a kind of spiritual protection during their period of fragility. Additionally, a period of postpartum seclusion enables elders within the community to guide and transmit important knowledge to new mothers— knowledge about important ancestral and religious customs. Sometimes this transmittance of knowledge feels like an invitation into a greater community of belonging. At other times, ritual obligations can feel burdensome as women must learn to embody the fady and fomba (customs) not only of their own family but of the baby's paternal kin as well. In any case, there are often many choices to be made: about rituals of blessing, about food taboos, and about which ancestral customs to observe in order that children are properly rooted and integrated. All of these choices have implications not only for children but also for their mothers' sense of belonging in religious and ancestral communities.

Most of my informants spoke favorably of post-childbirth rituals and lamented the fact that some of these customs are fading. As Nadima, a grandmother who lived behind the bazaar kely explained to me, "Nowadays people do not cook the special food for the mother so they do not do *mampiravaka* [the haircutting ceremony] either." She went on to explain:

> Life is changing now and not everyone can stay for a long time to take care of the woman after she has given birth. If the person has the time to stay, they can cook for the woman, but she probably also has her own house so she is busy with her own cooking. People just come to visit but they usually don't stay for long.
>
> When *all* customs are followed, then the person who takes care of the mother must stay for two weeks. That means two weeks day and night. And nowadays because people are busy, it is easier to cook food [any kind of simple food, not special food] at the mother's house and then return home. It is easier when everyone eats the same food instead of one person eating one kind and another person eating another. No one can [prepare the special food] now because they are busy with their own stuff [*azon'ny jaly*].[2]

According to Nadima, the disappearance of postpartum customs in the early decades of the twenty-first century, resulting from people's busyness with other things, represented a loss for women.

Similarly, Mireille Rabenoro argued that the customs and laws in place in what she referred to as "traditional Malagasy society" afforded women significantly more protection, and a higher status, as compared with contemporary society. She wrote, "As in many early human societies, where life was precarious and child mortality rates were high, in traditional Malagasy society life was precious, and mothers, being a source of life, were venerated as an essential factor in the perpetuation of the family, and hence of the very social group."[3] This veneration of women, she argued, was especially apparent in the customs people observed after the birth of a child.

Outsiders sometimes frame seclusion rituals in terms of the oppressive effects they have on those forced to abide by them. Moreover, it is sometimes assumed that postpartum seclusion exists exclusively in societies that view childbirth as polluting. Several of my informants did describe childbirth as a dirty affair (*maloto*: literally, dirty) and spoke of the necessity to either wash or shave the baby's head to cleanse it after birth, but they did not describe postpartum rituals as oppressive. In fact, the majority of the women I interviewed spoke fondly and nostalgically of this special time, where family members guided them through the healing process, cooked their meals, and enabled them to have a break from their normal household responsibilities. This is not to say that women never felt constrained by these rituals, however. One younger woman I interviewed, whose story is told in this chapter, found the food restrictions, ritual bathing, and words of blessing she received arbitrary and cumbersome. Moreover, she did not feel as though these rituals granted her, or her newly born son, any kind of greater belonging within the family. That said, the vast majority appreciated the focused attention and care they received postpartum, deeming this nurturing time critical to their transition to motherhood.[4]

Following most of my informants' urge to see postpartum rituals as a welcome, appreciated, and even endangered practice, I will focus on the protective and caring properties of such rituals over and above the emphasis on pollution.[5] To the extent that these rituals can feel oppressive, or overwhelming, it typically has more to do with competing family agendas than with pollution. For while it is true that parturients in African societies are often marked as polluted or contaminated by the birthing process and thought to pose a potential threat to those with whom they come in contact, parturients are also understood to be *in need* of protection themselves.

According to Bodo Ravalolomanga, for Tañala mothers of southeastern Madagascar, the period of postpartum seclusion serves multiple functions, all of which afford women and the newly born rest, protection, and strength. Women and babies are kept inside, in a warm room by a fire, for several weeks or months and given nourishing foods like chicken, rice porridges with milk, and shrimp, which is thought to increase the production of breast milk. This period of isolation not only offers women a chance to rest and regain their strength but also protects mothers and the newly born from harmful spirits (*lolo*), from people who have had recent contact with the dead, and from women who've recently lost children, all of whom may threaten the emerging fertility of the new mother-baby pair. The warmth of the room serves both to strengthen mothers and babies who were weakened by the birth and to offer a symbolic source of light, or blessing, on the birth.[6]

Rita Astuti describes something similar among Vezo mothers of southwest Madagascar, noting that after childbirth, both mothers and babies are considered weakened and vulnerable, and even penetrable, because of the wounds incurred from the separation of mother and child—the wound where the placenta separated from the mother, and where the umbilical cord detached from the baby. These wounds leave babies and mothers vulnerable not only to infections but also to wandering ghosts who may try to disturb them. Thus, babies and mothers need to be kept inside in a warm environment, and enveloped with blankets, before they are able to safely leave their homes and move about their daily lives again.[7] Rebecca Popenoe notes analogous customs among the Saharan women she works with, noting that "[postpartum seclusion rituals are] a chance for the mother to close herself off again from the dangerous forces childbirth has opened."[8] Similarly authors Blystad, Rekdal, and Malleyeck point out that *meeta* and *metida* rites, as observed by Iraqw and Datoga peoples, respectively, are not just about the isolation of "people and substances perceived to be dangerously contaminating, but in similar ways may seclude the fertile element in order to protect it."[9]

In addition to offering mothers and babies vital protection during their period of fragility, postpartum rituals also enable children to connect with their ancestral roots (*foto*). In Karen Middleston's research among Karembola of southern Madagascar, Karembola informants explained to her that in a woman's last few months of pregnancy, her husband is urged to take her back to her "father people" so that the baby can be connected with his or her "hearth of origin." Middleton went on to write, "the mother's people are the baby's *foto*, its 'origin' and 'cause.' If a man fails to acknowledge his wife's rootedness by failing to pay homage to her kin, the latter grow so angry that their malice is likely to kill the child." Maternal uncles are sometimes even referred to as "mothers" in this context because, as wife givers, or those who give their sisters (in marriage) to bless another family with the gift of children, they are understood to be the root, "the hidden but effective cause of growth, the power that makes others give birth."[10] Thus, it is important for babies to be connected to uncle-mothers and to all their maternal kin who connect them to their ancestral roots. Once a child is born, ideally mothers will continue to be cared for in this same hearth of origin. During this period of postpartum confinement, Middleton writes, "a woman is housed by her father-people and nurtured with vast quantities of the finest body-building foods they can afford, for instance, millet cooked in milk rather than plain boiled manioc."[11]

Given these examples, it might be more helpful to view postpartum rites as less about maintaining boundaries between polluted versus nonpolluted categories and more about preserving the fecundity of the new life that has just emerged; connecting mothers and children to their ancestral source, those who make their lives possible; and equipping women with the tools they will need to protect that new life in culturally appropriate ways. In different circumstances, and in different regions throughout the island, mothers need either heat, cold, or both to protect and strengthen them as they emerge from this period of fragility. Warm enclosures can be protective, but cold-water ritual bathing, discussed in greater depth in the following paragraphs, can also be protective, especially for individuals who are ranginaly. Cold-water bathing cools women's bodies from the inflaming energy of childbirth and marks mothers and their children as ranginaly, a collective identity inherited and performed through ritual bathing.

In addition to warming and cooling remedies, herbal medicines, like African basil and ravintsôha, in the form of teas and sitz baths, slow postpartum hemorrhaging and ensure that the flow of blood out of women will eventually be stalled and contained. And retaining the baby's first excrements, wrapped carefully in banana leaves, inside the home until the baby's first outing serves to keep mothers and babies safeguarded until they are more equipped to intermingle with the outside world. Marilyn Strathern describes practices such as these as about the management of "flows" based on what others have described as an understanding of bodies as "open and dynamic systems that mingle with other bodies in social interaction and in intimate exchanges of bodily fluids."[12] In other words, postpartum rituals in Africa at large, and in Madagascar in particular, serve in part to help ensure that the "flows" of breast milk, blood, food, excrements, and spirits move in and out of people's bodies appropriately in ways that preserve the health and fertility of all involved.

In sum, postpartum rituals provide women rest and support, which is especially welcome given the modern struggles Malagasy women face to balance mothering, work, and household responsibilities. They also manage "flows" by drawing things out of the body, closing things up, and offering protection against germs and from harmful spirits for young babies and mothers who have been opened up by childbirth, are not fully equipped to ward off. Finally, I hope to make clear in the following stories that postpartum rituals in Madagascar also serve to prepare women for the greater task of raising children in accordance with the prescribed guidelines of the communities they inhabit, so that the next generation will come to embody legacies of those who have come before. In this way, postpartum rituals help mold women into the kinds of mothers who will bless their babies.

Of course, guiding mothers in this way is not always a straightforward process. When women return to their natal home for the birth, as is customary, women are ushered through the birthing process by grandmothers and elder kin who can instruct them in the steadfast ways of their forebears and within the generative spaces of their ancestral lands. If children are understood to grow from ancestors, then it is necessary for their mothers to return home to the ancestors to give birth as doing so grants babies a connection to, and rootedness in, the people and land spaces that will continue to sustain them. Children are further tethered to these lands through the ritual burying of their placentas, and sometimes other materials from the birth, all of which tethers them to the land and to other people who are similarly tethered.[13]

When women give birth elsewhere, as is becoming more common, the relatives, friends, and neighbors who are most proximate will step in to support women through the process. Sometimes, this means the babies' paternal kin will have more influence in the birthing process than they would otherwise. Karen Middleton notes a particular type of ritual care, called *couvade*, that fathers of babies sometimes perform; this form of postpartum care is traditionally performed by women, or by the brother of the woman who has just given birth. However, in this case, it is performed by the woman's partner or husband in order for him to make visible his contribution to the child's emergence and growth. She writes, "In the context of an ideology of exchange that diminishes his reproductive contribution in favor of the mother's brother's agency, the groom puts visible effort into documenting his own consubstantiality with his wife and child."[14]

Women's bodies are contested sites. Women are often used as instruments in the perpetuation of both matri- and patrilineages and sometimes also in the construction of competing religious identities within their families. As the stories of motherhood in this chapter demonstrate, the transition to motherhood can be a time of discernment and choice, an opportunity for women to be guided and mentored, and a chance for women to negotiate and deepen their place within their families and in the larger society. For others, the transition to motherhood can be a precarious time, surrounded by rituals that feel arbitrary and constraining and that have more to do with the agendas of others than with their own growth and transition. Pregnancy fady and postpartum bathing rituals are prime examples of how rituals can both empower and constrain depending on the circumstances.

In Madagascar, people follow fady for many different reasons: sometimes because they feel pressured to do so, sometimes because they fear what the repercussions would be if they did not, sometimes to gain legitimacy in the eyes of certain relatives, and sometimes as a conscientious act of responsibility. Observing taboos binds people together in families or as members of a religious or ancestral community committed to certain food and behavioral restrictions. However, when mothers observe fady during pregnancy or during the postpartum period, the action does something even more profound; it is her way of signaling not only her commitment to her community but also her intention to raise her child according to the behavioral restrictions of the child's collective kin. This intention has the potential to integrate both her and the child into multiple communities. This means that during pregnancy, the fady that women observe multiply as they learn to avoid not only the foods that are prohibited within their own families but also the foods prohibited within the baby's father's family as well. In this way, women's bodies become the means by which multiple ancestral legacies converge and continue in the life of the child.

Postpartum ritual bathing does something similar. By observing cold-water bathing, for example, ranginaly mothers perform their inherited identities or the inherited ranginaly identities of their children. Their motivations for doing so might stem from a sense of respect, fear, or obligation or from a willingness and desire to belong. Regardless, doing so serves to mark and integrate children into community while also strengthening mothers' statuses and sense of belonging within these same communities. Moreover, postpartum bathing rituals' resemblance and relationship to other kinds of bathing rituals in Madagascar increases the meaning and potency of these postnatal rituals, shedding more light on their significance in the context of childbirth.

Ritual Bathing in Madagascar

In Madagascar, the transmittance of blessings through water is a customary practice for which there is a long historical precedent. One of the words for blessing in the Malagasy language is *tsodrano*, which literally translates as a blowing on, or sprinkling on, of water.[15] Maurice Bloch demonstrates water's central role in blessing rituals from circumcisions to the highland Merina's famous ritual of the royal bath.[16] This royal ceremony, as practiced during the late nineteenth century by the Merina of Madagascar's central highlands, was one whereby royal power was transmitted from rulers to subjects through an annual New Year's bathing rite.

> The central part of the ritual which gave it its name consisted of the King's taking a bath in pure water in which had been mixed "earth" obtained from the royal tombs of the royal ancestors. After the bath the king sprayed this water on to his subjects by way of blessing. The elements of blessing and of continuity are therefore identical to those found in the *famadihana* and the circumcision ceremony. As for those rituals, the blessing requires contact with the ancestors on the part of the legitimate head of the group and then the spraying on of water.[17]

In Madagascar, royalty are among the human mediums through which blessings from the divine are channeled. Thus, in the ritual of the royal bath, Merina royalty would bathe their bodies with fresh water and then offer this bath water, mixed with bits of dirt from ancestors' tombs, as the means by which to transfer ancestral blessings on their subjects. This practice enabled the transmittance of ancestral blessing (hasina) from royalty to commoners.

In the contemporary setting of Diégo Suarez, communal bathing occurs more frequently not as part of a royal ceremony but as a weekly or periodic practice of residents, some of whom visit the sacred mountain Nosy Lonjo, a practice that is discussed in the second chapter of this book. There participants arrive early in the morning to invoke their ancestors, request blessings of them, make vows, and perform a ritual bath in the waters that surrounded this sacred site where royal ancestral spirits are known to reside. It is important to note that Malagasy care about being on good terms both with their own kin ancestors and with royal ancestors more generally, even when they are not direct descendants. Even people with no kin-based connection to the site of Nosy Lonjo found bathing in the ancestral power of the spirits who reside there an auspicious act.

Water is also an important component of domestic religious rituals, especially in rites of passage. In haircutting ceremonies for babies and at circumcision ceremonies for young boys, water for blessings is fetched from a natural source before sunrise and also before the birds fly across the morning sky. Such water is then sprinkled on the initiate(s) and others present by a ritual head of the family or invocation leader (mpijoro) who channels the hasina and bestows it on participants. Interestingly, these contemporary practices, in which heads of families sprinkle water onto new members as a way to bless and incorporate them, appear to be modernized versions of family rituals that predated and also served as a model for the ceremony of the royal bath. As Gillian Feeley-Harnik describes,

> Both the ritual of the royal bath and the circumcision ritual [that the Merina nationalized] seem to represent royal appropriations of common Merina rituals (Bloch 1986: 116–118; 1987; Kus and Raharijaona 2001: 117–120). At the heart of both, for example is the transference of blessings downwards from elders to juniors via the use of water associated with the *Vazimba* ancestors. Merina royalty were inserted into this chain of blessing by organizing and centralizing these rituals such that the sovereign served as the initiatory of a national chain of blessing. In the case of the royal bath, the washing of the king's hair on the New Year initiated the replication of this ceremony down a line defined by status and seniority. It was also the occasion of annual visits to family tombs, linking in this way ancestors, descent and royalty.[18]

By appropriating domestic ritual bathing and then nationalizing the practice, the nineteenth-century Merina monarchy sought to conjoin ancestral power and political power. However, despite these attempts to monopolize and standardize ritual practices, there is evidence that suggests that communities throughout the island, especially coastal groups, continued to perform blessing rituals according to the various regional customs with which they were familiar.[19]

Moreover, Merina monarchical attempts to create annual, national versions of domestic rituals actually inspired some people along the coast to transform and/or hide what had previously been more communal or public celebrations in order to avoid scrutiny by Merina officials.[20] These concealed rituals celebrated local relationships with ancestors and privileged regional identities such that local contributions would not be lost in the modern composite national identity the Merina sought to create.

Thus, the contemporary use of water as a means by which to channel ancestral power for the purpose of blessing the living has a long and complicated history, one that predated, and subsequently became a response to, Merina politicians' attempts to wield and conflate divine authority with royal authority. Blessed water, bits of earth from ancestors' tombs, and gold and silver coins (which are associated with the auspiciousness of full moons, the open mouths of ancestors speaking, and also royal taxes and royal gifts) are the material means by which Malagasy maintain, produce, and reference the hasina they possess as members of particular descent groups. Though not the same as the royal bath, or even necessarily related, today's practice of postpartum bathing can nevertheless be understood to be part of a larger phenomenon in Madagascar of conferring ancestral power on individuals via the mediums of water, bits of earth, and relics from the ancestors.

As mothers' accounts in this chapter reveal, sometimes women are agents in this conferring of power on their children, as they take it on themselves to observe ranginaly on behalf of their children and themselves, sometimes they are vessels, made to heed the advice of relatives with regard to the fady they are expected to follow while carrying babies who are the continuation of particular lineages, and sometimes women are made to feel like mere instruments in the agendas of others, as they are forced to adopt practices and convert to religions that are not their own in order to further the traditions of their husband's families.

Hot and Cold Postpartum Bathing

The majority of women in Diégo Suarez describe themselves as ranginaly (cold-water bathers) as opposed to the *mafana* (hot-water bathers) of the central highlands, and they insist on the need to follow the appropriate washing style postpartum to recover effectively from childbirth. Unlike some postpartum customs, which are understood to be more optional, countless informants warned that ignoring these ritual baths could lead to illness, seizures, paralysis, or even death. In general, followers of ranginaly are expected to bathe with cold fresh water, preferably from a natural source, at least three times a day during times of sickness or transition, and it is especially important that water is poured over the head.

One notable informant, "le médecin inspecteur" of the Dispensaire in Diégo, Dr. Hanitra, likened ranginaly to the experience of being baptized. He said, "With ranginaly, women first have to take a dip in a river and then take a bath with cold water. It's especially important that water gets poured over the head; it's kind of like a baptism." Despite some doctors' ignorance of or ambivalence toward traditional practices, there were others like Dr. Hanitra who were quite knowledgeable about and supportive of birthing and postpartum customs. He asserted, "It is very important to respect peoples' fomba, unless they interfere with their health."[21]

Although my informants gave birth in a variety of settings—in their homes, in their midwives' homes, in birthing clinics, and in hospitals—nearly all of those who wished to practice postpartum bathing found a way to do so regardless of the setting. For example, I was told on numerous occasions that if a woman had a cesarean surgery and could not be bathed with water over the head, her family members modified the practice by simply trying to keep cloths of cold water on her head.

In addition to the three daily cold-water baths, postpartum women in Madagascar typically bathe with an herbal infusion of either ravintsôha (lemon leaves) or rômba (African basil). Female relatives splash the parturient with this hot remedy one week postpartum and then again two weeks after the birth.[22] Parturients are also encouraged to drink some of this medicinal concoction in the form of a tea. These herbs are said to speed up the recovery of the woman's internal wounds, while the daily cold-water bathing is said to both harden and strengthen her body, making her less vulnerable to biomedical and spiritual illnesses. Nadima described the grave necessity of ranginaly:

> NADIMA: After a woman gives birth, once she is able to stand up, they take her and give her a cold-water bath pouring the water from head to toe. If they don't do it, the woman will be paralyzed or dizzy. You should not try it [tsy mety feky]; it is forbidden to risk not bathing the woman. Even now when people do not follow all of the customs; they still do cold-water baths. If they can't give the woman a bath, they at least wet her head.

> ÉDITH: Who helps the woman bathe, her mother, or someone else?

> NADIMA: You don't have to choose, but it should be someone who knows about fomba, and they should follow the woman to the hospital. If there is no one who knows the customs, any of her family can assist her. When she goes home, [the new mother] has to take a bath three times a day. She has to bathe in the morning, at noon, and in the afternoon—three times a day. During the bath, the head must be wet and then after one week, she bathes with ravintsôha. The ravintsôha should be hot, and when it's still hot, she takes a bath with it. It [the ravintsôha] should be very hot, but not burn the woman, so you should wait until the skin can touch it. The second week she repeats the process. And then after she is finished with the ravintsôha, she continues with the ranginaly. For three months after the birth she should do cold-water bathing. After two weeks and the second bathing with lemon leaves, she can go outside with the baby (afaka miboaka an-tany miaraka tsaiky).[23]

The expressed purpose of postpartum bathing rituals is to help women heal and to provide them with a period of rest and preparation for the demands of motherhood; however, they also serve to link women with others who observe the same customs. These inherited, kind-specific rituals, much like fady, are central to people's sense of identity and belonging in the world. As Kwame Appiah argues, identities, though fabricated (i.e., socially constructed), matter to people because they both give you reasons for doing the things you do and give you a sense for how you fit into the world.[24] The majority of women I interviewed echoed these sentiments insisting that the danger in not following postpartum bathing stemmed largely from the fact that failure to do so amounted to a breaching of contract with one's ancestors, which could lead to a shattered sense of one's place in the world.

Like all customs of the ancestors (fombandrazana), ranginaly is an inherited practice. It is also a dominant practice, described as stronger than the custom of mafana, and as such becomes a means by which a now less powerful group preserves its existence in the face of the more numerous and more powerful customs of the central highlanders.[25] Or alternatively, as a dominant trait, ranginaly practice can be the means by which mothers assert influence over their children despite a father's more principal claim due to the privileging of patrilineages. Typically, when a couple produces children, they follow a combination of both the mother's and the father's ancestral customs, with priority given to the male side of the family, but in the case of ranginaly, if either parent is ranginaly, it is this trait that takes precedence. As Lesley Sharp described,

> Structurally, the choice to observe the cold over the hot practice has a number of effects. From the point of view of the male Sakalava parent, it is straight forward. Having the child's mother follow the cold practice provides him with a means to assert his paternity, since it symbolically illustrates that the child is with Sakalava qualities. (The child is already recognized as such by the bureaucratic rule that stipulates that a child shares the ethnicity of its biological father.) Since the mother must use the cold system, her offspring—as well as future generations of children—will always be considered cold. If the mother is Sakalava and the father is not, however the effect is different. It serves to label the child as being partly Sakalava and endows it and its progeny with coldness, a Sakalava trait. As a result, here it works to assert the *maternal* tie to the child, regardless of the bureaucratic rule.[26]

Thus, according to Sharp, because ranginaly has precedence over other inherited characteristics, cold-water bathing enables Sakalava mothers to mark their children with the trait even when custom compels families to favor the child's ties with his paternal kin.

Additionally, according to one informant, ranginaly can also be a process by which women assert the paternity of their children. Take, for example, Nadima's account of the practice. Nadima described herself, by virtue of her mother, as Anjoaty and indicated that this is where her practice of ranginaly comes from: "Anjoaty people are from Bobaomby and Vohemar, but they have since moved all over, which is why you get the differences in the ranginaly customs. Once a woman gives birth, there is another phase to do. At first the woman is lying in bed still wearing her sarong [*lambahoany*], but as soon as she is able to stand up, they take her and give her a cold-water bath, pouring the water from head to toe." Nadima then went on to describe the processes involved in, and the importance of, cold-water bathing. According to Nadima, bathing helps mothers recover and feel less faint after childbirth; it also enables mothers to mark their children as descendants of Anjoaty, and in some cases, ranginaly can also be the means by which mothers discern or assert the paternity of their children. She explained,

> If she doesn't know who the father is, there may be many problems during her pregnancy and during the labor like bleeding. If the woman is mafana and the father is ranginaly and she covers herself up with too much clothing, she may become paralyzed. She is paralyzed because she has too much heat. She needs cold water. Sometimes she is dizzy, and she faints, and then by chance the person next to her will pour water over her head, and then she gets better. That is how she sometimes discovers she is ranginaly. The ranginaly gives her a signal about her baby and her baby's father. Ranginaly does not let you go like this if the father is not ranginaly. Take this example. Sometimes the woman is *malemy* [weak] and cannot do anything. They take her to the doctor, and the doctor says there is nothing wrong and the person next to her doesn't know what to do. They just put water on her and then discover that it is helpful. Or sometimes, they decided to do a cold-water massage. They do a massage with cold water on her feet, and it helps her stand up and get stronger. And some people even suggest outright that they try cold-water bathing because maybe the baby's father is ranginaly. Ranginaly does not accept for people not to follow it even if you do not know you are ranginaly. It will give you a signal. Ranginaly doesn't let you [*tsy magnambela*] disregard it. Ranginaly is difficult. People in town do not follow all customs associated with being ranginaly, but they still follow cold-water bathing after childbirth. And

even when they do circumcision, they do not follow all of the customs, but they do pour cold water over the child's head before they do the cutting.

Generally speaking, ranginaly is more than a description of a particular kind of bathing practice post-childbirth. It is a part of people's identities as descendants of ranginaly ancestors, and it can also be used as a tool by which to resolve questions of paternity and compel fatherly involvement.[27] For although postpartum rituals mark babies with particular religious identities and ethnic histories, as Gillian Feeley-Harnik notes, sometimes what is more difficult than negotiating the multiple identities that maternal and paternal kin wish to imprint on descendants is encouraging a father to claim his child.[28]

When asked about the origins of ranginaly, most informants described it as a regional custom, insisting that southerners and highlanders are mafana as compared to northerners, mainly people from Diégo, Vohemar, and Mahajanga, most of whom practice *ranginaly*. Though Nadima described the practice as having originated from the Anjoaty, an Afro-Arab ethnic group from the regions of Vohemar and Bobaomby in northern Madagascar, Lesley Sharp and Michael Lambek both link ranginaly with the more prominent Sakalava, in particular the northern Sakalava as opposed to Sakalava of the west and southwest coast.[29]

Although it is not entirely clear when or from which kinds of people cold- and hot-water bathing first emerged, what is clear is that for the people who practice this style of bathing, it is considered obligatory (tokony) and vital to one's health, from both a religious and a medical standpoint. For people with ranginaly ancestry, coldness brings health and healing, whereas warmth can cause sickness and even death. Therese, a retired nurse-midwife from the teaching hospital in Diégo explained it this way: "We have to follow cold-water bathing post-childbirth because our ancestors knew that heat dilates the veins."[30] She went on to explain that people have known for a long time that cool water can speed recovery and that warm water sometimes inflames, whereas cool water helps a wound to contract and heal. She described both heat and cold as important elements for healing; sometimes heat is necessary, sometimes cold, but for childbearing women who are ranginaly, cold water is essential.[31] For Therese, her biomedical understanding of health and healing add new layers of meaning to these inherited practices from her ancestors.

Ranginaly is an inherited practice that confers blessing on those who abide by it, but it is also a weighty custom, especially for women who find themselves in the position of having to adopt customs that had not previously been theirs. Most hot-water bathers, for instance, really disliked the idea of having to become ranginaly. As one woman expressed, "I'm glad I'm not married to a ranginaly because I would hate to do the cold bathing."[32] Women, seen as the primary caregivers, are often charged with the responsibility of guiding infants on the journey from the spirit world to the human world and from having an ambiguous place in their communities to having a defined social status within their families. This role carries both privileges and burdensome responsibilities. Holding her grandson in her lap, Nadima described to me the responsibility she had in raising her son as a Muslim even though she herself is not religious and was not Muslim at the time of her son's birth:

> AUTHOR: Do you practice religion? Are you Muslim, Christian, or just Malagasy?[33]
>
> NADIMA: I am just Malagasy [Gasy fo] but the baby's father [Nadima's son] is Muslim [Silamo]. Truthfully, I don't have a religion [za, teña marany, za tisy], but when I raised my son I followed Muslim customs. The mother raises the child and if the child sees that the mother doesn't follow any customs, he won't either so I felt a responsibility to raise him as a Muslim. When he was a child, I followed Ramadan. I followed all customs that I could follow until he was nine and then he started to do Ramadan and some customs on his own. And then I did the customs whenever I wanted to but it was not compulsory. [Nadima's sister who was sitting in the room with us interjected to say that they are Christian.]
>
> NADIMA: Our parents are Christian. We are Gasy—but I had a child with a Muslim (Zaho niteraka amin'ny Silamo).

In a sense, Nadima became a practicing Muslim, even if only temporarily, in order to raise her son as a Muslim in accordance with her husband's family wishes, just as non-Sakalava women who marry and bear children with Sakalava or Anjoaty men must become ranginaly in order to raise their children accordingly. Though Nadima did not disclose the processes through which she became a practicing Muslim, it is quite possible that she went through a formal conversion given that she now goes by a Muslim name (Nadima), a name her Christian parents would not likely have given to her at birth. For it is common practice, among women in East Africa and among converts the world over, to receive a Muslim name upon one's formal conversion to the faith.

Anita Hannig notes a tendency among Orthodox Christians in Ethiopia to describe postpartum mothers as Muslims, but for a different reason. In the

Ethiopian context, mothers are not converting to Islam in order to raise their children as Muslims, as was the case with Nadima. Rather, Hannig refers to a phenomenon in which mothers temporarily lose their Christian identities by virtue of their being associated with their not yet baptized (read: non-Christian) babies. She writes, "During childbirth and its attendant dangers, a laboring woman is immersed in the loss of self, the ambiguous mother-and-child being, and the bloodiness of the not fully human. In her intimate linkage with the child she brings into the world, she temporarily shares in her offspring's ambiguous religious status. She thus slips—at least symbolically—outside the margins of Orthodox Christianity."[34] In this example, parturients in Ethiopia have not converted to Islam, rather by virtue of temporarily losing their Christian identities in order to bear children, they are simply described as Muslims. For Orthodox Christians in Ethiopia, "Muslims constitute the principle religious 'Other'"; thus, the term "'Muslim' becomes a catch-all phrase for non-Christian."[35]

In Madagascar, as in Ethiopia, and indeed many other African societies, one of the ways in which women gain status is by adding to their husbands' lineages through the procreation of children. So, a significant part of their responsibility as mothers entails abiding by and incorporating their husbands' customs (*manaraka fomba vadinazy*) into their own bodily habits and familial customs so that they might be better equipped to raise children with particular kinds of ethnic and religious identities. Such a task sometimes requires women to adopt new sets of ancestral practices; take on a new name, a teknonym that refers to the mother by the name of her child; or convert to another religion or at least become adept at observing that religion while their children are young.

Postpartum rituals, especially when women are guided through them by other relatives, give women clues about the kinds of mothers they are expected to become and the kinds of children they are to produce. This does not mean that women cannot teach their children of their own matrilineal or patrilineal customs. Many women do, and ranginaly bathing is a particularly interesting example of how northern Malagasy mothers are doing this. It does mean that women's places in society are more ambiguous and require more negotiations as compared with men's social positions. When couples produce a child, women more frequently than men adopt their spouse's family's traditions in order to raise the child accordingly. And as Jennifer Cole notes, Malagasy are taught not to simply remember their histories and religious identities discursively but also to care for them viscerally.[36] Thus, women, more than men, find themselves embodying practices and identities not previously their own in order to raise their children according to the traditions of their ancestors.

Historically, this was especially true for some enslaved women in Madagascar, who through the procreation of children and the adoption of various religious and ancestral rituals were able to integrate themselves into the dominant culture in ways that enslaved men could not. Of course, producing children with a master in no way guaranteed one's integration into a lineage-based community. More often than not, children of such unions were understood to *not* belong in the same way that children produced by legitimate wives were. That said, there is some evidence that some enslaved women, over time, were able to find their place in society by adopting the ritual practices of their masters.[37]

What's clear from my own research, even though slavery did not factor heavily in it, is that the northern region of Madagascar allowed for the integration of enslaved peoples into society in ways that were not always possible in other parts of the island.[38] What's also clear is that women played an important role in this process of integration. As Gwyn Campbell describes, enslaved women, more than enslaved men, served in domestic capacities as weavers, clothes washers, servants, and sexual companions, affording them more opportunities to integrate themselves into Malagasy society than enslaved men had.[39] They did so by bearing children, who most of the time were not considered legitimate descendants but who nonetheless overtime became integrated into families in ways that made one's slave status less pronounced.

According to Gwyn Campbell, female slaves in Madagascar were highly preoccupied with efforts to "secure a niche within the dominant society for themselves and for their children" and with efforts to acculturate. He writes, "Acculturation was essential for the slave concerned, but it also enabled female slaves to transmit local belief and value systems to their children."[40] In other words, enslaved women, because they worked in domestic capacities and bore children, had resources available to them that enabled them to strategically integrate themselves into local ancestries and into the dominant culture, efforts they pursued not only for themselves but also for their children.

Though northerners seem to disclose slave descent more readily than other groups in Madagascar, it was not clear if, or to what extent, twenty-first century descendants remembered this history in the lives of their children or if the rituals they observed during birth and postpartum bear witness to the traumas of slavery.[41] What *is* evident is that historically women, through the procreation of children and likely through the observance of various other kinds of rituals, were able to integrate themselves into collectives that sometimes mitigated their status as slaves, not always in their lifetime, but for generations to come.

Women in Madagascar have been charged with adopting and embodying cultural and religious practices for themselves and on behalf of their children for a long time and for a variety of reasons. The birth of a child can unsettle women's status in interesting ways, opening the door to various kinds of opportunities for inclusion into ancestral families, religious communities, and the like. Practices like ranginaly have the capacity to both remember and re-member ancestral families either by acknowledging and strengthening someone's already established connection to those who have gone before or by incorporating new people into these webs of ancestral descent.

Camellia's story of motherhood bears witness to the kind of social strengthening that can occur when mothers observe the postpartum rituals that are specific to their families. As she describes, the fady and rituals she observed during pregnancy and the postpartum period were difficult, but she also understood them to be an important part of her identity and an important means by which she remained linked with relatives who had observed the same customs.

Camellia

Camellia moved to Diégo to attend the University of Antsiranana.[42] There she completed her undergraduate degree in biology and stayed to obtain her *maitrisse* in the same program. During her many years of schooling, she often moved back and forth between Diégo and Ambanja, a coastal town south of Diégo, where she grew up. She was there, in Ambanja, when she discovered that she was pregnant. She did not feel ready to be a mother, but her own mother reassured her, "You'll find a job. You can handle this." She found a job at the chamber of commerce that Camellia described as a "blessing from God." It was a part-time job and thus not quite sufficient to meet all of her financial needs at the time, but Camellia nevertheless managed to piece some other work together by serving as a private tour guide for a company in Diégo. As Camellia described with a grin, the baby was unexpected, but she also "brought good luck (*misy anjara*)."

Camellia observed a lot of fady during her pregnancy, and although she found them difficult to stick to at times, she also appreciated their importance. She recalled, "Every family has different fady. I couldn't drink milk or eat any milk products like cheese, butter or yogurt, which was very hard because I sold yogurt during my pregnancy and I couldn't even taste my own yogurt! I could never be sure if the yogurt had the right sweetness, but throughout my pregnancy I remained disciplined and my clients assured me that the yogurt's flavor was sweet and good." According to Camellia, who is of Sakalava, Antankarana, and Anjoaty origins, the fady she follows are not based on these karazana (kindedness, or ethnic distinctions). Rather, as she described, she observes the fady of her family, of those whom she is related to, some of which are pregnancy specific and some of which are more general, like her mother's family's abstention from pork.

During pregnancy, Camellia preoccupied herself with all kinds of advice from strangers and neighbors and medical professionals, some of which she heeded and some of which she ignored, but when it came to fady, she observed them as a deeply held commitment toward the people with whom she is related. She did not have to comply; rather, she chose to. For all the women I met in Madagascar who observed pregnancy fady, there were just as many who did not, and still others who were selective about which fady they deemed critical and which were expendable. As Andrew Walsh explains in his essay on the importance of fady in Madagascar, it is "the freedom to do otherwise" that makes a person's observance a powerful and responsible act.[43]

As I state earlier in this book, beliefs about who babies are and where they come from can have profound influences on how parents care for them.[44] Camellia's commitment to observing fady during her pregnancy proves that this premise holds true even before babies are born. If Malagasy believe their babies to be a "continuation of the ancestors" (ny fitohy raza), as some do, then certainly pregnant women would want to be careful not to feed the babies in their wombs foods that their ancestors have long since abstained from eating. On the flip side, observing certain dietary and behavioral restrictions can also be an act that sends signals to the developing baby about what kind of person they are expected to become. For behavioral restrictions within families and religious communities not only bind people to those who have come before; they also shape babies into the people their families imagine them to be. In other words, infants, the mysterious spiritual creatures Malagasy affectionately call zaza rano, are at the apex of Malagasy remembrances of the past and the visions they have for their and their children's future. They are, as Annie Paul writes, "a mix of influences" shaped by their ancestors and their mothers' actions just as much as they are shaping their mothers into bodies who must pay attention to the lives growing inside of them.[45] Pregnancy fady may seem arbitrary to outsiders, but within their proper cultural and religious contexts, they help create a sense of belonging and connectedness that stretches across wombs and tombs. Fady shape the future of fetuses within the womb, *and* as one informant described to Jennifer Cole, "they are the ancestor's stones," or the ways by which we remember those who have gone.[46]

Camellia's observance of fady and other birth-related rituals did not end with her pregnancy. When her labors began, she was surrounded by many support persons including her sisters, her mother and grandmother, and her midwife, Yasmina, a retired nurse from the Hôpital Be, all of whom led her through rituals that facilitated healing, blessings, and guidance as she transitioned into motherhood. She recalled,

> My labor started at around 1:00 in the morning. My mother, grandmother, my sister Hortensia and another sister were all with me. They had come to stay with me a few weeks prior to the birth so as to ensure that they would be with me and could help me when the baby arrived. My mother was worried, even though she had had six daughters of her own with no trouble or complications during pregnancy or childbirth. But, she knows childbirth can be dangerous sometimes and found it hard to watch me go through the process. Yasmina lived near me, so when the labor began, we all moved to Yasmina's house for the birth. We went there when my contractions became too painful, when I felt the need to go to the toilet. When we arrived at Yasmina's house, she made me walk around as much as I could; she said it was important to exercise during labor. So, I walked around in the yard, which was very difficult. The baby came out a few hours later, at 5:00 that morning.
>
> During my labor, they poured warm water on my back to help the baby descend. After the baby emerged, Yasmina pushed on my abdomen to help me deliver the placenta. Then Yasmina took the baby, cut the cord and wiped her off, and gave her to me for nursing. After that, she sent us home.

According to Camellia, there was much support after the birth and many rituals to follow. She described,

> After my daughter was born, I followed ranginaly. It made me feel better. You must pour the water over your head. That especially made me feel

better. If I started to become dizzy, the water would make me feel better. And then after one week, and again after two, I bathed with ravintsôha.[47] It was really hot. [*Laughing as she spoke*] It's not fair!

Two weeks after the birth, we brought my daughter Corinne out of the house in a formal way with a ceremony called *mampiboaka tsaiky* [to make the baby come out]. We bring the baby out to see the sun. Before this ceremony, the baby and I stayed in the house, not strictly speaking. We left the house for vaccinations, and of course, I moved with the baby from my midwife's house back to my own house right after she was born. And I also left my house to bathe, because we bathe outside, but otherwise I remained indoors with my baby.[48] When we bring the baby out, this is when we officialize the baby and the birth. It's a simple party. We did it early in the morning in my yard. Everyone went out and sat on lamaka.[49] My mother, grandmother, and two sisters, who were present for the birth, were all there for the ceremony as well. We went out early in the morning, sometime between 6:30 and 7:00, and sat down. I wore a good lamba, not just any. I wore a nice one that was relatively new, and it had a matching second piece that I draped over my head.[50]

My grandmother held the baby and my mother gave the baby a joro. My mother asked for health and strength for the baby and for me. She thanked Anjanahary [God] and the razana [ancestors] that we had survived childbirth and were doing well. We always thank and speak to God first and then to our ancestors. We cooked and ate sabeda, a special rice porridge made with milk and honey, and at that time all of the fady I had been observing during my pregnancy were lifted [*magnadoso fady*]. I was really pleased about this. I could eat milk, eggs, and *sakay* (spicy peppers) again. I was happy. I was very excited to eat these foods again.

The postpartum rituals that Camellia performed not only afforded her protection and helped her "feel better" and heal but also served to link her with others who observe the same customs. For example, by observing ranginaly, she acknowledged an inherited identity that connects her, and her daughter, to her own mother and grandmother and to a lineage of others who have observed the same customs. Last, the weeks of bathing and seclusion leading up to her baby's first outing afforded her a chance to bond with, and learn from, her mother and grandmother, to receive their wisdom and, through her mother's joro, receive the blessings of God and her ancestors.

At the time of the interview, Camellia had not yet given Corinne any kind of formal haircutting. As she explained, "Really, it's the father's family who is

in charge of this, and I have to respect the father's family because it's customary for the father's family to do this. They are the first to cut the baby's hair
and it is they who know how." She did however have plans to baptize her at
her hometown church in Ambanja in line with her family's Catholic faith. The
birth rituals Camellia observed during pregnancy and the postpartum period
are only the first of many in which her daughter will participate, but they are
also somewhat foundational as they represent the beginnings of her inclusion
into both the Catholic and lineage-specific communities to which she will belong. In subsequent months and years, baby Corinne will participate in other
rituals, some of which will be orchestrated by her father's family, which will
help set the stage for her connection to, and inclusion within, the network of
relationships important to them.

Camellia's daughter Corinne was sixteen months old when I first interviewed Camellia. She was still breastfeeding, learning to use the toilet, and
running all over the place. As Camellia described, "She crawls all over the
tables. She climbs! She runs! She gets into everything and you have to watch
her carefully. She also likes to sing and dance. She watches television and
learns how to dance from the television." Camellia and her boyfriend had
not anticipated that they would have a child when they did. Both were finishing school and in the early stages of their careers. Moreover, Camellia and
her boyfriend were not living in the same city. He was working in Tamatave
while she worked in Diégo and finished her degree at the university there.
But the birth of their daughter was a surprise that Camellia interpreted as
fortuitous.

For at least half of the women I interviewed, one or more of their pregnancies came to them as a surprise, but as will become clear in the story
that follows, not all interpreted these experiences as fortuitous. The following story of a young woman by the name of Adeline illustrates this point.
Becoming a mother at seventeen, and far from her natal home, left Adeline
feeling alone, and at the mercy of her boyfriend's relatives. Though she
was encouraged by her boyfriend's family to observe specific pregnancy
fady and postpartum rituals, none of these practices felt like something
that granted her greater belonging, nor did she understand the intentions
behind them. Instead, she simply felt obliged to observe them, in order to
please her boyfriend's family. At the time of my interview with Adeline,
much was up in the air. What was clear was that she loved her son and was
still finding her way as his mother.

Adeline

When Adeline became pregnant, she was only seventeen and living far from her hometown and her parents in Diégo Suarez.[51] She came from a family of eleven children in which she was the ninth. A pregnancy had not been in either her or her boyfriend's plans. And like most young Malagasy couples struggling to make ends meet, they had to rely on their families to help them navigate this new juncture in their lives. I met Adeline through my research assistant Édith, who was Adeline's neighbor during that year. Like Édith, Adeline was a young woman who had moved to Diégo for better schooling and work opportunities. And like Édith, Adeline was living with her boyfriend. Together, the two couples earned enough money to rent small makeshift houses, but each was far from ready to bear children or marry, according to their own estimations. When Édith approached Adeline about the possibility of us interviewing her, Adeline readily agreed, affirming that we could come anytime as she was "always at home."

Adeline was washing clothes when we arrived at her home for the interview and asked that we give her a few minutes before beginning. So Édith and I walked across the dusty dirt path that separated Adeline's house from hers, a path that was big enough for bicycles and motorbikes to pass but too small for a larger vehicle. We waited inside Édith's newly built house made from sheets of corrugated iron, and that wait afforded me a brief window into both women's worlds. It was hot inside Édith's house, and there was not a lot of furniture or any electricity, but there was a bed, bookshelves filled to the brim with books from Édith's and her boyfriend's respective college courses, a couple of chairs, a nonworking refrigerator used for storing food, a portable gas burner, a table with some spices and pots on it, a bicycle, plastic buckets in which Édith hauled water each morning for the daily washing and cooking, and a single chicken.

Édith and her boyfriend had been trying to set up electricity for months, but there was a long waiting list, and as she explained, "one would have to bribe the company [JIRAMA] to be moved up on the list." Édith offered me a chair and some litchis as we waited for Adeline. She fed the chicken a handful of dry rice and then took her outdoors and tied her to a tree. "We mean to eat her," Édith explained, "but we keep buying other things for dinner and putting it off." "Now," she said, "I don't want to kill her because I have grown to like her." A few minutes later, Adeline crossed the dirt path separating their homes and arrived at Édith's home, cradling her eight-week-old baby in her arms.

Adeline began her story by sharing with us what it was like when she became pregnant, how she decided to keep the baby, and what it was like trying to observe all the pregnancy fady her grandmothers encouraged her to follow.

> My "grandmother" [*dady*], that is, my boyfriend's great-aunt, lives next to us and she was the first to notice when I became pregnant.[52] When it happened, I asked my boyfriend and his family what I should do—whether I should keep the baby or abort the baby. They told me to keep the baby and offered to help, so that's what I did. During the pregnancy, it was fady for me to eat sour foods as well as wrapped foods [*raha mofogno*] like egg rolls and sambos [samosas]. And it was fady for me to have sex beginning around the seventh month because the baby's head was on bottom and sex at that stage would have made the baby impure. But even though my relatives cautioned me about these fady, I disregarded them often. My grandmothers on both sides warned me that my legs would tremble during labor if I ate too many sour things. I was not supposed to eat cold food during the pregnancy either. My grandmothers told me, "If you break the fady and don't get sick, then you might lose the baby [*mangadoso tsaiky*]. If, however, you break the fady and do get sick," then they explained, "the baby will be fine." When my legs trembled during my labor, I knew it was because I had broken the fady. That is why my legs were weak and I needed an injection during the labor.

Adeline did not care to observe the pregnancy fady her grandmothers encouraged her to follow. Instead, she disregarded them more than she followed them and attributed her weakness during her labor to this very indifference. Adeline observed many of the same birth rituals Camellia had, but unlike Camellia, Adeline did not express feeling nurtured or blessed by any of it. Instead, she expressed mostly sadness. She disclosed, "The day before I gave birth to Alain, I was very sad. I had wanted to go home to see my family. The pregnancy had worn me down and I longed to go home, but my mother-in-law encouraged me not to leave. 'Go home when you are happy,' she said. 'You are sad now, and it is not good to go home when you are sad. Besides, we have already given you a joro for the birth; there is nothing you need to go home for right now.'" Adeline heeded the advice of her boyfriend's relatives and stayed. She gave birth to her son Alain, a name the baby's father chose, at an "*hôpitaly an trano*" (house hospital) near the fish processing plant at Place Kabary. A retired *rasazy* (midwife) who used to work at the Dispensaire works out of her home there.[53] Her boyfriend, mother-in-law, and dady ("her boyfriend's grandmother") were all there for the birth, which was helpful, but it did not fully mitigate the sadness she felt being so far away from home.

Adeline received many blessings: a joro before the birth and a joro two weeks after the birth, when the baby was brought out of the house in a formal way. In addition, she was led through the rituals of ranginaly (cold-water bathing) after Alain was born. She bathed this way three times a day, one week after the birth with rômba and ravintsôha leaves as well; this was repeated after the second week to slow her hemorrhaging and more quickly facilitate the contracting of her uterus. On the advice of her mother (from afar) and a midwife, she also drank a tea right after the birth called *anamaganan-jangahary* and later another tea called *agnamafana*. All of the aforementioned rituals helped mark her, and her baby, as ranginaly and created an atmosphere of care around her healing process, but despite being led through similar rituals as Camellia, Adeline did not remember her birth story as a joyously as Camellia did her own. She shared how much she loved her son but also shared that "life is more difficult now." She went on to say,

> Before things were a lot simpler, whereas now my work is never done [*tsy vita asa*], and I am always in a hurry. And my work is always interrupted by the baby, who cries often and needs to be held often. My house is dirty now which is why I did not invite you in and asked for you to wait for me at Édith's house instead. What I want to tell you is that I had not wanted to have a child. I was counting my cycles, but I must have miscounted and gotten pregnant anyway. I never planned to have a child this young.

As the interview ended, I thanked Adeline for sharing her story with me and asked, "Can I help you with any of your housework?" "Do you know how to hand-wash clothes?" she inquired. I replied that I did. "Even clothes for adults?" she asked incredulously. "Yes, especially clothes for adults," I answered enthusiastically. Still skeptical of my handwashing competence, she agreed that next time I came, I could wash the baby's clothes but not the clothes for the adults.

Édith and I accompanied Adeline back to her house and took turns holding Alain as Adeline finished washing clothes. Édith was surprised that I knew how to hold a baby. She had heard that American women did not know how to hold babies. She had seen a movie with Ben Affleck and Jennifer Lopez, and the mother in the movie did not know how to care for a baby. I conceded that this was sometimes true but also explained that it depends. My status as an American in Diégo Suarez often granted me a kind of celebrity status because of the associations Malagasy have of Americans, but it was also true that I was sometimes regarded as childlike or assumed to have childlike skills, presumably because some vazaha (foreigners) have very little know-how in the kinds of everyday skills with which Malagasy are familiar.

As an outsider, I was privy only to a minuscule snapshot of Adeline's life, and even that was likely tainted with a few cultural miscommunications on both of our parts. That said, what I understood from what Adeline shared with me was that her journey to motherhood had been a struggle and had brought more sadness, uncertainty, and work into her life than she felt ready for. Her boyfriend's family encouraged her to go through with the pregnancy. They promised their support. Yet there Adeline sat in his family's courtyard, at seventeen, washing her boyfriend's pants. In that moment, when no one else was around, I wondered how much of the burdens of parenthood she shouldered alone. I let her in on my judgment of the situation when I asked, "Does your boyfriend ever help out with cooking?" "Yes," replied Adeline. "He does when he's around and sees that there's work to be done." Then Adeline asserted to Édith and me, "You know if you want to have children, it gets increasingly difficult with age." Her statement offered an alternative angle from which to view her surprise pregnancy and evidenced a more critical perspective on what she understood as mine and Édith's respective decisions to delay parenthood. Moments later Adeline's grandmother passed through the yard accompanied by several other people, which offered a slight correction to my initial assumption that Adeline spent most of her days at home alone. Indeed, after subsequent visits to Adeline's house, I would see that Adeline often had company as she and her boyfriend lived side by side many of his relatives.

Adeline's story reveals both the joys and uncertainties that sometimes follows a young woman's journey into motherhood. Her story also reveals the ways in which rituals can be used to coerce women rather than to simply heal and protect them. In particular, when Adeline's mother-in-law insisted that the joro her family provided was the *only* blessing Adeline needed, she signaled to Adeline that she either did not need to return to her own for the birth or would not be permitted to do so. Rituals of care postpartum can impregnate with meaning the otherwise ordinary transitions people move through, but they also restrict behaviors and send subconscious messages to the body about the social expectations one is expected to follow. In Adeline's case, the decision as to whether she should keep her baby was one she had to make in concert with relatives, as she did not have the resources to make this decision alone, nor did she have the ability or means to return home for the birth, as is customary, to root her son in the traditions of her own family. Instead, she was subjected to the agendas of the baby's father's family, which is not to say that she had no agency as a mother, only that her agency is limited and that the very postpartum rituals that helped some women deepen their connections to family can be used by others to isolate and diminish a mother's influence.

Despite the challenges she faced, Adeline repeatedly expressed how much she loved her newborn son, even with all the uncertainties that hung over her about whether she and her boyfriend would stay together or part ways and about who would keep Alain if they did. And if she later became involved with another man, would that man love Alain as she did? Would another man want to be with her even though she already had a child? These were the questions that weighed on her. In earlier generations, Malagasy men were known to find mothers desirable and adopt the children they had had from a previous relationship, but in contemporary times, Malagasy note that the opposite is sometimes true.[54]

Adeline's story is not so different from the struggles other Malagasy face when they become mothers at a young age. When young Malagasy women become pregnant, they do not always have much say as to whether they should keep their babies. Many also do not have the financial means to return home for the birth, leaving them at the mercy of whatever relatives happen to be proximate to them and interested in the upbringing of their child. Adeline ended up seeing her pregnancy through, but there were certainly other women I interviewed who had abortions when they became pregnant at a young age, sharing stories of how they had kept their pregnancies secret to make the decision to terminate their pregnancies privately. Some of the latter were students who feared that their unplanned pregnancies would disappoint their parents who had sent them away "in order to have a better life, not to come home pregnant." And of those who had faced abortions, some did so alone.[55] One young woman described how her doctor had driven her back to her dorm room and helped her into bed before leaving her under the care of a roommate. Some of the young women I interviewed took birth control pills to avoid an unwanted pregnancy. Others used alternate means of contraception. Several managed to delay motherhood to obtain a university degree or pursue job training. Of these, a few later regretted this decision. For they later found themselves older and out of place for not having a child and felt envious of the joy their peers' children seemed to bring.

Pregnancy does not always afford young Malagasy women a newfound sense of status and worth. Parenthood brings both joys and sadness, and uncertainties, not only financial but also social ones. For Adeline, her lack of financial resources made becoming pregnant at an early age especially difficult, and left her especially vulnerable to others' decision-making at the expense of her own. Birth rituals and pregnancy fady, even though empowering for some, can be taxing and constraining for others and do not always serve as a means by which mothers are further integrated into their respective communities. Sometimes mothers are simply made to, or at least strongly encouraged to, observe fady, and participate in rituals that mark their children as descendants of someone else's lineage. In other words, sometimes, they are merely instruments in other people's agendas. More often than not, though, women still find a way to assert some influence in the lives of their children.

Embodying Motherhood

Rites of incorporation for infants including joro, first haircuttings, baptisms, and circumcisions all serve to make babies into humans, or in the least, mark them as new initiates of certain lineages or religious communities, granting them the kind of identity and belonging vital to their becoming human. What stories like Camellia's and Adeline's demonstrate is that integral to the process of turning babies into humans is the shaping and making of women into mothers who will raise babies accordingly. But childbirth in and of itself is not enough to transform women into mothers. Even as Malagasy recognize childbirth as a marker of womanhood, Malagasy are also quick to point out that childbirth does not always or automatically turn women into mothers nor does one have to give birth in order to become a mother as fostering and adoption are also common and important ways by which women become mothers in Madagascar.[56]

There are many social circumstances that have the potential to shape women into mothers. Rituals play a role, but they are certainly not the only determining factor. Rituals that turn "water babies" into "real human beings" do not necessarily guarantee a baby's firm placement in their social milieu, but they *do* increase the likelihood that babies will begin to embody the kinds of habits and markings that will grant them inclusion into a greater collective. Similarly, postpartum rituals for mothers do not guarantee her full acceptance or success as a mother, but they can serve as a powerful means by which women can come to understand and embody the practices that might lead to their and their children's inclusion into certain kinds of communities. Of course, the same kinds of rituals can also serve to control women or to wrest influence away from them in order to set children on a trajectory toward greater patrilineal affiliation.

Childbirth, and the rituals that surround it, is a rite of passage like no other. Arnold van Gennep's three-phase structure of rites of passage offers some insights, especially when considering a woman's customary return to her natal home (the separation period) and her eating of special food and observance of fady during the period of postpartum seclusion (the liminal period), culminating with a reentry into her husband's household (the reintegration phase).[57] Collectively, these practices form the ceremonial processes that have the capacity to transform women into mothers and render childbirth momentous. But reducing childbirth and motherhood to a three-part ritual schema is misleading because women do not always return to their natal homes and reenter their husband's households with a child in hand. Women's transition into childbearing is significantly less prescribed or fixed as compared with, for example, the way boys are forcibly and sometimes violently separated from the "maternal" spaces they inhabit during the circumcision ceremony in order that they are reborn into the social hierarchical worlds of men.[58] Instead, childbearing women are often guided by the competing agendas of multiple families who perform rituals differently or who perform no rituals at all.

Ironically, rites of passage, which have long been modeled after physiological birth, do not necessarily help elucidate women's passages into motherhood. Women's experiences of childbirth and the transitioning role from young women into mothers do not necessarily fit with the predominant literature on rites of passage which emphasize abrupt separations from the old habits and spaces and reentry into new spaces transformed. Women's experiences of life's transitions may be significantly more fluid, experienced more as a deepening rather than as a rupturing and renewal.[59] Bruce Lincoln proposes the metaphor of the chrysalis as a more appropriate model of women's experiences of transformation. He writes,

> Without a clear enactment of separation, one might question whether there can truly be a liminal period or a process of reincorporation, for

nothing has been left behind and there is nowhere to which one can
return. Thus, although women's initiations regularly conform to a
three-part structure, the three stages cannot accurately be described as
separation, liminality, reincorporation. Something different seems to be
at work, and in place of van Gennep's terms I would suggest three others:
enclosure, metamorphosis (or magnification), and emergence. . . . The
seclusion chamber is her chrysalis, where she acquires her new mode of
being.[60]

Lincoln's model, at least in terms of imagery, seems a more apt description of
Malagasy women's evolution into motherhood. For after the birth of a child,
Malagasy women enjoy a flexible period of seclusion, or enclosure, at home
(in their chrysalises), followed by a gradual introduction to new mode of being, where relatives guide her until she is ready to emerge (read come out of
her house) on her own.

That said, as discussed in the first chapter of this book, women in Madagascar sometimes refer to childbirth as a spear battle (ady antsaboa), describing
childbirth as women's battle with the sword, comparable to circumcision for
men.[61] While the notion of a spear battle may seem to connote a rupture or
clean break more than it does a gradual metamorphosis, in fact women do
not experience a symbolic exposure to death, as neophytes do during the
liminal phase of puberty rites in order to make the transition feel more powerful. Women use the metaphor of spear battle because they know that some
among them may literally die or come close to death during childbirth. Thus,
no three-part ceremony to make this life experience seem real is needed,
precisely because it *is* real. The moment Malagasy women become pregnant,
they are instantly charged with the responsibility of becoming mothers who
will grow, birth, and transition their water babies into the kinds of hardened
bodies their descendants might one day remember.

In short, no singular rite of passage exists to transition Malagasy women
into mothers in the way that circumcision readies young boys for their journey
toward manhood. Malagasy women nevertheless have claimed childbirth
as a transformative battle, as *their* rite of passage, though it may at times be
significantly less ceremonious and considerably less scripted. As the stories
in this chapter have demonstrated, ritual and regalia are no doubt involved,
in the blessings that women receive, in the fady they follow, and in the ritualized baths they endure. However, it is not the pouring of water over women's
heads that gives them the sense of having crossed over, despite Dr. Hanitra's

proclamation that ranginaly represents "women's baptism." Most women rather described ritual bathing as more discipline-like than spiritual. Even those who take pride in these inherited customs describe bathing with cold water and with hot herbal medicines as "difficult" and "unfair."

There is a reason why religious communities have modeled rites of passage after childbirth and not the other way around. The act of giving birth becomes a powerful act not because of the structured ceremonies that surround it but more often from the harrowing physiological experience of having another being come out of one's body. The rituals are there not to make the experience more powerful but rather to give voice to what is already profound about that experience. Of course, women often do desire their experiences of childbirth to be marked as sacred, which is why their families give them joro before they go into labor and why loved ones visit them after the birth bringing them gifts of *rôm-patsa*.[62] It is also why Malagasy women say to one another, "Congratulations for you have made it over to the other side." This need to have what is momentous about childbirth recognized is why North American women give each other gifts and words of blessing at a baby shower or the purpose behind the Native American prenatal ceremony called Blessingway. Rites of passage help consecrate the transitions in our lives that we have deemed sacred—our births, our comings of age, our unions, our entrances into religious communities, and our deaths.[63] They also help give meaning to these experiences by offering up symbols, metaphors, and scripts for how we might come to interpret the experience.

And rites of passage also function as a way for communities to shape initiates into new kinds of people. Sometimes this goal is achieved through ritual but not always in the tripartite structure we imagine, which accounts for the diversity of experiences that people profess. Sometimes women are made into mothers, for example, the kinds of ranginaly or Muslim mothers who will raise their children as such; other times they are not. And rituals are sometimes part of the equation. Malagasy use postpartum bathing to ensure that women's bodies are protected, healed, and hardened post-childbirth but also, and perhaps primarily, as a way to ensure that new mothers will know something of their ancestral and religious heritages that they might impress them on their children.

Adeline's story falls more in the realm of the latter, but Camellia's story of motherhood highlights what is perhaps the more common story—the tension between agency and constraint that mothers must navigate in their efforts to situate their children, and themselves, within lineages and religious com-munities that will grant them identity and belonging. In the case of Camellia, she proudly observed her family's postpartum fady and bathing practices (ranginaly), and together with her mother and grandmother planned her daughter's first ceremonious outing (mampiboaka tsaiky) and baptism, but with regard to haircutting, a ritual that has the potential to shape babies in important ways, it was clear to her that this fell in the domain of her baby's father, although this is not always true of haircutting ceremonies. Whether to empower, to constrain, or both, postpartum rituals are a powerful means by which to solemnize the birth experience and also to orient those involved, especially mothers, toward the task of raising children who will embody the habits and traditions of their ancestors and of those with whom they are in community.

FOUR

TURNING "WATER BABIES" INTO "REAL HUMAN BEINGS"

Outside the city of Diégo Suarez, on the way to Ramena Beach is a hill where dead babies, wrapped in special cloths called lamba, hang from the trees in handwoven baskets.[1] This hill, near the mangroves and old salt marshes, is just meters from the main road and contrasts with the flatter terrain that surrounds it. On a walk from Diégo in search of the hill, my research assistant Zafisoa and I wove our way through the University of Antsiranana neighborhoods to the junction that leads toward Ramena. Most of the houses near the university were either new or under construction, and many of them were owned by vazaha (foreigners). The houses on the opposite side of the road were multiplying rapidly and threatened to eclipse what is arguably the most beautiful public view of Diégo's bay. Residents were concerned about the growing number of houses, especially given that the panorama of the bay that these homes obstructed is one of the most sacred spots in Diégo, the ancestral site of Nosy Lonjo.

As we continued past the crossroads, in search of the hill, Zafisoa spoke quietly and cautiously and advised me to do the same. "It's a discreet topic," she said. We spotted some fishermen and made our way from the road to the sand below to speak with them. Leaning against their canoes near the mangroves that bordered the bay, they were jovial and leisurely in their conversation with us. We asked about the hill with the babies' remains. The fishermen explained that people leave zaza rano in baskets when they die before they have teeth or while they are still nursing, because babies of this age cannot be buried in the family tomb. "It's because they are not yet full of bones," Zafisoa remarked while holding up her arm as if to demonstrate the bone-filled nature of her own limbs.[2]

We asked people all along the road about this hill and thus managed to collect several fragments of information before we reached our destination, a description of which can be found at the very end of this book. Some, like Zafisoa, were unaware of the hill's whereabouts; others knew where it was but had never experienced the misfortune of losing a baby whose body would need to be brought there. We stopped to buy some *mofogasy* (rice cakes) from a woman at the top of the road. She did not know where the hill was, but she believed that the location had been moved because "authorities now discourage the practice." Another man, who ultimately pointed us toward the right hill, explained that it was not fady to go there and look around as we wished to do but that though it was his family's fomba to leave water babies there, he would rather not accompany us. He indicated that he did not want to "see their bones." This fisherman's statement was intriguing, given that most of the people we met along the way insisted that these deceased babies did not have bones. In fact, the very man who was afraid to see their bones had previously described them as *mbola rano* (still full of water).

The affirmation by some that young babies are still soft and watery and without bones does not stand in place of scientific understandings of babies' physiology—how they are conceived and grow and that they have skeletons and organs. Instead, it speaks to the vulnerability of young infants, who are more susceptible to both biomedical and spiritual illnesses and who have less of a stronghold in the world. Sometimes, the spirits of these young babies decide not to stay in the human realm but to return to the watery spirit realm from which they came. Or perhaps, as others have described, conditions were not yet right for that child to flourish, and so the ancestors "took the child back."[3] Even when parents blame congenital abnormalities or an infection for the child's death, they may simultaneously understand there to be an underlying spiritual cause. For these reasons, zaza rano, as young infants are often affectionately dubbed, are handled with extreme care until they have successfully transitioned into bone-filled, fully arrived-in-the-world humans. And when some fail to transition, parents attend to these losses with a special kind of care.

The arrival of teeth in infants represents a hardening of the bones and is a highly anticipated event that marks the child's successful transition from the spirit world to the human world. This occasion is often celebrated with a

joro (ritualized blessing), a haircutting (*mangadoso fagneva*), and an adorn-
ment of heirloom jewelry on the child (*mampiravaka tsaiky*). In addition, by
virtue of his or her ability to consume solid foods, the baby is declared a "real
human being." These ritualized activities—all part of the larger haircutting
ceremony—signal that the child has crossed over (*tafitsaka*). That said, it is
probably more appropriate to see these acts of consecration as initiating a
process of social hardening rather that marking their culmination.

Haircutting ceremonies offer communities a chance to gather together
in celebration of a new child's life. They are opportunities to remember (and
re-member) what it means to be part of a particular family or religious community. Common throughout Madagascar, practiced by Muslims, Christians,
and the nonaffiliated, haircutting ceremonies are performed in various manners, with specific foods eaten, inherited family customs (fombandrazana)
undertaken, and prayers uttered enabling orchestrators to shape initiates into
particular kinds of people. In this chapter, I examine three such haircutting
ceremonies and the rituals associated with them that parents in Diégo employ
to instill in their children "bones," or a sense of enduring social worth. I argue that the process of instilling bones in children is an incremental process
that begins at birth, or even earlier when children are still in the womb, and
then later as well, when children are first overcoming the malleability of their
infancy. Moreover, this process of incorporating the young into community
is often taking place in environments of pluralism where, rather than passing
down a set of unchanging traditions from one generation to the next, it is
people's engagement with difference that helps them formulate their sense
of who they are.

The Malagasy Life Trajectory: From Water into Bones

Northern Malagasy use a variety of names to describe infants, including *tsaiky*
(child), *zaza kely* (little baby/child), *zaza mena* (red baby/child), *vao-teraka*
(newborn), and, as previously mentioned, zaza rano (water baby).[4] Of these,
the term *water baby* is unique in its reference to babies' spiritual or metaphysi-
cal composition.[5] Families describe infants as "still full of water" (mbola rano)
and lacking in bones because they believe young babies come into the world
bearing a special connection to the spirit world, a spirit world that is often spoken about in terms of its proximity to and association with water. As discussed
in the previous chapter, water is an important medium of blessing in many
Malagasy rituals. It is also a spiritual realm where magical creatures, and even

some ancestors, reside. Most ancestors dwell near their cold, dry bones, but a
few populate warm watery areas, such as Nosy Lonjo, or inhabit the bodies of
jewelry-wearing crocodiles like those sighted near Lake Anivorano. Or take,
for example, the sacred waterfall within Montagne D'Ambre National Parc,
where, according to park guides, Malagasy Merina are forbidden from going,
lest they be drowned by angry ancestor spirits still protesting nineteenth-
century Merina invasions into the north of the island.

That ancestors are associated with both bones and water is not a contradic-
tion but rather speaks to the complex relationships that descendants have with
ancestors, whose legacies endure as surely as bones and who simultaneously
possess a murkiness, fluidity, and potential from which new legacies surface.
According to northern Malagasy mythologies, water deities and mermaids
dwell in water; certain animals, such as *aomby* (cows), materialized from
water; and water bears the memory of those who, because of war, accident, or
illness, lost their lives in water. This is illustrated in Michael Lambek's description of a type of water-dwelling tromba called Antandrano who possess people along the western coast of Madagascar from Mahajanga to Diégo Suarez.
According to Lambek, Antandrano evoke a "dramatic and sentimental story
with strong political implications."[6] After being pushed back to the banks of
the Loza River by Merina invaders, they jumped in the river and preferred to
drown themselves rather than submit to Merina rule. Because Merina still
play a dominant role in national politics on the island, some northerners continue to harbor resentments, which get viscerally remembered in incidences
of possession by still angry water spirits.[7] Legacies such as these, regardless
of how literal they may actually be, speak to people's sense of the continuous
arrival and departure of peoples, goods, and animals in northern Madagascar
by way of water.

Water possesses mysterious spiritual properties, both creative and destruc-
tive, and serves as a medium through which life is both taken and given. Consider the following legend recounted to me by a young Malagasy man about
Antankarana, an ethnic group at the tip of northern Madagascar:[8]

> A long time ago, the Antankarana broke a lot of fady, causing the
> Mahavavy River to dry up, and lots of people died because there was no
> water. In a dream, a moasy[9] received a request from the ancestors that a
> woman sacrifice herself, but all the villagers refused. After several weeks, a
> woman of around sixteen years decided to sacrifice herself, so the villagers
> cut her head off and put her blood in the riverbed. After the sacrifice, the

river filled with water once again and that is why it is called Mahavavy, which means "to become a woman."

Unpacking the full meaning of this particular *angano* (fable) would take us beyond the focus of this chapter.[10] Yet we can see two themes integral to our understanding of the Malagasy life course: women's vitality, as those who sacrifice in order to bring new life into the community, and the power that water holds as a material medium through which life is both given and taken. Communities in Madagascar are heavily reliant on water for all sorts of essential activities from washing and bathing to fishing to crop irrigation. But such reliance creates a vulnerability that often manifests as a reverence toward the unpredictable and sometimes life-destroying fluctuations of water. This reverence compels Malagasy to be ever mindful of their actions, especially with regard to the breaking of fady, which can disrupt right relations with the earth and with the sacred powers that govern the earth.

In the case of the angano previously mentioned, the breaking of fady disrupted the Antakarana people's relationship with their ancestors, thereby cutting off the flow of ancestral blessings, which often come to the living in the form of swelling rivers, fertile landscapes, and pregnant wombs. And only a woman's sacrifice was able to restore the relationship between the ancestors and the living. In this fable, the woman's sacrifice to restore the Mahavavy River to its proper water levels is particularly ripe with meaning given that still today, Malagasy understand ancestors to work through the wombs of women to bestow blessings of fertility on their descendants. Moreover, women are understood as vessels of ancestral fertility, but under such conditions, they suffer and sacrifice much in order to be so. For they currently lack access to clean water, and their children are dying of diarrheal infections. This is due in part to the lack of access to clean water, and the exploitative takeover of their land by irresponsible companies, often foreign mining companies, who ignore the ancestors' pleas to respect the fady of the land.[11]

The softness of babies relates to the life journeys all Malagasy expect to take from water into bones, a path by which one begins as a warm malleable body and progresses to the cold and hardened corpse of an ancestor with a discrete identity whose legacy will be remembered in bones. Scholars have described this Malagasy understanding of human growth in both progressive and gendered terms as a journey from one's mother's womb to one's father's tomb, a life course that moves from soft to hard, from maternal lines to paternal lines, and from warm viral blood to the cold social order of the tomb.[12]

In other words, Malagasy understand people to come into the world with an impressionable, indeterminate status. However, over the course of a lifetime, as people marry, reproduce, and contribute to society, their status within their families solidifies to the extent that, when they die, they can leave an enduring legacy symbolized by their bones in tombs, which their descendants can remember and care for.

Malagasy trace descent bilaterally, recognizing ancestors from maternal and paternal relatives. However, given that patrilineal lines of descent are slightly more privileged, one of the more effective ways to ensure that one leaves a legacy is to align oneself as an important person, or relative of an important person, within a patrilineal ancestral family. This explains the use of the phrase *womb to tomb*, which refers to a person's increasing attachment to their paternal relatives toward the end of a lifetime.[13] For example, while rooting children in maternal ancestries may be important at the beginning of one's life—facilitated by mothers returning home to give birth in the babies' hearth of origin and by burying babies' placentas on these lands—facilitating connections to one's patrilineal kin may be more important toward the end of life to ensure one is buried on the lands, or in the family tomb, of one's paternal kin. In Madagascar, one becomes an important person in a patrilineage in a number of ways. One should produce children, learn to abide by the customs of one's father's family, help finance marriages and funerals, and possibly become a mpijoro or spirit medium who can channel ancestral blessings to family members in the event of an illness, birth, or death. However, strengthening relations with paternal relatives toward the end of one's life is not the only way to acquire bones or ensure that one leaves an enduring legacy.[14]

Increasingly, in Madagascar's postcolonial society, and as has been made clear in the preceding chapters, there are many different kinds of communities—ancestral and religious—that provide people with a sense of transcendence. Moreover, one's affiliation in such groups is not exclusively contingent on adulthood activities but also on the rituals one undergoes as a young child, for example, in haircutting ceremonies that begin to link children with both paternal and maternal kin. Unfortunately, most of the detailed analyses of the Malagasy life course have focused prominently on "the acquiring of bones" that occurs in adulthood and in death and are based on men's movements along the life cycle.[15] To the extent that women's lives are considered, they are more often described as mere symbols of biological fertility that descendants must overcome in order to be born into the more enduring social order of the patrilineal family tomb.[16]

In reality, women exercise a great deal of agency in enabling their infants to acquire bones. They do this by entering into relations of reciprocity with midwives and other kinds of healers, by observing fady that help strengthen connections within their family, by returning home to give birth so children might be connected to their ancestral roots, by observing a style of cold-water bathing called ranginaly, and in many other ways. The decisions that women make around the birthing and blessing of babies, although demonstrating a form of agency focused on the life of their children rather than on themselves, nevertheless have the potential to alter their children's as well as their own life courses in fundamental ways. Moreover, an investigation into women's movements along the life course, which are often less straightforward when compared to men's, has the potential to bolster the growing notion that Malagasy move through life and find a sense of belonging within their communities in layered and vacillating ways.[17]

Maurice Bloch provides a description of the ritual activities that Zafimaniry parents, of Madagascar's southern central highlands, are supposed to perform when a child is born.[18] He outlines the postpartum activities that women observe and the communal rituals performed for the child—naming, placing soot on the forehead, and rubbing chalk on the bodies of others present when the child is brought out of the home.[19] He concludes, however, that these activities bear little significance for the identity of the child in a society whose kinship is largely centered on a "house based" and "tomb based" system rather than a "birth based system."[20] Bloch argues that birth rituals matter only insofar as they enable Zafimaniry couples to solidify their place as productive members among their kin, by virtue of their ability to produce children and maintain a house together. He writes, "As children are born to the couple, this flimsy permeability [that the couple once had] diminishes. The Zafimaniry say that the house is then gradually acquiring 'bones.'"[21] Bloch goes on to say, "It is therefore not through birth as an individual but through marriage as a couple with a hardening and beautifying house that the person becomes a fixed and permanent element of Zafimaniry moral society."[22] Bloch's assessment that birth rituals are highly important to *parents* rings true. Parents have their children baptized, dedicated, or blessed and host haircutting ceremonies for all kinds of self-serving reasons. However, it is also true that in certain places in Madagascar, what happens at one's birth and during one's childhood also has bearing on one's inclusion (or exclusion) within the moral fabric of society.

While birth in and of itself does not serve as a determining factor for people's inclusion into various kinds of lineage- and religious-based communities, birth *rituals* do serve as one of the means by which children are marked, initially, as worthy human members within their communities. This is especially important in pluralistic settings like Diégo, where parents have more options in terms of the rituals they use to incorporate children into various religious and ancestral communities. From the perspective of northern Malagasy, it is in the moment that babies cut teeth that they are understood to be "acquiring bones" (deciding to stay and anchoring themselves within the community). Parents respond to this milestone by performing haircutting ceremonies that mark these babies as "real human beings" and new members of their communities. Not all babies, however, are equally marked. As one father explained, it is not uncommon for a man to have children with multiple women. He went on to say that not all of these children will be seen as equally legitimate. Those who are less so may be given a simple joro, but formal celebrations are reserved for children who belong in the household.[23] Thus, birth rituals have the capacity to mark a child as fully belonging, a marking that could potentially follow a person throughout a lifetime and have an impact on his or her ability to "acquire bones" in later years.

Granted, the understanding of when and how people acquire bones likely differs across regions. Certainly, the Zafimaniry village context, where Bloch's research took place, is different from the urban context of Diégo, but at least according to northern Malagasy accounts, a person's inclusion in a community is gradual and incremental, beginning when children first begin to overcome the malleability of their infancy. Gillian Feeley-Harnik makes a similar claim, insisting that childbirth rituals are "critical to the emergent identities of the 'mother' and 'father' of a child" and *also* "critical to the emergent identity of the child as having both a mother and a father, who is both—to use the Malagasy idiom—the 'child of women' who are sisters among siblings and the 'child of men' who are brothers."[24] Thus, while Bloch sees birth rituals as relatively inconsequential for children, at least among Zafimaniry, Feeley-Harnik's research and my own suggest that this might not be true for all Malagasy. Moreover, while discrete identities are often finalized at death, social hardening is a process that begins much earlier, often shortly after birth or even before, and requires a careful negotiating of family customs as well as religious obligations.[25]

In urban areas such as Diégo, parents face many choices and constraints as they seek to ritually protect and dedicate the newly born. There are many ceremonies and rites of blessing that parents use to protect and integrate the newly born into larger communities, including naming ceremonies, first outings, and baptisms, but haircutting offers a particularly illustrative example of the ways in which children are made to acquire bones through ritual. Throughout Madagascar, it is common to cut or shave a young child's hair. Sometimes, haircutting is part of a ceremony or rite of passage; other times, it is simply part of an infant's conventional everyday care. While the origins are unclear, we know that in Madagascar, ritual practices that honor birth are more than a few generations old.[26] Haircutting traditions of Madagascar's early Indonesian, East African, and Arab Muslim inhabitants likely contributed to contemporary practices. Some parents trim their children's hair a few days after birth as part of a joro or in conjunction with the Islamic practice of holding a sacrifice seven days after a birth (aqiqa); others shave babies' heads at multiple points during infancy, and some perform haircutting ceremonies once a child has cut its first teeth, at a ceremony called mampiravaka tsaiky (literally, to bejewel the child) where children are adorned with heirloom necklaces that link them to those—both alive and gone—who have worn the same jewels.[27]

In rituals, haircutting cleanses the child of any pollution (maloto) she or he might have acquired while passing through the birth canal, socializes the child, and transitions infants from something ambiguous (watery) to a fully integrated human (bone filled). In this way, haircutting humanizes the child and marks the child's full transition into the community. Thus, even though hair may on the surface seem to have nothing to do with bones, the act of cutting a child's hair serves to mark that child's solidifying status, symbolized by bones, within the community. Haircutting rituals appear across religious communities and ancestral lineages, with specific prayers, food, and ritual objects shaping the child in distinct ways. Haircutting is rarely performed in isolation from other cultural and religious practices, such as naming ceremonies, baptisms, sacrifices, circumcisions, and joro, which also shape children's identities, but it is nevertheless an important means by which Malagasy instill what it means to be a member of the community.

In addition to hosting haircutting ceremonies, many of the families I interviewed performed more than one kind of blessing rite from more than one religious tradition. Parents combined both maternal and paternal family customs in innovative ways. In Madagascar's postcolonial and neoliberal economy, many no longer live near their ancestral lands, which means most experience greater freedom in deciding whether to observe religious rituals and fombandrazana, some of which are family specific (i.e., observed only by descendants of a particular ancestral lineage) and some of which are more widespread (i.e., practiced by the majority of Malagasy who venerate and maintain ties with their ancestors). Some choose to abandon family customs, like haircutting ceremonies or family fady against eating certain foods during pregnancy, deeming these observances irrelevant or superstitious. Others choose to modernize these practices. For example, the latter may send money home in lieu of always traveling to their homelands for marriages and funerals, and they may invoke the deceased not on their ancestral homelands but in ceremonies performed in the courtyards of their urban rental properties, where children's placentas are sometimes buried today. Certainly, some of these ritual innovations alter the meaning of practices like placental burying. Burying a child's placenta at a rental property is not likely done in order to beckon that child's spirit back to the rental property in the same way that burying placentas on ancestral lands is meant to root, or link, someone to these lands. Sometimes burying placentas in these new locales, far from one's ancestral lands, might be the beginning of a family's efforts to begin anchoring themselves to a new location, on new lands that will one day become ancestral lands, but other times these innovations simply help people engage in practices that connect them with one another and that sacralize the places where life's important moments occurred. In all cases, these choices to uphold, update, or even sometimes abandon family customs have implications for the social worlds of mothers and babies.

In Diégo, these reckonings with modernity and pluralism have played out more in the domestic sphere than the public sphere. Especially when compared to other areas of the country, such as Mahajanga or Ambilobe, large funerary gatherings, spirit possession ceremonies, and rituals of sacrifice, made famous by ethnographers, are slightly less common.[28] Instead, ancestors have a pervasive presence in the quiet, informal domestic practices of young mothers who are abiding by, or ignoring, the family-specific pregnancy fady and fomba their relatives urge them to observe. In Diégo, conversations about what charms, amulets, or growth medicines (aody be) one should place around one's child's neck or wrist; what medical and spiritual practitioners one should consult; and what fady one should observe (or not observe) were ubiquitous.

These family-specific fombandrazana around pregnancy and birth have been largely overlooked in the scholarship that deals with ancestors in Madagascar. However, as I argue at the beginning of this book, an investigation into the prevalence of ancestor spirits and ancestor-related customs around the birthing and blessing of children shows just how crucial birth is, as a rite of passage, for women and children in their efforts to secure a sense of identity and belonging within the communities. As has been long recognized, and as the following story demonstrates, Malagasy invoke their ancestors not because they are preoccupied with death or even a remembrance of the past but because, perhaps primarily, they are invested in the future, and birth is a crucial moment when this process of navigating belonging begins.

Asmara Becomes a "Real Human Being"

When baby Asmara's teeth came in, her mother, Genevie, shared the news with those around her. The decision to hold a haircutting ceremony in Asmara's honor was neither inevitable nor automatic. When Genevie ultimately decided to have the ceremony, and to do it in Diégo as opposed to Nosy Be, where her extended family lived, she waited to set the date, checking first to see if any of her relatives from the countryside would be able to attend. After hearing from them, she waited yet again, this time for a full moon since life-giving religious activities are believed to be more successful if performed when the moon is reaching its fullness.

When family and friends arrived for Asmara's haircutting, the dirt courtyard where the family's two-room, metal-frame rental house stood bustled with the energy of an impending celebration. Genevie's coworker Jacqueline grabbed baby Asmara from one of her aunts and cajoled her by saying, "Did you know this is your day? Did you know that as of today, you are a real human (*une vraie humaine*)?" Genevie busied herself with preparing the sabeda (rice porridge mixed with milk and honey) in a large aluminum pot that seemed to anchor the family's excitement. Genevie's *vady* (partner) Rabo, the baby's father, went to buy more canned milk for the porridge as baby Asmara's paternal aunt bathed her in the shared yard in an orange plastic bucket and dressed her for the occasion.[29] Jacqueline repeatedly stepped in to offer advice, instructing Genevie on the appropriate amount of milk and honey to add to the porridge and on how to dole out the meal in even numbers onto the serving platters.

Genevie and Rabo had wanted an elder to perform the joro, but none of the elders from their community were able to travel the distance to attend.

Those present reassured Asmara's father that under the circumstances he was perfectly suitable to do the joro himself. Rabo wore a red-and-green Rastafarian T-shirt and athletic shorts for the occasion. His casual attire, juxtaposed with the women's elegant *salovana* (northern-style lamba) and head scarves (*kisaly*), gave the ceremony a mosaic feel as formality collided with informality and structure was offset by improvisation. Without the guiding hands of elder relatives, the young crowd pieced together a haircutting ceremony marked more by its extemporaneity than its scripted nature.

Rabo, a thin young man, appeared nervous but spent time rehearsing his words. Some of the women who had more experience attending haircutting ceremonies advised him on what to say. It was not clear to me why he was chosen, rather than them, to give the joro, except that elder men are typically chosen to give the joro at haircutting ceremonies. When we gathered inside the intimate space of the family's home, the room grew quiet as Rabo grabbed his baby daughter and sat her down between his outstretched legs. He took a palm leaf, dipped it in a bowl of water that also contained a coin, and waved it over his daughter's head, as he asked ancestors (razana) from all cardinal directions to come and bless his child. Asmara was reacting to the water that fell on her head by pursing her lips, blinking her eyes, and flapping her arms. She did not appear at all disturbed by the water droplets that landed on her face and once caused her to sneeze as her father blessed her with his improvised joro.

At the completion of the blessing, Asmara played with the palm leaf as her father fastened what appeared to be a brand-new silver necklace around her neck. Rabo then held the bowl of water up to his baby daughter's lips, offering her a drink, and then pouring some of the water over her head. He and Genevie then drank from the same bowl and poured the remaining liquid over their heads. Following the joro, everyone went outside to eat sabeda in the shade of the large trees that decorated the courtyard. The family invited the neighbor children over, and everyone kneeled down around two platters of porridge.

Asmara's paternal aunt held her and fed her overflowing spoonfuls. Jacqueline kept trying to hurry us along, indicating that we were only to have a few symbolic bites and then turn the platters upside down to share with the ancestors, but Genevie countered, arguing that if we turned them over too quickly, we would give the ancestors all of it. "There will be too much left," she said. She instructed the children to eat quickly. When everyone had eaten more than a token amount, we turned the platters over and stood up from the woven mat on which we had eaten, which was now covered with overturned platters of sabeda and silver spoons.

Rabo went back inside the house and returned with bowls of cookies and candy. After the candy was passed out, especially to the children, we stood around the lamaka (reed mat) and watched as Asmara's father cut her hair and placed several locks of it into a bowl. Asmara watched with wide eyes as wisps of her curls fell on her face and arms, amusing her and the little girl who stood in front of her. Once Asmara's curls had fallen to the ground, those of us who were friends and guests at the ceremony, as opposed to family, left for a couple of hours to give the family time to prepare the lunch we would all consume and to watch Asmara eat a chicken leg, the final part of the ceremony. Some sat in chairs and others on an eating mat inside the house as we all watched Asmara struggle to hold a chicken leg. According to custom, the haircutting ceremony is not officially over until the baby is able to grasp a chicken leg in both hands and take a bite.

Even though the symbolism of such a ceremony is that babies are supposed to enjoy their first food only upon the arrival of teeth, Asmara was eight months old and had been sampling food for several weeks prior to the ceremony. Most babies are fed sips of herbal teas, homemade broth, and packaged rice cereals long before the ceremony marks their transition from suckling babes to humans who eat solid foods. Adults celebrated with a feast of two separate chicken-and-rice dishes, one with a coconut sauce and the other in a curried tomato sauce, washed down with Fanta and other colas.

It was not clearly explained to me why a chicken leg in particular was given to babies as the final part of haircutting ceremony; participants simply knew that it was tradition to do so. While the practice has many potential meanings, Bloch's description of a ritual performed during pregnancy among Zafimaniry families offers some potential clues: "This is the custom called *tolotra harina* or 'given food.' The ritual consists principally of the giving of a chicken which has been cooked whole to a mother of an unborn or relatively young child by a man. This gift is intended to ultimately feed the child and makes the child of the woman resemble the giver physically and psychologically. The giver is usually the father but it may be any other man, for example the mother's brother." Drawing from this related practice, we could surmise that haircutting ceremonies are not just about marking children as human; they also serve as a means by which to connect babies to the multiple affiliations, both living and dead, that give their lives meaning. This is done orally through blessings and tangibly by placing heirloom jewelry around babies' necks, by feeding them special foods, and by cutting their hair so that they can be shaped in particular ways by particular people. As several women described it to me, when someone cuts a baby's hair, it is believed that the child's hair will come to look like the hair of the one who did the cutting. Thus, the child's haircutting and feeding serve to shape the child spiritually, physically, and psychologically.[30] That Asmara's *paternal* aunt was selected is likely significant given that haircutting ceremonies are sometimes the first chance for paternal kin to begin to vie for influence in the life of the child. While childbirth is largely, though not always, a chance for the mother's family to root the child in the mother's father's hearth, at haircutting ceremonies, relatives from both maternal *and* paternal kin begin to help shape the child, or make visible the multiple affiliations present in the child.[31]

The use of water is another important element within the ceremony. In this particular ritual, as well as in other blessing rites throughout Madagascar, as is discussed more extensively in the previous chapter, water serves as a medium through which ancestral blessings are transmitted to the living. The pouring of water on babies' heads blesses, protects, and sustains them, and also integrates them into a particular lineage. In this way, babies are given "bones" as their lives become connected with the enduring legacies of their forebears. However, the process by which parents draw children out of water is equally important since ancestors are associated not just with bones but also with the life-giving properties of water. Thus, we can say that haircutting ceremonies demonstrate that life trajectories can sometimes have a circular rather than linear quality. People move from having an indeterminate status to becoming part of an enduring collective, which in turn serves as the source from which new people and legacies emerge.

Genevie had been particularly intent on holding this ceremony for her first child not only to mark Asmara as a worthy, acknowledged descendant within her and her husband's lineages but also to celebrate what had been a long-awaited journey into motherhood. Genevie had struggled to get pregnant for several years, changing partners multiple times in an attempt to find the right match.

> Before I was not with Papa Asmara, I was with another person who was a lot older than me. I wanted desperately to have a child [*miteraka*], but

I could not get pregnant. . . . I decided to visit a gynecologist [*gynéco-logue*]. . . . She asked me lots of questions like how old is your partner [*va-dinao*]? Is he white or black [*malandy sa joby*]? Has he had kids before? . . . She said, "You should change partners and find someone younger." So, I found someone younger, a man around the age of thirty. We were together for a year but nothing changed. So, I returned to Madame Gynécologue, and she put me on a treatment plan to help regulate my periods, . . . but still nothing changed. When I returned again, she advised me to find someone even younger. . . . I had had abortions before when I was younger. That's the consequence, you see? Now when I want to have a child, God punishes me, I think. . . . Then I found Papa Asmara. . . . He's twenty-five or twenty-six I think. So, there's like a difference of five [years] or [a] six-year difference between us which is too much for me! So, we were living together. He was working and I was working. And after a month like that, my cycle didn't arrive [*cyclenaka tsy navy*].[32]

With everything that Genevie had gone through to get pregnant later in life and at the right time, she felt it especially important to honor the occasion of Asmara's teeth coming in. She found it imperative not only for her child who had crossed over (tafitsaka) but also as a celebration of her transition into motherhood, which granted her a kind of newfound status within her family and among her peers.

As the celebration came to an end and guests began to leave, someone commented that Jacqueline, Genevie's coworker at the lycée who had helped organize the ceremony, knew a great deal about Malagasy customs (fombagasy). Genevie added, "It is normal because she already has children." However, Jacqueline corrected her, "No, it's because I was raised by my grandmother." Jacqueline had encouraged Genevie to give her daughter a haircutting ceremony, both because she was a friend who was invested in Genevie's happiness and also because she saw herself as someone who wanted to continue in the footsteps of her maternal grandmother, a woman who had been an esteemed spirit medium and guardian of Malagasy traditions.

Jacqueline often spoke of her close connection with her grandmother and of her desire to become the next great spirit medium within her family, a position for which she found herself well poised given that she, unlike her cousins, fastidiously observed her family's fady, including the restriction against eating pork. Moreover, she abided by the good habits her grandmother had taught her. She tried to rise each day in accordance with the sun in order that she might receive the blessings of the day; she shared her knowledge of medicinal plants with her children and neighbors, including me, a knowledge bequeathed to her by her grandmother; and she performed the costly, but auspicious haircutting and circumcision ceremonies for her children.

For Jacqueline, helping orchestrate a friend's haircutting ceremony assisted her in her own efforts to maintain a close connection with the spirit of her maternal grandmother, and gave her standing, or bones, within her family as one who knows about, and promotes, fombagasy. Thus, haircutting ceremonies serve many purposes inclusive of the opportunity to bless and incorporate water babies as real, fully arrived-in-the-world members within their respective communities. Asmara's parents' decisions about whether or not they will stay together, something Genevie indicated was uncertain, as well as the additional decisions they will make regarding her care and upbringing will eventually add more layers of meaning to the haircutting ceremony they performed. For the time being, the ceremony served as an opportunity to immerse a newly minted human being into the traditions of her family, from both paternal and maternal sides, mark Genevie's transition to motherhood, and give their friend Jacqueline an opportunity to demonstrate her knowledge of Malagasy customs.

Zafisoa's Nephew Tovo Is Adorned with an Heirloom Chain

Though haircutting ceremonies are less prolific in urban areas as compared to surrounding rural areas, they occurred with enough frequency in Diégo that I was able to attend three and collected accounts of half a dozen more during my nine months of research. Tovo's haircutting ceremony, much like Asmara's, offered his family a chance to bless and incorporate him into the web of ancestral relations that give his life meaning. It also provided an opportunity for my research assistant, Zafisoa, to reflect on the significance of "traditional" ceremonies such as these, and their changing expression and purpose in urban spaces like Diégo.

One Saturday morning, I attended a haircutting ceremony for a cousin of Zafisoa's. The observance was to take place at dawn, several kilometers outside of Diégo in the suburb of Ambalavola. According to northern Malagasy ideals, water used for such blessings should come from a fresh source, not salt water, and be fetched in the early-morning hours before the birds have flown across the morning sky. In reality, however, parents sometimes perform ceremonies when it is convenient and with less-than-perfect materials. As one woman once explained, "There are no rivers in Diégo, so tap water will suffice."

When we arrived at the auspicious hour at which the ceremony was to commence, preparations were still underway. Zafisoa and I waited at another house across the yard, where more of her cousins lived. There, children crouched with sleepy eyes on the concrete veranda of their home as their mother and grandmother prepared them for the morning washing. Zafisoa and I watched through the sun-filled open doorway as one of the little girls on the porch unbraided her own hair. The girl's mother then undressed her and poured cups of water over her, scrubbing her hair and body with a bar of brown soap until the girl was deemed clean. Another little girl who appeared to be around the age of three came over to us wearing nothing but her underwear and purple, soft-plastic, high-heeled sandals. Zafisoa teased her, speaking to her as though she were a grown woman. The grandmother of the house brought us some bread and citronella tea.

When the ceremony commenced, about ten to fifteen adult relatives were present. The room was relatively empty of furniture. A lamaka had been placed in the center of the room on which we all sat, and several aluminum pots rested in a far back corner. Baby Tovo sat in front of his mother with his paternal grandfather on one side and his paternal grandmother on the other. The others present sat facing the sunrise. Many of the women and men were wearing salovana, but Zafisoa and I were dressed in casual attire. The baby's grandfather gave the blessing while waving two green palm leaves, just as Asmara's father had done. A necklace had been placed in the bowl of water that Asmara's grandfather used for the joro. The necklace appeared old, as though it had not just been bought for the occasion as Asmara's necklace seemed to be. The family remarked that the necklace had indeed been in the family for a long time.

When the joro was finished, the grandfather began snipping baby Tovo's hair with scissors until others told him, "That's enough [bas]," as though a few symbolic cuts were all that was needed. Tovo was alert but somewhat fussy until someone placed two piles of food in front of him, each wrapped in a single folding of banana leaves. One portion contained rice and the other a chicken leg, which he was encouraged to hold and eat. As the formal aspects of the ceremony came to a close, one of the women took the bowl with the water that had been used in the blessing and now fragments of the boy's hair, and poured it into the crevice of a tree's trunk. Everyone agreed aloud that the water and hair should be disposed of in a cool place and far from where stray dogs might disturb it. The adults in attendance were older and appeared more confident and also more somber than those who witnessed baby Asmara's haircutting. As they shared a meal of chicken and rice, a younger man held Tovo in the doorway and began shaving off all of the baby's hair with an electric razor.

On our walk back into town, Zafisoa remarked that haircutting ceremonies "are a much bigger deal in the countryside" compared to the one we had just attended for her cousin. "It's a big party," she said, "and people don't use scissors; they first take a few pieces of the hair in their mouth and pull it out with their teeth."[33] Zafisoa seemed almost disappointed by the lack of fanfare at her baby cousin's haircutting. Indeed, many residents of Diégo had commented to me that such ceremonies were performed in a more prescribed and formal manner in the countryside no doubt in part due to the fact that more elders and extended kin are often present in these rural locales.

Zafisoa's estimation that the ceremony had failed to live up to her idea of what it should look like gave voice to her concern that something was missing from these urban celebrations. Although many of my informants strove to be more "modern" (*moderne*)—as one woman shared with me, she wanted "to give her child a pure Christian environment" that would have nothing to do with the "darker" (*maiz-maizana*) cultural customs one finds in the forests of the Malagasy countryside—others, like Zafisoa, regretted what was seemingly lost in her modern, urban world. She spoke nostalgically of a sense of community and reverence for traditional ways of doing things. Zafisoa lamented the casualness with which scissors had come to replace the ceremonial way in which grandfathers had traditionally pulled out seven pieces of hair with their teeth.

With elders present, in particular paternal elders, Tovo's haircutting bore more formal qualities than Asmara's. The ceremony certainly appeared to function in the way that haircutting ceremonies are said to function. By invoking their ancestors, adorning Tovo with an heirloom rather than a newly purchased silver chain, and cutting his hair, the boy's paternal relatives began to interweave him into their lineage. That said, from the perspective of at least one witness, the ceremony had still failed to meet the minimum measures of formality. In urban port cities like Diégo, observing family traditions can give people a sense of identity and grounding in a world that is otherwise abounding with multiple languages and a cosmopolitan mix of customs. For Zafisoa, abiding by family-specific rituals and food restrictions gives her a sense of identity and belonging in an otherwise endlessly fluctuating world. Still, haircutting ceremonies are changing more rapidly than she would like and that felt unsettling.

The sense of fixity and tradition that urban dwellers like Zafisoa associate with Madagascar's countryside represents a sense of security many felt was absent from their lives in Diégo, where there are almost as many "right" ways to perform a ceremony as there are families. For some Malagasy, like Zafisoa's cousins, simply performing such a haircutting ceremony was enough to give their children roots or bones (i.e., a sense of security and enduring social worth). For others like Zafisoa, doing it "right" was as important as doing it at all. Either way, performing haircutting ceremonies enables families to construct a legacy around the blessing of children that both honors and updates the fombandrazana, a way that may or may not look starkly different from their modern and cosmopolitan life in the city. What life in the countryside, or during the time of the ancestors, was actually like matters less than how it is remembered, imagined, and then appropriated and imprinted on the newly living in the present.

As we made our way back to Zafisoa's house, we walked past the FJKM (Fiangonan'i Jesoa Kristy eto Madagasikara) church that Zafisoa had attended as a child. A woman from the churchyard called out to her and the two spoke briefly. It seemed that no matter where one went in the city, Zafisoa always knew someone in whose home she might stop for a drink of water, a chance to use the bathroom, or an opportunity to catch up on the latest gossip. For women like Zafisoa, who are not from Diégo, the landscape of the city has nevertheless become invested with meaning. Zafisoa felt connected to her ancestral lands in Vohemar but slightly less so than her mother did. Through relations formed in the urban spaces of Diégo, Zafisoa, like many other second-generation migrants to the city, has found a new kind of belonging that relies less on shared ancestral lands and more on friendships, diverse religious affiliations, and rituals performed in urban courtyards even when such rituals have less of the traditional trappings than they might in the countryside.

On another such walk through the city, this time along the high road that borders Diégo's bay, Zafisoa and I once again caught a glimpse of the sacred island of Nosy Lonjo, one of the city's more famous landmarks. Down the hill from where we stood, Zafisoa and I could see people wading in the water and walking out into the tide toward Nosy Lonjo—the sacred conical-shaped island mountain where some of the region's most powerful ancestral spirits are thought to reside. Zafisoa reminded me that this was the place where we had taken a ritual bath back in 2008 when she was consulting a spirit medium about a problem she was having. "I remember," I said to her. "I would not do it again," she replied. "It's not of God, and besides, when I was in Lebanon working as a maid, the problem I was having returned, so I could see that it was less of a spiritual problem, and more of a microbial problem."

Like many Diégo residents, Zafisoa has delved into a variety of cultural, religious, and medical practices over the course of her life. She describes herself as Sakalava, given her mother's descent from a royal Sakalava lineage, but also claims several other ethnicities and recognizes the many religious heritages of her family, which include Christian, Muslim, and those who "tsy mivavaka" (literally, "do not pray"). Raised Christian in the FJKM church, she became a Muslim (Silamo) in college but remains connected with many in her former church community and also sometimes engages in fombandrazana.[34]

For Zafisoa, life in Diégo has brought exposure to a rich array of cultural and religious practices, but from an economic perspective, it has not brought her family the prosperity and good fortune they imagined it would. As she put it on one of our many walks through Diégo's neighborhoods, "normally my father would have given me land by now on which to build a house. . . . Normally he would have remained married to my mother, but he did not, and he is raising baby twins now with another woman, and there is no money left for me." Ideally, Zafisoa's boyfriend would not have left her shortly after she gave birth to their first child, and she would not have been trafficked for two years to Lebanon in her quest to earn enough money to raise her daughter. Pluralistic cities like Diégo offer a wealth of potentialities, but they can also become places where residents struggle to find their way and become vulnerable to things like the dangers of human trafficking, which is why "traditional" rituals that offer spiritual and social capital to people are enjoying a certain resurgence in urban locales, even when they are performed differently and with modern accoutrements.

In the midst of these changes, people nevertheless find meaning, worth, and security. Perhaps precisely because these rituals are different, participants find new ways to honor the past or to stray from the past in order for the life they build to be closer to the vision of life they have in mind for themselves, their children, and their children's children. In northern Malagasy discourse about rituals, the countryside represents more than just a place where ceremonies are performed correctly; it is also a remembered place where families stayed together, honored their ancestors, and bequeathed land to future generations. For urban residents of Diégo, alongside their quest to be "modern" is the quest to recultivate something of the visions their ancestors fought for, which they remember as better, more stable, and more harmonious, regardless of whether they actually were.

Though haircutting ceremonies in urban spaces like Diégo look different from those that take place in rural Madagascar, they are no less real. In fact, haircutting in Diégo borrows from a multitude of religious and regional influences in ways that offer a truer picture of the hybrid realities of urban Malagasy, Malagasy who have migrated to cities for better work and educational opportunities and have been doing so for quite a long time. What's unique about northern Madagascar, and urban spaces like Diégo in particular, is that they have attracted diverse populations for centuries—populations of people who have intermarried with one another, produced children together, and generally speaking learned to live together as neighbors. This kind of cosmopolitanism shapes daily living but it also informs the kinds of rituals parents perform for their children—the often hybridized rites of blessings parents use to consecrate and incorporate their children into various kinds of ancestral and religious communities.

Hakim's aqiqa, described in the following paragraphs, offered his family more than just a chance to immerse him in a set of rituals that have sustained their ascendants; it was also a chance to draw together diverse community members who bring differing culinary, cultural, and religious traditions to the gathering and who offer up differing opinions as to what it means to be Muslim and Malagasy. Nonetheless, these attendees found themselves gathered for a common cause: the blessing and integrating of this newest life into their diverse community. In the ceremony, Haqim was marked blessed and marked Muslim, but what it means to be Malagasy—or to be a Malagasy Muslim for that matter—is a process born out of centuries of interfaith relations with Swahili and Comorian Muslims, with Indo-Pakistani Muslims, and with Christians from the central highlands. In northern Madagascar, when parents "instill bones" in their children (read: mark them with discrete identities), they are not marking them with identities that will go unchanged from one generation to the next; rather, they are drawing together a diverse array of influences that have momentarily come together in the life of this child, a hybridized identity subject to further hybridization as a result of the pluralistic environment in which the child

Tovo's haircutting. *Photos by author.*

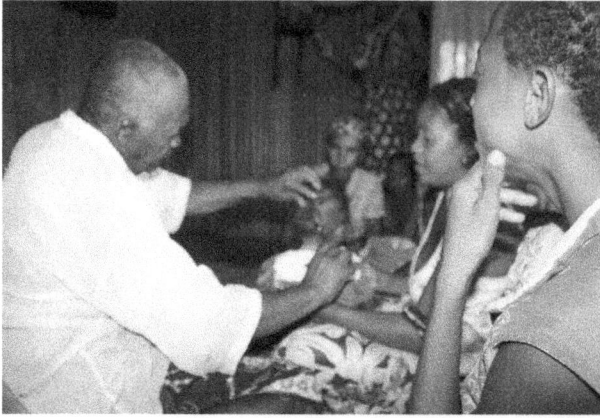

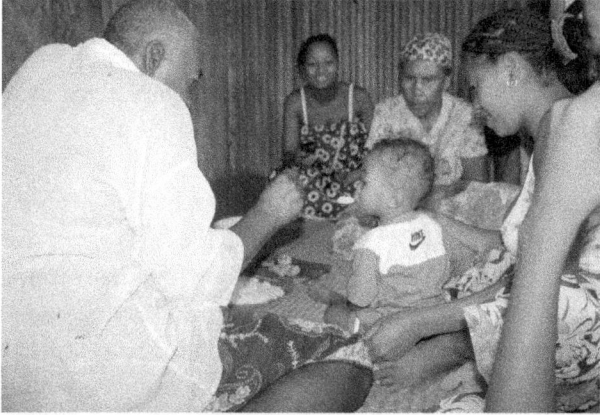

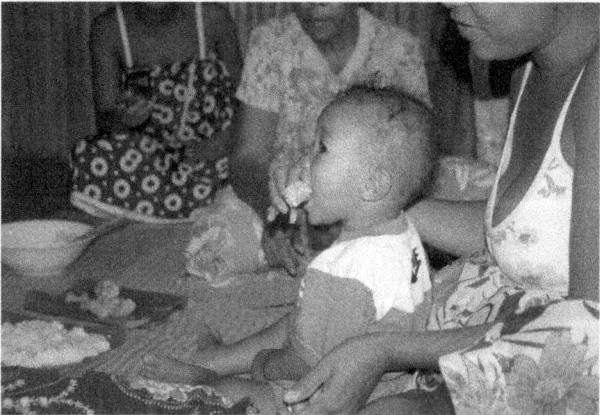

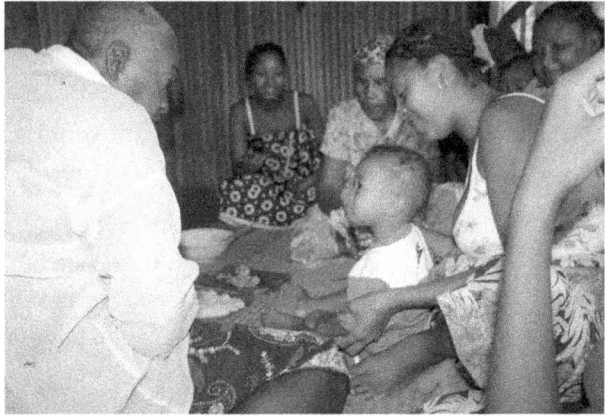

is being raised but a distinct identity nonetheless, even if evolving and momentary, that helps the child to understand who they are amid this diversity, amid the tangle of relationships and religious and ancestral influences that give their life meaning.

Nasreen Hosts an Aqiqa

At 7:00 a.m. on a Saturday, Nasreen, whose story of motherhood is told in chapter 2, and her neighbor Khalisah were preparing food for the aqiqa, an Islamic haircutting ceremony for the newly born. On the concrete porch that encircled their dormitories, they sorted rice, looking for tiny stones. Later, more women arrived to slice cucumbers for a salad, to scrape out the insides of a coconut to make coconut milk, and to cut up potatoes for a goat meat stew. As more and more guests arrived, women congregated around the rice, children played tag in the courtyard, and men readied the space for the slaughtering of the goats. In anticipation of the killing of the goats, Nasreen's five-year-old son, Aasim, began to cry, which prompted Nasreen to escort all the children inside for a *dessin animé* (cartoon). Outside, in accordance with the customs of halal, the prescribed method of slaughter for Muslims, men prayed over the animals, laid the goats to face Mecca, and, with a quick slice of a knife across their jugular veins, spilled their blood on the ground—at which point, young Aasim reemerged, quietly observing his father's work.

At midmorning, the newborn guest of honor, asleep and bundled in blankets, arrived and was brought into an interior room where the haircutting would take place. Rahimah held her tiny infant, Hakim, as Nasreen cut his hair by gracing his scalp with ordinary household scissors while he slept. Few observed this intimate procedure, save a couple of women and a handful of children. Only once did the baby cry, provoking his mother, who wore a long dress and hijab, to pull her clothing aside to console him. As he suckled, Nasreen removed the remainder of the downy hair that covered his head.

Nasreen gathered the handkerchief she had used to collect the hair, shook it into a piece of white paper, rolled it up, and handed it to a male member of the community who stood in the doorway. The hair would be weighed at a local épicerie (small grocery), and gold would be bought in proportion to its weight. They would give the gold to the poor, as a token of gratitude for the child's birth. Though the baby was unaware of the ceremony on his behalf, other children were not. They were in and out of the room, trying to touch the baby, observing him with infectious grins.

The meal following the haircutting was served unceremoniously. Unlike some haircutting events, no ritual speeches (joro) or requests for blessings from the ancestors were made. Instead, the gathering was casual. The sixty or so guests were relatives, friends, and schoolmates—part of the community to which baby Hakim now belonged. The attendees were diverse in age, religion, and nationality. Members of the community who were Muslim ate indoors in separate spaces according to their gender, while young children, regardless of gender, shared their own space outside.

Children changed from their casual attire into the gorgeously decorated religious dress, complete with hijab and hats (taqiyah). My husband, Ben; my research assistant Édith; and about a dozen of Nasreen's non-Muslim friends gathered around a table on the outdoor thatched patio. We sat in chairs and were given plates, forks, and spoons, while Muslim participants ate on the floor with their hands from communal silver platters atop traditional Malagasy eating mats (lamaka). The rice tasted of the fire on which it had been cooked, a taste distinct from that of rice cooked over gas or charcoal for more common, nonreligious occasions.

Those at our table discussed the goat meat. Some did not typically like goat because "it smelled," but they liked how Muslims cooked it in a curry sauce with turmeric, onion, garlic, tomato sauce, and potatoes. Osman, a gregarious Muslim and an international student from the Comoros, an island country to the northwest of Madagascar, sat at the table with the non-Muslims. Telling jokes, he switched between Malagasy, English, French, and Comorian Swahili. Some found his use of Comorian Swahili amusing, given that the northern dialect of Malagasy has enough Swahili borrowings to make his language sound simultaneously strange and familiar.

Osman complained about burqas, loose outer garments some Muslim women wear to cover their entire bodies in public (as opposed to hijabs, which typically cover just the hair and neck) and about Malagasy perceptions of Comorians. He argued that Muslims who dress in burqas are "adding to," or perhaps altering, the traditions of the Prophet and his wives. He seemed well versed in the theological arguments against wearing burqas but less so in the religious rationale behind some Muslims' decision to do so. He appeared embarrassed that Muslims who wear burqas in Madagascar are usually thought to be Comorian, since he viewed such garments as sinful. "Sometimes," he countered forcefully, "they are pure Malagasy." He also complained that most Malagasy think Comorians are "very black." Others concurred that they used to think this too, but agreed that Comorians come in all shades and dress in various styles, "just like Malagasy." "Though, to win the Miss Comorian contest," Osman explained, "you have to have very black skin and you have to have curly hair. We have to stand up for ourselves," he proclaimed, designating dark skin as a source of pride.

"What about in Madagascar?" Ben inquired. The Malagasy students agreed there were no criteria for skin color for the Miss Malagasy contest. However, conversations I had overheard and my knowledge of tensions between lighter-skinned Merina, an ethnic group of mixed-racial origin from the central highlands, and darker-skinned coastal groups made me wonder otherwise. While staying in Antananarivo, the capital of Madagascar in the heart of its central highland's region, I remember one Merina mother's concern that her children might look "black like the father," a disappointment to her, given that her family had been so careful to preserve their lighter skin. By contrast, while walking around Diégo, I recall students who boldly spoke of the beauty of blackness.

Osman's concerns about Malagasy impressions of Comorians were evidence of the tensions between Malagasy and migrants to the island, including Comorians, who make up one of the largest migrant groups in northern Madagascar. In Diégo, interaction, and even intermarriage, is common among people of diverse backgrounds. Yet stereotypes still exist about the city's Comorian and Indo-Pakistani migrant communities, and about Malagasy highlanders versus northern coastal groups. Communal gatherings provide opportunities to confront these stereotypes. Osman's assertion that burqas are worn by both Comorian and Malagasy Muslims sheds light on the complexity of religious identity in both the Comoro Islands and Madagascar. The discussion about the criteria for winning beauty contests speaks to the racial hierarchies and racial pride that exist in both countries. It is within these multifaith, multiethnic spaces that people assert and question boundaries in terms of nationality, ethnicity, and religion.

In sum, this aqiqa ceremony served multiple purposes. First, Hakim was surely blessed. He was declared worthy of a sacrifice and feast, socialized with the blades of scissors, and fully welcomed into the life of his community. Second, the ritual also made an impression on the older children present who, in their donning of religious garb and witnessing of a child's haircutting, observed what it meant to be Muslims in Madagascar. Similarly, adults, in gathering and feasting together, created and reflected on their bondedness as members and friends of a particular religious community. On that day, being in this community meant gathering in the courtyard on a rainy day, with young and old together, Muslims and Christians alike. Third, the ceremony was an opportunity for Nasreen to invest in her community. As we learned in chapter 1, Nasreen's devotion to Islam has waxed and waned through the years, but her faith community has become increasingly important to her.

Last, the ritual provided space for conversation and social merriment that highlighted how gathering and eating together can be a sacred act. Ordinary acts of slaughtering an animal, cooking, eating, and haircutting can become sacred when they are done before witnesses and with a spirit of intentionality. When Malagasy women wake early to sort rice and prepare the coconut milk, spices, and vegetables, they help to cast the day with its proper investment of meaning. When men say prayers over a slaughtered animal, they offer something to God, that God may in turn bless the community. Similarly, ordinary tools can be transformed into sacred instruments when used with a spirit of intentionality. As part of the necessary tools of sacrifice and other rites of passage like circumcision and haircutting ceremonies, spears, knives, and scissors not only mark moments as sacred but also provide for those present a sense for the seriousness of the occasion, as participants simultaneously remember the past and shape initiates into new members of their community. It is the purposefulness with which normal everyday activities are performed that make them transformative for all those involved.

Guests at this ritual came from varying backgrounds but were unified as members or friends of a specific Muslim community in Diégo Suarez. The ritual provided space for discussions about the appropriateness of certain religious acts and modes of dress within Islam, about what it means to be "purely" Malagasy or "purely" Comorian, and about ethnicity, skin color, and religious orthodoxy. Rituals such as this one are spaces where questions of one's identity are worked out, not only among the in-crowd but also with and among those external to the religious community. In pluralistic settings, both engagement with difference and immersion in a cohesive community give us a sense of who we are. And while such conversations can and do occur anywhere, the birth of a child serves as a particularly salient moment to think about one's own religious heritage and markings.

Hakim's aqiqa. *Photos by author.*

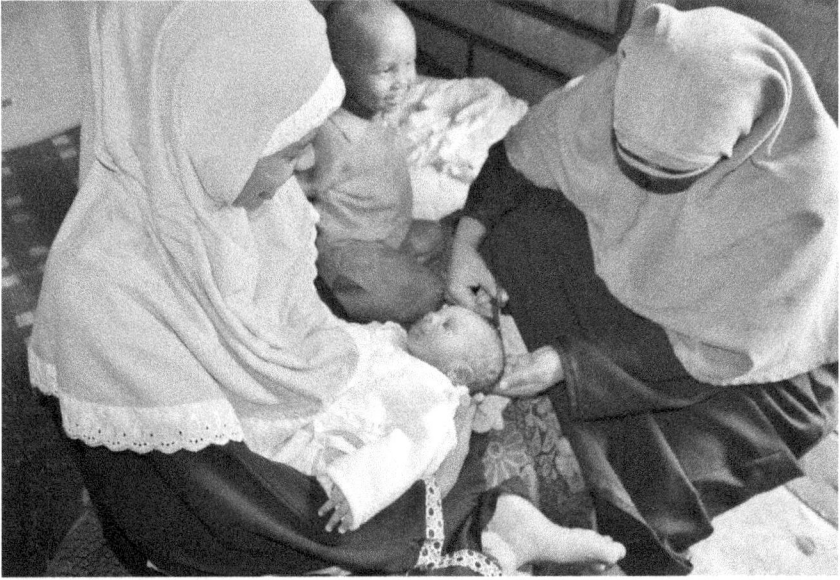

Webs of Connection

First, and in the broadest sense, haircutting ceremonies, like infant rites the world over, are performed as a rite of passage to celebrate the life of a newly born child and to mark that child's transition from a state of liminality to a state of solidity within a human family.[35] Parents give thanks that the child has crossed over (tafitsaka). They call on their ancestors to come and bless the child that she or he might continue to grow into the full life of the community. Within such rites, children are deemed worthy of a feast, worthy of their ancestors' blessings, and valuable new descendants in a long line of ancestors.

Second, these ceremonies are also performed because they are tradition or, as one man described, because "the ancestors dictate that we do so." In other words, in keeping fombandrazana, relatives maintain ties with their ancestors, but more than this, they also forge powerful links with one another through their shared experiences and through the common commitments required of them as members of this particular family versus another. While haircutting ceremonies are common across Madagascar, the particular ways in which families celebrate haircutting, the precise foods that mothers avoid during pregnancy and postpartum until their children have officially crossed over, the kinds of heirloom jewelry that is placed on children, and whether joro are combined with either Muslim or Christian prayers are unique to specific families.

Third, Malagasy parents use haircutting ceremonies as a form of nondiscursive collective remembering. Through such rites, parents, and other invested relatives, reflect on the ways in which their forebears have shaped them and instill these memories in their children. By adorning babies with jewelry and objects from the ancestral past and pouring consecrated water over their heads, parents, aunts, uncles, and grandparents collectively piece together the foods, special objects, and words of blessing that make children who they are. Babies do not need to have an intellectual understanding of how these objects come together to form them into bone-filled human beings any more than an infant need be awake during a baptism. What makes these celebrations transformative is the manner in which they penetrate us and become rooted in us, in a deeper, subconscious, preverbal way. When Malagasy parents adorn their children with heirloom jewelry and teach them to turn their plates upside down and share their food with the ancestors, they are sowing in the young an embodied and unremitting awareness that their lives are interconnected not only with those whom they can see but also with the histories and legacies of those whom they cannot see but to whom they nevertheless belong.

Fourth, when Malagasy parents encourage their children to pay attention to their ancestors as they do in haircutting ceremonies, they are also teaching them about what is sacred, held dear, and set apart in Malagasy society.[36] In Madagascar ancestors have a pervasive spiritual presence. They possess vital hasina, the life-sustaining energy that Malagasy cultivate by engaging in right relations with God (Zanahary); with their ancestors (razana); with neighbors, relatives, and friends; and with the land (tanindrazana) on which they live. When the ancestors are pleased, their blessings are apparent; when they are not pleased, their wrath is palpable. Babies, no less than other persons, must learn about the ancestors and the special presence they inhabit in Malagasy society. Babies grow into the life of the community by learning to honor, fear, and occasionally tune out the cacophony of voices from their ancestral past.

In essence, rites of blessing for the newly born facilitate webs of connection or ties to numerous ancestral figures and their living descendants across multiple lineages. As the newly born make their transition from zaza rano into "real human beings" (vrai humains), heirloom necklaces are placed around their necks that both literally and symbolically link them to others who have worn the same jewels. In Madagascar, descent is an important part of identity, but as Bloch and others have indicated, the simple act of being born is not enough to grant one inclusion into the community.[37] Rather, inclusion and identity must be constructed around such things as lineage, one's relationship to land or place, religious affiliation, and one's willingness to observe inherited ancestral customs. As Andrew Walsh describes, among Antakarana people, "the freedom to do otherwise" is precisely what makes the observance of family-inherited fomba and fady such a powerful act.[38] The decision to not eat pork or to host a haircutting ceremony is a relatively free choice. As evidenced in the earlier stories of this book, Malagasy ignore these regional and family-specific customs all the time, which means that, when people do choose to observe these customs, either because of pressure from family or because of a more personal drive, there is a weightiness behind them. Andrew Walsh, Michael Lambek, and Rita Astuti all argue that performance in rituals and in regional occupations like fishing can be as important as place and descent in marking people's identities as Antankarana or Vezo.[39] Similarly, in Diégo, observance of certain family-inherited taboos during pregnancy or in everyday living represents a willingness to be linked to others, to be bonded to others by certain habits of living, and to reap the benefits of this type of bondedness. The decision to host a haircutting ceremony is tradition not in the sense of it being unchanged or of it being a custom that everyone must do (plenty of families do not), but in the sense of it being a ritual that, when performed, grants people belonging by way of their bondedness with one another.

According to historian Nancy Rose Hunt, the challenge is to see traditional rituals not as "static articles of culture" but as tools people employ to heal and restore. In her discussion of *libeli*, a male puberty ritual performed in the Congo during the Belgian occupation, Hunt describes the challenge "to imagine *libeli* as history, as the work of healing and restoring, or recomposing wealth and power, and calming the anger of the ancestors in the face of unspeakable violences and humiliations."[40] Hunt imagined libeli as it was practiced during the Belgian occupation of the Congo less as a lingering tradition and more as a very timely way for Congolese families to maintain control over the making and shaping of their boys into men at a time when many felt they were quickly losing their children to a colonial regime that sought to turn them into low-wage laborers and colonial subjects. Libeli was restorative because it enabled families to regain control over the reproduction of their children in both tangible and symbolic ways.

In light of her interpretation, we might understand haircutting ceremonies in Madagascar to be tools that heal and restore and claim children for certain kinds of purposes and legacies. Rites of passage for the young are a timely means by which families claim their children, etch identities into their newly emerging bones, and ordain them for the task of living according to the ideals their ancestors established. In this way the contributions of their ancestors are remembered in rituals—not restored to some original primordial moment, but made new and relevant again, despite the many ways in which fombandrazana have been disrupted by colonial interventions, the pressures of modernity, and Malagasy desires to innovate. Ceremonies that invoke ancestral blessing on the newly living are religious acts that recall the past as abundant and fertile or at least recall the past as something worthy of partial "continuation" (*ny fitohy raza*). Even as Diégo mothers struggle to have access to a way of living that is far more "modern" than that of their ancestors, they also sometimes lament the loss of what their ancestors were working for. They lament the loss of a time and place where reciprocity (fihavanana) and community were emphasized, where land was owned by one's ancestors and not by vazaha, and where fathers bequeathed land to daughters and sons.

When mothers in Diégo perform traditional blessing rites on behalf of their children, they do so not in a conscious or calculated desire to become more securely integrated into enduring ancestral lineages but in an effort to lay the groundwork for a more hopeful future, a future that will be filled with the kinds of dreams and ideals their ancestors worked for, alongside the more modern aspirations they have as urban mothers. They long for a Madagascar where farming has not become a form of cash-cropping that makes people too poor to feed their children; where land is owned by those Indigenous to it, not by foreign mining companies or by Chinese investors; where hospitals are actually full of the kinds of medicines and labor-support persons that make women feel safe during childbirth; and where women do not have to turn to prostitution or indentured servitude in faraway countries in order to finance a viable future for their children.

While it may not be possible to pinpoint the exact origins of haircutting ceremonies, sources indicate ceremonial haircutting in Madagascar to be more than a few generations old.[41] Yet despite professions that the practice is an ancestral custom, the ceremony as it exists today can be described as much by its contemporary trappings as by its traditional ones. Scissors have come to replace knives and grandfather's teeth, cans of evaporated milk and plastic-wrapped candies have made their way into the sacred meal, fathers wearing Rastafarian shirts can perform the ritualized speeches (joro) in lieu of their elders, new rather than heirloom necklaces are sometimes used, and imported Asian-made lambas form the attire of those present.

Nevertheless, some continuity exists, and it is this continuity that in part gives the ceremony its legitimacy and weight. When Rabo invoked his ancestors and blessed his daughter, he both continued and updated a well-established custom and thereby linked himself and his daughter with others who have observed the practice before them. As Feeley-Harnik notes, "the practice of invoking ancestors by saying their names dates back to at least the 1840s if not earlier . . . 'When Sakalava *mijoro*, they call on the ancestors and sprinkle water' (*Mijoro Sakalava—mikaiky razana, mitsipiky rano*). A white dish (*sahany*, from Swahili *sahani*)—Clean!, as people most often describe it—is used to hold the water. Fresh green leaves are added and sometimes silver coins."[42] In addition to the long history of *mijoro*, a long history also exists of marking birth in ways that bear continuity with contemporary Malagasy birth rituals. In two separate accounts, one from a nineteenth-century foreign secretary to the London Missionary Society and another from an early twentieth-century explorer, both make mention of elements that exist within present-day Malagasy birth rituals.[43] These descriptions are a testament to both the ways in which birth rituals have changed over time and the ways in which they have maintained some continuity, as rituals are known to do. The tradition of giving gifts to the baby and mother postpartum, of dancing and feasting with relatives and friends, of decorating people and spaces with heirloom silver chains, and finally of having a playful competition between maternal and paternal kin over the affiliation of the child continues into the present.

Malagasy rites such as this one become traditional not when the details of how they are performed remain unchanged throughout the centuries (for they never do) or when the meanings associated with the ritual become uniform (for they never are) but when the act of holding such a ceremony enables families to create links between the traditions of their ancestors and the emerging customs of their children. As Paul Connerton proclaims, the repetitive and repetitious nature of rituals implies continuity with the past, but "[rituals] do not simply imply continuity with the past by virtue of their high degree of formality and fixity; rather, they have as one of their defining features the explicit claim to be commemorating such a continuity."[44] Although sometimes repetitive and often based on a model, rituals are also often as marked by improvisation and invention as by a static state.[45] Most fombandrazana, at least in their current manifestations, are more recent than ancient preoccupations, but it is their nod to the ways of the past that gives them their authority, relevance, and weightiness in the present.

Complex Belongings

When parents speak of children "acquiring bones," they are referring to a process of social integration that begins at birth, and sometimes even earlier, when babies are fed certain foods (of their ancestors) and nourished by the blood of their mothers and the "ordering" structure of their father's semen. As Peter Metcalf and Richard Huntington describe, "In terms of the Bara phenomenology of the person, life is maintained by a tenuously balanced combination of what can be referred to as 'order' and 'vitality.' As a biological being, a person is formed when the fertile blood of the mother's womb is ordered and arranged by the sperm of the father during sexual intercourse. To be socially and economically successful, an individual must balance out his or her relationships with his mother's and father's families. A person's life is seen as a journey leading gradually from mother's womb to father's tomb."[46] The

Bara of southern Madagascar have distinct birthing and mortuary rituals, but their understanding of the Malagasy life course—of people moving from a close affiliation to their mother's kin toward an increasing affiliation with their father's kin—is widespread throughout the island. That said, vacillation is also common, which is especially evident in the life courses of women and the rituals they employ to integrate their children into communities. An investigation into these kinds of practices—pregnancy fady as well as postpartum bathing rituals and haircutting—allows us to nuance some of the claims that have been made about the life course in Madagascar, claims about the "soft to hard," "maternal to paternal," and "blood-filled to bone-filled" life journeys that some have described.[47]

Most analyses of the Malagasy life course, especially in earlier decades, focus prominently on "the acquiring of bones" that occurs in adulthood and in death and are based primarily on masculine models.[48] Unfortunately, these overly masculine and linear models have become dominant in the literature. Although scholars have accurately portrayed the life journey as progressive— people move from a state of social ambiguity toward a state of social fixity—it is important to bear in mind that such social progressions do not always follow normative or linear trajectories, nor does a person's hardness or social fixity arrive suddenly in adulthood and once and for all. As Michael Lambek points out, even the last movement along the path (one's placement in the family tomb), which is understood to finalize discrete identities, may have more ambiguity than was once thought since people often "take the body to whichever family tomb is nearest, as long as people are buried with their ascendants rather than their spouses."[49]

If we turn our attention to include women, we realize, too, that vacillation is especially common. If acquiring bones is about finding one's sense of place and worth within one's family and lineage, one could argue that for many women, the act of becoming a mother invites them to reflect on their place in society in new ways. In northern Madagascar, women often return home to give birth and to be buried in the family tomb, but in the intervening years, many live far from home, adopting the cultural practices and inherited customs of their partners' families. Women gain immense status in motherhood and in having their children recognized as important members within a family, but it is also often said that the act of giving birth makes women soft again or weak (malemy), which is in part attributable to their shifting status. Ranginaly (cold-water bathing), an inherited practice, and other forms of postpartum care can harden them again as they become reintegrated into their communities, but this reintegration is rarely as straightforward as it is for men. When women carry the next generation in their wombs, they are bearing the continuation of multiple lineages within their bodies and must incorporate the customs, pregnancy fady (taboos), and religious habits of all of these lineages in order to best transition themselves and their babies from a watery to a "bone-filled" place within their social milieu. Sometimes this involves conversion to another religion or permanently adopting the habitus of the lineage into which one's children are becoming integrated.

Women set the stage for their and their children's progressively solidifying identities. They do so not only by hosting haircutting ceremonies that recognize the child's worth within the family, despite the fact that such ceremonies are sometimes said to be the father's family's prerogative, but also by baptizing babies or, as demonstrated in chapter 3, by observing Ramadan so that their children may someday understand what it means to be a Muslim (Silamo); by helping their children foster important relationships with elder kin; or by observing particular styles of postpartum bathing.[50]

In understanding how humans are shaped into particular kinds of people in Madagascar, many have emphasized the power of burial place as a beckoning force in people's lives. In reality, through their observance of birth rituals and other means, Malagasy parents lay the groundwork for various kinds of ethnic and religious identities, instilling bones in their children from a very young age. Metaphors of human growth (e.g., womb to tomb) express an ideal, but we should not stretch them too far. Rarely do such metaphors square with the real-life experiences of women and men, many of whom follow life paths that are less than conventional. For example, it has yet to be determined if Genevie will remain with Asmara's father or whether Zafisoa will find another vady with whom she will bear siblings for her only daughter, Sera. Some Malagasy find love in multiple partnerships, bearing children from more than one union, and some bear no children at all. Some choose to cultivate their prominence primarily within a maternal line, as was the case with Jacqueline, whose story is told in the next chapter. Of course, the notion of choice must carry significant qualifications within these contexts. Romantic relationships, the arrival of a child in one's womb, whether one's parents stay together, and the way spirits speak to you are often driven by forces out of one's control.

Women are not the only ones in Malagasy society for whom the womb-to-tomb metaphor does not always neatly or easily fit. Feeley-Harnik emphasizes that childhood affiliation in Madagascar is not always as clear as customary dictates would have us believe. Whom children, whether male or female, belong to is more complicated than the narrative that northern Malagasy tell about how God came to decide that children would belong to their fathers (paternal kin) and not their mothers (maternal kin).[51] In reality, families do not always remain intact and children move back and forth between relatives. People do not always grow from having a closer connection to their maternal kin to a closer connection to their paternal relatives, even if this is the stated ideal.

When families have playful contestations over whom their children belong to in haircutting ceremonies, something I did not observe but that is documented in the literature on haircutting in Madagascar, they are demonstrating not that fathers always win but that a person's connectedness to maternal and paternal ancestries is always negotiated, which is often evidenced by the number of relatives who show up for these occasions. Over the course of a lifetime, people often move within a network of family connections and obligations, and this process begins at birth. As I have demonstrated here, it begins when mothers choose to observe or alternatively ignore the pregnancy fady of their particular lineages; when women observe certain styles of postpartum bathing, such as ranginaly, that will mark them and their descendants as that heritage for generations to come; when parents elect to perform haircutting ceremonies, circumcisions, and baptisms on behalf of their children; when mothers convert to new religions in order to raise their children in those traditions; and when maternal grandmothers cultivate relationships with their granddaughters that may someday transcend earthly ties. New life emerges from water, but it is often through ritual that all the various potentials are constituted in a particular way. In deciding who will be present, how they will participate, and what elements will be used, ritual orchestrators determine how and to what extent mothers and babies will become "hardened" members of their communities.

Children's lives are caught up in all kinds of family struggles, yet in ceremonies of blessing, parents, together with extended kin—including grandparents, aunts, uncles, and the like—try to preserve the hope that some kind of harmony may take root within children's tenderly emerging lives. Rites of incorporation for the newly born are performed so that children may be blessed and grow up to lead lives firmly grounded in their families and firmly poised to leave an enduring legacy in the memories of their descendants. These religious child-rearing efforts are creative and hopeful and, at the same time, bear a sense of urgency in the face of looming threats to children's survival. In urban areas, where many feel that they have lost their social safety nets, parents are searching for new ways of belonging for themselves and their children.

The families I spoke with in Diégo led dynamic and pluralistic religious lives. Many were invested in family/ancestral traditions, but they were also busy finding new ways of acquiring bones in moments of birth, marriage, divorce, and death. Moreover, they were investing in various kinds of ancestral and religious communities among those already endogenous to their community as well as in pluralistic urban contexts where their engagement with diversity helped them formulate their sense of who they were. In our efforts to understand the unique and provocative ways that Malagasy remember their ancestors, we must not forget to incorporate stories of birth, which are the continuation of the ancestors (*ny fitohy raza*); rites of blessing, which are among the ways by which parents, and extended kin, create connections between the living and the dead; and the manner in which families handle the death of an infant, which represents not the loss of a life well lived but the loss of what might have been. Although all emerge from a woman's womb, not all will necessarily find a place in the ordering structure of one's father's tomb. Some will lead lives whose worth will be lost and forgotten. Others will be remembered as good churchwomen or men or as great healers or spirit mediums (tromba). Regardless of the means employed, all are anxious to find security—spiritual, social, and otherwise—in an unstable and pluralistic world where babies, sometimes tragically, slip back into the watery realms from which they came.

FIVE

BEARING BABIES IN DYNAMIC
RELIGIOUS LANDSCAPES

As increasing numbers of Malagasy move to urban centers like Diégo Suarez in search of work and educational opportunities, they face new decisions about how they will bring their children into the world. They find themselves in urban contexts far from the support (and sometimes critical gaze) of their extended kin and far from their ancestral lands, in cities haunted by unfamiliar spirits, with novel specialists, medicines, and religious communities on which they will learn to rely. In Madagascar, as is the case in much of East Africa, and indeed throughout the Indian Ocean world, land has a sacred value. The land on which one's ancestors were born bears a kind of power over one's moving, marrying, and decision-making. Many Malagasy understand the land on which one's ancestors farmed to be impregnated with a kind of sacred power (hasina) and to be a source of social security in one's family by virtue of the land's ability to produce the kinds of plants, medicines, and food crops on which one's descendants will rely.

People are born belonging to places, both maternal and paternal, and are beckoned back to those places when they die. But increasingly, as a result of colonial labor policies and other economic circumstances that compel people to migrate to cities, people's sense of belonging is no longer as tied up in ancestral lands (tanindrazana) as it once was. Amélie, a mother we met in chapter 3, persuaded her father, who was struggling to move away from his ancestral lands, with these words: "We're your family, and the plantation is fine. You need to stay near us." Parker Shipton explains it thus: "If we cannot easily hold onto or preserve the land we are on, we may find strength in remembering that others have come before us and that others will follow. If humans make up the continuing life of their ancestors, perceived as spirits or conduits to the divinity, these may in turn help humans cohere, and to find and accept their places on shared ground."[1] In other words, ancestral lands have sacred value not because of the lands themselves but because of the people who farmed and lived in community with one another on those lands. In this way, even when one is far from one's ancestral lands, belonging can be established in people through ritual processes that remember these connections to one another and to the common lands from which people descend.

This chapter is about broader changes regarding people's access to, and relationship with, ancestral lands, ancestors, and the rituals that bind descendants of these lands together. In this book so far, I have highlighted the importance of ancestors in Malagasy religions and, in particular, the unique ways that women engage with ancestors upon the birth of a child to secure for themselves and their children the kind of social and spiritual resources necessary for their children to acquire bones and flourish. I would be remiss, however, if I did not also share stories of how people are beginning to sever ties with their ancestors or, at least, beginning to question and reconsider the roles that ancestral legacies play in their daily lives.

Sometimes mothers are severing their ties with their ancestors for practical reasons. They simply cannot keep up with the obligations required of them as members of descent groups, and the benefits of upholding these obligations are not always apparent when one has moved away from extended kin and thus cannot as easily reap the benefits of these support systems. Sometimes, these practices feel antiquated and out of line with parents' twenty-first-century agendas, where aspirations might be more individualistic than communal in nature and efforts to secure a future for their children might be more focused on investments in education than in lineage-based social support systems. And sometimes, too, people's changing relationship to ancestors might be attributable to changing religious commitments.

As I mentioned in the introduction to this book, the rise of Pentecostal and charismatic forms of Christianity are changing the religious landscape of the island. Though it is not entirely clear what the outcome of all these changes will be, what is clear is that these changes will matter not only for the lives of women and men who are themselves both driving and being driven by these changes but also for their babies. When mothers opt to dissolve their ties with their ancestors, for religious reasons or otherwise, children may lose access to certain forms of community, especially lineage-based kinship networks, but they may also gain access to new forms of community. None of this means, however, that people's engagement with ancestors will disappear entirely or that traditional religious specialists who broker access to the ancestors will become obsolete. In fact, while some are distancing themselves from ances- tors and lineage-based commitments, other urban dwellers are prompting a resurgence of traditional customs precisely because they are less proximate to their ancestral lands and have a greater need to hold on to ethnic- and lineage- based identities in these new urban contexts.

Given these newer religious alternatives, and because of the religious proclivities of women like Marie and Jacqueline, whose stories are told in the following paragraphs, some scholars have recently turned their atten- tion away from traditions of ancestor remembrance in African societies in favor of new focuses on the growth of Pentecostal churches and charismatic forms of Christianity. Indeed, the rapid growth of charismatic Christianity throughout the global south represents a fascinating religious phenomenon that warrants scholarly attention. That said, even when Malagasy discover new forms of religious practice in charismatic and neo-Pentecostal churches, the struggles and dreams of their ancestors pervade in new and innovative ways. Their legacies beg for acknowledgment, pressing on their descendants as a force that must be reckoned with. For even when Malagasy sometimes wish to forget, forgetting is still a process by which hasina is acknowledged, however conceived, as a sacred force, a burdensome legacy, or a potentially malicious element that must be either exorcised or negotiated, appropriated, and restrained. In other words, engagement with ancestors remains central to most Malagasy practices, even among Pentecostals, who, through rituals means, strive to ward themselves of ancestral connections.

Citing a sentiment expressed by John McCall, Jennifer Cole and Karen Middleton wrote, "The disappearance of ancestors from Africanist literature since the 1970s owes more to a shift in anthropological paradigms than to changes in African practices on the ground."[2] The importance of producing timely relevant scholarship cannot be overstated; however, scholarly trends that overlook ancestral traditions simply because they are unfashionable must be reexamined. Among those who have sustained their attention on ancestors, most rightly position Malagasy concern with their ancestors as a historical re- sponse to the struggles they have endured, struggles caused by the hegemonic rise and fall of the Merina Kingdom, whose reign during the late eighteenth and early nineteenth centuries threatened the political autonomy of coastal groups, and by the French colonial government during the late eighteenth and early nineteenth centuries, whose settlements disrupted local economies and threatened Indigenous access to land and vital resources.

Perhaps more than anyone, Gillian Feeley-Harnik has revealed the extent to which preoccupation with ancestors, at least in modern manifestations, is a relatively recent phenomenon owing as much to the historical disturbances of slavery, colonialism, and neocolonialism as to people's concern for observing timeless traditions of the dead.[3] As I have noted in an earlier chapter in this book, Nancy Rose Hunt observes a similar phenomenon in the Congo when she discovered that "traditional" initiation ceremonies for boys actually augmented during the Belgian occupation of Congo as colonial officials sought to increase the population of schoolboys who would be prepared to work in rubber plantations.[4] Congolese fathers both imagined and sought to claim another future for their boys and tried to maintain influence over them by creating traditional religious rituals that preserved the values and ways their ancestors instilled in them rather than submitting to having their sons recruited into exploitative foreign labor markets.

In sum, in northern Madagascar, there are at least two trends regarding ancestral engagement. In one, mothers and the specialists with whom they consult are seeking to preserve traditional rituals and medicines of their ancestors. The other is a trend away from traditional medicines and rituals and from the customs of one's ancestors, influenced both by the rise of charismatic forms of Christianity and by mothers' own proclivities about religion, health, and what it means to be modern. In the midst of these trends, mothers in Madagascar, like mothers everywhere, are struggling to make the right decisions for their children.

Marie's story provides one such example of this struggle to determine which kinds of customs felt like the right ones for her daughter. Marie was in the middle of completing a maîtrise degree at the University of Antsiranana when we first met in 2011.[5] That year, she spent a portion of her time living with her toddler-age daughter in her parents' house in Diégo, but she and her daughter also traveled frequently back to Madagascar's capital, Antananarivo, where she stayed with one of her sisters. Of all the women I interviewed, Marie had some of the more exceptional social and financial resources available to her. As the daughter of two professors, both of whom received degrees abroad, she had many opportunities available to her. However, as she saw it, these opportunities did not make her transition to motherhood any easier. In fact, both her social position and her somewhat detached relationship to the cultural and religious customs of Madagascar often meant she felt distanced from her peers, and ignorant of the traditions of the dominant culture. Upon bearing her first child, Marie felt even more disconnected from the societal norms as she and her boyfriend struggled to put their lives together in ways that both families deemed acceptable. For Marie, this disconnect was inspired not by an interest in Pentecostal or charismatic forms of Christianity but by her family's social status and experience abroad.

Marie's Ambivalence toward Malagasy Customs

"Being a mother was not at all in my plan," answered Marie as I began my interview with her.[6]

> And for my boyfriend,[7] I think he felt the same way. But it happened, nonetheless. You see, I had *un copin*. I had *un garçon* of about twelve years and I became pregnant. For me, it was a beautiful thing. I was surprised but also very content. I took my responsibility, and he did too. During that time, I left to go to France for some months to stay with one of my parents' friends who was a nurse and he stayed in Tana (Madagascar's capital).[8] So we were apart for a while. I was there for just five months while he remained in Tana. We continued to communicate very often. I kept him informed about the progress of the pregnancy. I sent him the sonogram pictures. And I thought that he was also content. But when I returned to Tana after five months of being away, I saw that things had become a little bit difficult for me.

Marie's pregnancy brought to the surface the differing values she and her boyfriend's family espoused with regard to welcoming this new child. In particular, Marie would come to learn just how important traditional customs were to her boyfriend's family, which was in stark contrast to her own family's more ambivalent relationship with traditional customs.

According to Marie, in her own family, they had a rather estranged relationship both to ancestral customs and to the dominant cultural customs of Madagascar. She described,

> In my family, we do not follow fombagasy, not when my parents are educated like they are. No one in my family follows *fombagasy à la maison* [domestic customs] because of my parents. Perhaps it's because they are

professors and have traveled a lot and have taken a lot of culture from elsewhere. So, they don't see the need to strictly adhere to what Malagasy culture dictates. Instead, they mix things. They've acquired a proper culture [*une culture propre*]. I don't know if it's a good or bad thing. There's a negative side to this because it's difficult to live in a society without truly knowing the culture.

She went on to describe, "For example, I have never been to the place where my dad is from. I think it's because again, my parents didn't want us to be involved in their traditions. They live in a small village, and they follow a lot of traditions there. This is especially true for my father's mother. Her family observes a lot of fomba. So maybe he didn't want his children to do all of that." Unfortunately, however, this distanced stance in her family with regard to ancestral customs proved difficult when discussions ensued with her boyfriend's family about the couple's plans to get married as well as the rituals of blessing for their daughter.

Discussions about both the date of the wedding and the rituals the couple would follow brought to the fore the family's conflicting expectations of ancestral customs. Marie described,

And for example, the father of my child, his family *does* follow the culture. Thus, when his parents came from Morandava in the southwest of Madagascar for the birth, they asked, "What is your culture? What are your customs?" I said, "No, we don't really know the culture, so it depends on you." But then they didn't really say anything about what their culture is. There were some words said between us and now things are a bit cold, and I regret that very much, but it is not easy.

With the date of the marriage, we had wanted to get married before the baby was born, but it was difficult to decide on a date for the marriage. But for my boyfriend's parents, before deciding to get married, it was necessary to first consult a wise person, a moasy [herbalist or healer-diviner]. They insisted that it's up to this man to decide if the day is good or not because there are certain days that are fady. My boyfriend and I, we had already prepared all the paperwork for the marriage. But when his parents came, they said the day we had chosen was not good for the two of us because that day was fady for them. And for me, right away, that shocked me. For me, all that is fomba, all the traditions, I'll consider all that. And because of my education, I respect all of that, but consulting a moasy, that's taking it too far; that's maiz-maizina.

Marie understood the cultural and religious differences between the respective families in religious terms, framing her own as more enlightened, frequently using metaphors of light and dark to contrast her own perspectives with that of her boyfriend's family. For example, when I asked her what *maizmaizina* meant, she described it thus: "It comes from the devil. It means dark. It comes from darkness. It's the opposite of light. It's the opposite of God. My parents are very pure. And because we're educated as we are, for me, I don't like to follow things that are *un peu sombre comme ça* [a bit dark like that]. For me, that seems a bit occult to consult *un mage* [a magician] to see if two people are compatible. So that's how things stand, and we still haven't arrived at a decision regarding the marriage." It is likely that Marie's boyfriend's father would understand the moasy he consulted regarding the date of the marriage to be not *un peu sombre* but rather an experienced herbalist, or healer-diviner, but because the two families could not reach a kind of mutual understanding of each other's customs, to Marie, his practices remained dark and mysterious in her mind.

Marie went on to describe other aspects of her father-in-law's customs that seemed shadowy to her and the rift these misunderstandings were causing. She went to say, "His father is still a mystery to me. He often goes into the forest, like I said before, and I don't know what he does there. I guess he goes to see *les gens sages* [wise people], like I said before, *les moasy*. And so, for now, my boyfriend and I have decided to take a break. I'm beginning to imagine that his parents have a real problem." At one point, the couple's parents tried to negotiate on the couple's behalf, but as Marie described, this conversation did not go well either. According to her account,

> My parents, when they were in Tana, they tried to talk with his parents. My dad is very good at being diplomatic, but my boyfriend's parents weren't interested in negotiating. They are angry because they have never met Malagasy who don't follow fombagasy. For people, like my boyfriend, who come from Morandava, just like with Indians, their parents are like a God. They are very sacred. You have to please them one hundred percent of the time. Everything that they tell you to do, you must do. I learned about this from friends, but I learned about it too late. For me, I'm not used to doing things without a reason. I'm not used to being forced to do something. I can't just do something if I don't believe in it; it would be like killing my personality. I asked his parents why we must we do this, and they responded simply by saying, "Fady les andry" [It's taboo for Andry people].

Finally, my mother said, let the father of the baby decide, and he said he needed a night to think about it, but then he decided he would wait until after she is born. When the baby turned a year, I asked him for an update, and he said it's still not the right time. So, I don't know what that means. Maybe he still needs a little bit of time. My husband's mom invited me to Morondava to bring the baby to show to the family, and I wanted to. But my mother told me not to go because, she said, "if you bring Clara there, they will do the fomba. You don't know what they will do to her. Maybe they will take her into the forest and do *les rites* [the rituals]." I agreed with my mother. I did not want to go there by myself. You see, I am no longer *la belle fille* [a single woman]. I am a mother, and now the situation is a bit more delicate. I do not want to go by myself. It should be the three of us if I am to go. I know my daughter is their child also, so I am not sure how to handle the situation. I don't follow fomba, but there are some things, some dictums. For example, there is this saying, this Malagasy belief, that the mother-in-law does not like her daughter-in-law so you should not go see her by yourself. That's why I told my boyfriend to come with me. But he always has excuses. Usually, he says he has to work. I truly don't know what's going through his head. I don't know if he's being influenced by his parents or if it's a cultural thing. Maybe there's just a difference in culture.

Two years into their daughter's birth, Marie and her boyfriend had not settled their disagreements but neither had they formally decided to end their relationship either. She was still living in Diégo, raising their daughter, while he remained in the capital city, Antananarivo.

Though the two families could not come to an agreement about the marriage, or the appropriate customs with which to raise baby Clara, Marie had her own thoughts regarding Clara's religious upbringing. She planned to baptize her daughter at the Anglican church where she and her parents were members and described her decision-making and the theology behind it this way:

Before I baptize her, I want to first study the Bible because according to the truth of the Bible, I should be better educated. So before baptizing her, I need to better educate myself. I don't want to baptize her right now because she's so small. She doesn't know anything. I want her to have the choice. I want her to know the difference between good and evil. I don't want the baptism to be just like a passport, just like that. And for me the fact that she is small means she is protected because God has said that children are without fault. So maybe someday when she is ready, I will baptize her.

Aside from her plans to baptize her daughter, Clara, Marie did not plan to observe any other kinds of religious rituals or cultural customs. She is ranginaly (cold-water bather), but despite this inherited identity, she opted not to follow it. She explained, "I have not cut her hair either. Well, I have, but not as part of any kind of ceremony. I just cut it because it is so hot in Diégo and the hair on her neck makes her especially hot. I had to wait until she was sleeping, because when she is awake, she moves around too much. Also, my father told me about ranginaly when my daughter was born. He told me that we, my family, we were ranginaly, but he was just telling me, not insisting that I do anything with that information." Marie was not alone in her reluctance to engage in ancestral practice, but she did acknowledge the difficulty this caused for her, and her boyfriend, in the raising of their daughter.

Despite the many familial discords surrounding their daughter's birth, Marie and her boyfriend were nevertheless able to find agreement on a name that celebrates the legacies of multiple personalities within their respective families. Marie proudly described this process:

> Well, the advantage of Malagasy names is that you can cut them into smaller parts. So, we decided on Clara-Élis for the first part because our mothers' names are Élise and Élisabeth, and her middle name Soafara comes from one of my names [soa] and one of my sister's names [fara]. And for the surname, we used both my boyfriend's surname and my father's surname. It's good because it saves our family name. You see, we have no boys in our family. My dad loves his name. When we told him the name we had chosen, he pleaded that we add his surname as well. So, we did. My dad's surname is long, like most Malagasy surnames, but we took off the first part and then added it together with my boyfriend's surname. I thought to myself, "Oh, the family name is too long." But I think it's OK. Malagasy have long names. And it keeps her connected to both sides of the family.

When our interview ended, Marie reiterated that she loved motherhood and that she wished everyone to have the chance at being a parent. However, she also indicated that her pregnancy had been a source of embarrassment at first given that it occurred before she was married. Because of her religious upbringing, she felt that she had "done things out of order." But her trip to France during the first part of her pregnancy afforded her a chance to reflect on how she would proceed given the pregnancy and also enabled her to receive high-quality prenatal care, under the care of a nurse with whom she lived.

When she prepared to come back to Madagascar and feared revealing her pregnancy to her community, her own mother reassured her, insisting that "people in Diégo do not care about that sort of thing." Marie's mother also assured her that her fellow parishioners at the church where they worshipped would similarly understand and support her.

Reflecting on these initial insecurities, at the time of my interview with her, Marie was sure of only one thing. She was committed to raising her daughter in "a pure and healthy environment" defined by her and her parents' religious and cultural commitments. Everything else in her life remained unclear as she waited for her boyfriend's decision regarding their marriage and regarding the customs they would (or would not) observe in the raising of their daughter. Marie confessed that she often struggled to find her way among friends and family because of her ambivalence toward fombagasy. Though she was not the first or only Malagasy to adopt such a stance toward so-called traditional and cultural practices, she reiterated over and over again that she felt it to be a difficult position. Ultimately, she wondered how she would raise her daughter given that Clara-Élis belongs to two families.

As Marie's story reveals, disagreements over how best to raise a child have the potential to forge an impossible divide between parents. Ideally speaking, Malagasy parents strive to preserve multiple aspects of their respective heritages in their children. And traditionally a child's father's customs are privileged more heavily than the mother's, but parents' religious commitments, social class, and educational background also strongly inform how parents will navigate these competing religious agendas and ancestries that vie for continuance in the lives of their children. Marie's story reveals that Malagasy mothers can sometimes assert just as strong an influence over the religious and cultural upbringing of their children as fathers when they want to, and when it is within their power to do so. Her story is also evidence that, for some, ancestral commitments are not always of upmost importance in decisions about how best to raise a child.

The birth of a child is one of the more quintessential moments to preserve and fashion anew family legacies, but sometimes this process simply cannot be achieved within a union of families. The parenting of Clara offered Marie an opportunity to think about her family history, how her parents emerged from a family of cattle herders to become professors. In doing so, they traded some of their "traditional customs" for what Marie referred to as a more "proper culture" that "mixes" and diverges from the cultural norm. It is important to note, however, that despite Marie's insistence that her parents wished to protect her from the ways of village life, her parents have in other ways remained connected to their rural roots. This was evidenced by her father's return to his natal village for the funeral of a relative, which occurred during my time in Madagascar. His presence and financial contributions at this important event speak to the fact that even when Malagasy turn away from the customs of their ancestors, most still maintain some ties with their natal villages. They do by sending money home and by returning for funerals, marriages, and births. Nevertheless, Marie's insistence that her parents have created a "proper culture" spoke to her evolutionist views regarding the various religious traditions in her country.[9]

In other words, Marie adopted a view of progress where village life and the Indigenous customs associated with it were, in her mind, darker and less rational than what she understood to be the more modern worldview she espoused as a highly educated, Anglican urbanite.[10] Because of this position, she found herself less concerned with bathing her daughter in the fombandra-zana. Instead, she strove to preserve in her daughter what she understood to be her family's progress—their move from the countryside to the city, from the observance of "dark" rituals performed in the forest to the more "pure" and luminous rituals of the Episcopal cathedral in which she worshipped. In doing so, Marie was also giving birth to a renewed story about herself, about her ancestors, and about her family.

Marie's story is unique in many ways, but the struggles she faced in the early years of parenthood were also illustrative of the challenges many Malagasy youth face as they strive to make their way in new urban contexts far from the supportive social structures their parents and grandparents knew. They are at a crossroads and are charged with the task of either continuing the ties their elders have maintained with their ancestral homelands or, alternatively, forging new paths and new identities that rely less on bearing the histories and customs of one's forebears and more on the sense of identity and belonging they find in the religious communities of the city and in other kinds of social milieus.

There were many personal circumstances that led Marie away from fombandraza, including her parents' educational experiences, their upward social mobility, and her family's Protestant religious inclinations. Even though her family attended a mainline Protestant church, rather than a Pentecostal or charismatic church, Marie still felt ancestral customs to be incompatible with her faith. While it is generally true that mainline Protestant churches and Catholic congregations are more accommodating of ancestral practices as compared with Pentecostal ones, this might be changing as a result of the broader influence of charismatic forms of Christianity, a phenomenon Laura Tilghman discusses in her research among residents of Tamatave.[11]

In Madagascar, the first beginnings of a charismatic Christian movement actually began a few decades before the global rise of Pentecostalism in the form of an Indigenous Christian healing movement called Fifohazana (awakening). This movement, often called the shepherd-healing movement, has had great influence over people's thinking with regard to healing and community. It was one of the first Malagasy-led Christian movements to promote a distancing or turning away from ancestral customs, and as will become clear in the stories that follow, the movement continues to influence women's decision-making around the blessings that children receive and the ways in which they are incorporated into religious community.

The Shepherd-Healing Movement

On an island populated by a multitude of spirits, West African *bori* spirits, *maishetani* from the Swahili coast, and Sakalava tromba among them, the religious communities that have been the most successful in Madagascar both acknowledge the presence of spirits and offer therapeutic means of dealing with these same spirits. Sometimes these spiritual therapies, for example, mediumship versus exorcism, seem like opposing responses. Without glossing over important differences, it is also true that people's experiences with spirits, and theological understanding of spirits, rarely emerge in religious silos but instead develop as a result of people's ongoing participation in and fluency within and across multiple religious worldviews. Sometimes these experiences might lead a person to convert from one way of thinking about spirits to another, but even professed conversions are often more fluid than it might at first seem and instead involve subtle negotiations. This is true in the cases of Jacqueline and Fita, whose stories of involvement in the healing movement are told in the following sections. It was also true historically, for the founder of Madagascar's Indigenous Christian healing movement, Dada Rainisoalambo.

The shepherd-healing movement began in 1894, when Dada Rainiso-alambo, a Betsileo healer-diviner (*mpisikidy*) converted to Christianity and founded the Fifohazana movement.[12] As a child, Rainisoalambo attended a mission school, served as a catechist, and even contemplated becoming a minister. Later, he left the mission school and began working as a healer-diviner in the village of Ambatoreny.[13] At the time of his formal conversion to Christianity, Rainisoalambo had been suffering from a relentless skin disorder and sought relief through a variety of means. On October 15, 1894, out of desperation, he prayed to Jesus that he would be healed of his affliction. According to the story, Jesus healed Rainisoalambo but demanded of him in return that he destroy the traditional medicines (*fanafody-gasy*) he had used as part of his practice as a healer-diviner. Grateful for his newfound health, Rainisoalambo complied, threw away his traditional medicines in a latrine, and created a village called Soatanana (beautiful land/village). Within the village, Rainisoalambo formed the first of many healing camps (*toby*) where he and his followers tried to live by the example of the community of Acts 4:32–35. They sought to heal the sick in Jesus's name, preach the gospel, and train others as apostles (*iraka*) and shepherds (mpiandry) of Jesus's healing powers.[14] He promoted literacy and the cleanliness of one's home and clothes and asked others to abandon divination and service to the ancestral dead just as Jesus had required of him in a dream revelation.[15]

Rainisoalambo came from a long line of traditional healers. His family were royal servants, and he succeeded his father as a keeper of the royal talisman or charms called *sampy*.[16] During that time, however, being royalty or servants of royalty meant that you were educated in the Christian mission schools (established by missionaries from the London Missionary Society) even if you also served as a traditional healer-diviner for the royal courts. So Rainisoalambo was very much engaged in both the Indigenous religions of the Betsileo peoples of south-central Madagascar and the Protestant Christianity observed by Merina royalty of the central highlands.[17] Even though Rainisoalambo's conversion to Christianity is often professed by members of the movement as a clean break from his older religious commitments, one could argue that his experience as a traditional healer informed the version of Christianity he created. And consequently, Rainisoalambo's creation of Christian toby represented not a total break from but an evolved continuation of his abilities to harness divine spiritual powers for the purposes of healing the sick.

What began as a small-scale community of Christians serving the sick and mentally ill in the highlands of Madagascar under the leadership of Rainisoalambo is now a global and transdenominational movement with a branch in the United States.[18] The incorporation of Fifohazana healing therapeutics into the liturgical structures of two mainline Protestant churches—the Malagasy Lutheran Church (Fiangonana Loterana Malagasy [FLM]) and the Church of Jesus Christ in Madagascar (Fiangonan'i Jesoa Kristy eto Madagasikara [FJKM])—is a relatively recent phenomenon, but it speaks to the growing interest and reliance on charismatic forms of Christianity both in Madagascar in particular and in the world at large.[19] Historically, leaders of the two Christian denominations previously frowned on what they considered the "syncretic" and "overly emotional" practices of the Fifohazana movement, but as Malagasy interests in Pentecostal and charismatic Christianity increased, mainline denominations eventually embraced and institutionalized shepherd-healing within their churches as a way to gain converts in the 1980s.[20]

Thus, despite the difficulty in classifying Fifohazana, a movement that certainly predates the rise of Pentecostal and charismatic forms of Christianity across the globe, the current iteration of the movement can be understood within the broader context of the rapid growth over the past several decades of other Pentecostal and charismatic forms of worship, which emphasize healing, the experience of being born again, and the power of the Holy Spirit. In April 2014, at the invitation of my shepherd-healer (mpiandry) neighbor Noémi, my research assistant Zafisoa and I attended such a service of healing and renewal for a young woman named Fita. Fita's story highlights a growing interest in Madagascar in charismatic Christian movements that offer healing and renewal upon one's turning away from ancestral practices.

Noémi and Fita

Before attending the service for Fita, Noémi described to us her story of becoming a mpiandry, recounting how her calling into the ministry came slowly to her after a long period of illness and discernment, followed by months of prayer, scripture reading, and training with other mpiandry. She portrayed the work of healing as tiresome but fulfilling, as she recalled the 140-kilometer journey she and other healers had recently embarked on over the Easter weekend to heal a woman who had been possessed of a *devoly* (devil), which she later called a *bori be*. Noémi's description of the woman as possessed by a "big" West African bori spirit speaks to her understanding that spirits travel transnationally and require experts, like herself, who are trained to identify and release people from all the evil spiritual forces that could potentially threaten their well-being. Noémi remembered the afflicted woman as "[being] sick, walking funny, and [being] possessed by a violent spirit." "But now," Noémi proudly proclaimed, "she is healed and will receive a new life [aina voavoa]." Noémi then had me kneel before her as she demonstrated just how the woman was freed of her spirit and given new life. She placed her hand on my head, uttered her prophetic words, and then assisted me back onto my feet.

Zafisoa and I witnessed this deliverance work firsthand when we attended the healing service Noémi invited us to. Noémi transported me on the back of her motorcycle to the FJKM church, and Zafisoa met us there. When we all arrived in the churchyard, we met the other mpiandry who serve that congregation. They were sitting in a circle in a back room of the sanctuary, talking with the young woman seeking care. Fita shared her struggles and her decision to abandon her reliance on traditional medicines (fanafody-gasy). The mpiandry then prayed with her and escorted her into the churchyard, which stood in proximity to downtown Diégo, near one of the larger clothing markets, where cars frequently passed. The mpiandry began singing hymns as they dug a hole in which they instructed Fita to place her traditional medicines. She did as they instructed. The mpiandry burned the bag of medicines, continued singing, said prayers, and then stomped on the fire, covering it at last with dirt. After the burning of medicines, everyone proceeded inside for a worship service. Inside the sanctuary, scriptures were read, songs were sung, and then congregants were invited to come and kneel before the shepherds who would bless congregants one by one. The mpiandry donned white robes inside the sanctuary, the traditional costumes of mpiandry, and began blessing and exorcising the people who came forward.[21]

At one point during the service, a congregant became possessed by a violent spirit. Thus, what began as a calm altar call grew into an ecstatic experience of possession that necessitated a rapid gathering of mpiandry around the afflicted woman. The mpiandry shouted and screamed to the spirit "out in the name of Jesus" (miala amin-ny anarany's Jesosy) as they laid their hands on her. Soon the woman collapsed on the floor, was then helped to her feet, and was declared free of the spirit that had been plaguing her.

The shepherd-healing movement, on which women like Noémi and Fita relied to "chase away the demons," offers an alternative religious solution to a problem nearly all Malagasy are striving to address—how best to protect themselves, and their children, from the forces of evil in the world and also how to integrate children into communities that will provide them with the spiritual and social resources they need to flourish. This alternative religious

Shepherd-healers offering blessings. *Photos by author.*

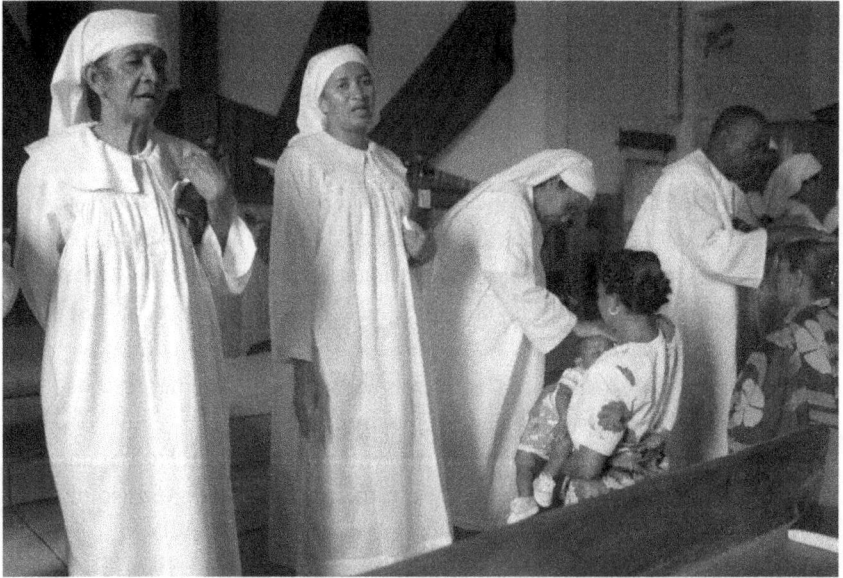

solution is appealing as much for its rhetoric of ultimacy as for its efficacy. As other scholars of charismatic Christian movements in Africa have claimed, the success of these variants of Christianity lies, in part, in their willingness to recognize the prevalence of evil or temperamental spirits, something that has always been emphasized in African Indigenous religions but has rarely been addressed in mainline and missionary churches.[22]

Pentecostals commonly use the language of rupture to frame their conversion from traditionalist, or mainline Christian practices, to charismatic ones.[23] In a similar vein, Malagasy mpiandry encourage participants to abandon fombandrazana and burn traditional medicines. However, more often than not, among people who profess dramatic change, few wholeheartedly abandon older religious commitments. This language of rupture and the rituals that accompany it (like burning medicines) enable Malagasy to envision new religious experiences as transforming and dramatically life altering, even when religious change is more fluid and continuous than these rituals of rupture suggest. Often those who embrace charismatic forms of Christianity undergo a subtler process of renegotiating of their relationships to their ancestors, as is evidenced in Jacqueline's story, which follows, even as they emphasize the distinctiveness of various other kinds of religious practices.

And at the institutional level, incremental change more than rupture is also the norm. Religious movements, like Fifohazana, emerge from a fabric of well-established and intricately connected religious traditions and, therefore, do not merely break away from the Indigenous religions or the missionary-based forms of Christianity from which they borrow. As G. C. Oosthuizen writes, "The office of prophet/prayer healer in the African Independent Churches fulfils a much felt need because of the traditional society's age-old role of the diviner and herbalist."[24] Moreover, as Cynthia Holder Rich explains, within the Indigenous religions of Madagascar, women often held prestigious positions as spirit mediums but were not allowed to hold these kinds of prominent positions in mission churches.[25] She, Céline Ratovoson, and Mariette Razivelo argue that Fifohazana made room for women religious leaders and prophets in a way that other Christian organizations did not and attributes the success of the movement partially to this factor.[26] In other words, these newer, alternative Christian movements may fill a spiritual need and offer something more or less unique and timely, but they also "develop alongside," "borrow from," influence, and are influenced by the mainline and missionary forms of Christianity that predate them.[27]

In the following story, Jacqueline, a mother of two, discusses her relation-ship with all of the various spirits in her life, highlighting both the complex relationship she has with a tromba, an ancestral spirit within her family, and her relationship to the Holy Spirit, which offers her an alternative way to engage in the spirit world and safeguard her family from harm. Jacqueline's story is representative of a broader shift away from venerating and channel-ing the spirits of one's ancestors in favor of charismatic engagement with the Holy Spirit, which offers deliverance from (rather than connection with) the spirits of the past. Her story is also representative of the sometimes complex relationships Malagasy have with the competing cosmologies of their reli-gious landscape.

Jacqueline's Struggles with Spirits

On a Saturday morning in early December, Jacqueline and I sat on the steps of the Alliance Francaise cultural center, where she worked part time as an instructor of Malagasy language.[28] Jacqueline, a teacher, wife, and mother of two, as well as one of my Malagasy language tutors, had been telling me about *tromba*, a word Malagasy use to simultaneously refer to ances-tor spirits, the experience of being possessed, and the human mediums that are possessed by such spirits. Jacqueline thought she might be next in line to receive her grandmother's tromba, the spirit that had possessed her grandmother.

At the time of our conversation, Jacqueline was still living in her grand-mother's house, and even though she had been working on building another home for herself, her husband, and their two children, every time she tried to leave, something bad would happen, as if her grandmother's spirit insisted that she stay. Unlike her cousins, Jacqueline observed a lot of the family's fady, including the restriction against eating pork, which Jacqueline thought made her a more suitable candidate to receive her grandmother's tromba.[29]

Jacqueline then paused to inquire about whether I wanted to learn more about tromba. I assured her that I did, at which point she offered to take me to see a spirit medium but expressed reservations about going herself because she also goes to church and tromba are forbidden for those who go to church. In fact, later that day, she planned to attend a shepherd-healing service at a Lutheran church, with her two young children in tow, so they might "chase away the demons" (*pour chaser un peu les demons*). "This is why I can't take you to see tromba, because I think they're a bit demonic," she explained. I asked,

"Does everyone think that? Do people who have tromba think they are demonic too?" Jacqueline clarified,

> No, they don't think that, and I didn't used to think that either. You see,
> I was raised around tromba and didn't used to think they were evil, but
> I changed my mind about it later. I knew someone in college who had
> tromba, and it was bad, and also my daughter had some trouble with bad
> spirits, and it was after these experiences that I decided tromba were no
> good. Actually, there are different kinds of tromba, the real ones and the
> false ones, and it's possible to tell the difference between the two. There
> are some that are actually ancestors, but most of them are devils. You
> can tell if they're true or not by going to Ambilobe. There are different
> methods, but one method is to go before the king, the one who lives in
> Ambilobe, who is the king of the Antankarana.[30] If the tromba *regarde
> le roi* [see the king], then they are true tromba, but if they don't, they're
> devils because devils are afraid to come out in front of the king. My
> grandmother told me that before there weren't a lot of tromba, at least
> not as many people with tromba as there are today. The traditional way of
> speaking with ancestors was in dreams and visions and only a few people
> had tromba, and the ones who did were those who had *un don* [a gift], like
> healers. Now, lots of people have tromba, but my grandmother said this is
> a more recent phenomenon.

As Jacqueline's grandmother expressed, historically in Madagascar, mediums
and other important religious figures were the ones predominantly possessed
by tromba. By contrast, in the late twentieth and early twenty-first centuries
more and more ordinary Malagasy find themselves afflicted by tromba and
other spirits. Some of the afflicted are interpreted to be victims of evil spirits, or "false tromba"; others are written off as charlatans trying to appear
possessed in order to earn money as healers; and still others are considered
authentic vessels of real tromba spirits.

According to some, the uptick in possession incidences, of which Jacqueline's grandmother spoke, probably occurred as a result of a variety of changing social circumstances and social turbulences. Colonization, urbanization,
and a move to a neoliberal economy engendered all kinds of new relationships with missionaries, colonists, expatriates, tourists, and Malagasy from
all parts of the island, all of whom prompted one another to understand, and
even experience, the spirit world in new ways. In Lesley Sharp's research in
the town of Ambanja, she attributes the rise in incidences of spirit-related

illnesses, particularly among disaffected women and youth, to societal disruptions caused by the creation of cash crop economies during the French colonial period, which left many people displaced from their ancestral lands and forced into new urban societies, no longer able to grow the foods and participate in the kinds of communal observances that previously sustained their families.[31]

In Madagascar, Malagasy divulge information about tromba to vazaha, foreigners like me, with great caution. Vazaha—who are missionaries, colonists, expatriates, students, researchers, Peace Corps workers, environmentalists, and tourists—hold all kinds of perspectives about tromba, ranging from viewing them with respect to viewing them as demonic to odd curiosities to objects of scholarly investigation. That Jacqueline framed her relationship with tromba as complicated might have had as much to do with the fact that she was talking to me, a vazaha whom she was still getting to know, as it did with her own mixed feelings on the topic.

While she viewed her grandmother, who had been possessed by an ancestral tromba, with great respect, she spoke more cautiously and even guarded herself and her children against invasion by false tromba. At the same time, a part of her hoped she would be an honorable enough vessel to receive her grandmother's tromba, something which would afford her a great deal of respect within her family, which is one of the reasons she diligently observed ancestral taboos, especially her family's fady against eating pork; performed the necessary haircutting and circumcision ceremonies for her two children; and regularly took them to church to be exorcised of evil spirits by Malagasy mpiandry.

For Jacqueline, shepherd-healing offered an important service to her family, a religious technique for ensuring that she and her children would not be possessed by false tromba or any other kinds of harmful spirits. And while Jacqueline framed her commitment to being a churchgoing Christian as one that prohibited her from engaging with the tromba, it's also true that a part of her aspired to follow in the footsteps of her grandmother and become a medium of tromba. Jacqueline was highly aware of, and well versed in, multiple religious worldviews of both the Indigenous and Christian varieties. Her life, and the rituals of care she constructed around herself and her children, required a kind of fluency between the two even as she obeyed the distinctions, working hard to discern the best ways to engage with tromba while also remaining faithful to her Lutheran community.

In a similar vein, the mothers we met throughout this book—Nasreen, Céline, Françoise, Amélie, Sylvie, Camellia, Adeline, Genevie, and Marie, as well as countless others whose stories were not told in full—work hard to preserve the traditions and legacies they deemed worthy of continuation in the lives of their children. At the same time, many also search for newer alternative forms of community and healing. In other words, their efforts are not holdovers from a previous era but instead creative strategies on the part of mothers, who often have a foothold in multiple religious worlds as they strive to provide their children with a sense of identity and belonging in a pluralistic city where multiplicity abounds and reproductive insecurities threaten to eclipse their ability to grow the next generation. As I also have demonstrated in this chapter and throughout this book, their efforts are not conducted alone but in tandem with the efforts of relatives and many medical and religious specialists, including aunts, uncles, grandparents, midwives, healer-diviners, and mpiandry. Some of these specialists offer newer forms of healing and deliverance from what ails their clients. Others are heavily invested in the preservation and continuation of older rituals and medicines, precisely because of the growing diversity of religious options in urban contexts. Abdel, a professor, herbalist, and proponent of ethnopharmacology, is one such specialist invested in preserving the wisdom of his ancestors on behalf of future generations of Malagasy children.[32]

"At Risk of Losing Everything"

At the time of this research, Abdel Cadère worked and taught at the University of Antsiranana in Diégo Suarez during the week and returned to a town outside of Ambanja, south of Diégo, on the weekends, where he owns a house and runs a Catecom clinic with a medical doctor. Together the two operate a lab and pharmacy and provide consultations to patients. Abdel in a moment's notice can provide a comprehensive list of traditional medicines used by women in childbirth and also name their pharmaceutical equivalents. His knowledge extends far beyond pregnancy and childbirth, however, into nearly all aspects of a person's health.

Abdel insisted that people are quickly losing this knowledge and that Malagasy are ignoring important health customs because they are not being advised properly. When women, for example, ignore the northern Malagasy custom of bathing with cold water after childbirth, they risk a splitting headache. "These days," he said, "doctors will tell you that a woman cannot give birth without the pharmaceutical drug Buscopan. That's nonsense," he contended, "for we have been giving birth without Buscopan for a long time, before modern medicines and before the doctors were here." According to Abdel, there are plant alternatives that produce the same results. Women have been using these alternatives and hydrating with coconut water during labor long before the introduction of intravenous fluids and pharmaceutical drugs. There is a mentality, he argued, that chemical products are better than plant products and this mentality is threatening the loss of an invaluable traditional medicinal knowledge system.

According to Abdel, traditional massage (manindry), which can help en-sure a baby's proper position, by experienced specialists is also in danger of extinction within Madagascar's modern medical economy. Abdel expressed that that renin-jaza (traditional midwives) know how to massage the uterus to promote the proper position of the baby inside, how to assess the position of the baby, and how to make adjustments when necessary. He recounted a story about a young sage-femme (medically trained midwife) who had just completed her training. She was assisting a woman in childbirth whose baby's foot presented first during the birth. The sage-femme immediately indicated that she could not handle the birth and that the woman should be taken to the hospital, but transportation to the hospital in the moment of a baby's imminent emergence would likely have meant the death of the baby. For-tunately, a renin-jaza was called to the scene and had experience handling breech deliveries. She managed to push the baby's leg back into the mother and was then able to deliver the baby safely. Although other outcomes might have ensued in a birth as difficult as this one, Abdel's recounting of this story is demonstrative of his, and presumably other people's, confidence in the knowledge possessed by renin-jaza and other kinds of traditional specialists. This story is also demonstrative of the reality that not all women live in close enough access to a hospital or medical clinic providing obstetrical care should an emergency arise during childbirth.

Abdel spoke of "traditional knowledge" (conaissance traditionelle) as both sacred and in desperate need of preservation. He said renin-jaza are starting to have a bad reputation, and he blamed this on "charlatans," on people who pre-tend to know what they are doing and who claim to have gifts and powers but actually have very little experiential knowledge. "They," he argued, "are giving renin-jaza a bad name." And according to Abdel, it is not just renin-jaza who are being accused but also people like him, those who specialize in traditional medicine as opposed to what he described as "modern medicine." Europeans (vazaha) will reportedly come to his clinic and then shy away when they discover that the remedies he provides are herbal rather than pharmaceutical.

According to Abdel, if these knowledge systems are not preserved, Malagasy people "risk losing everything." Currently, the Malagasy government and the international medical community are promoting the idea that modern medicine is a better alternative, rather than a complementary component, to people's knowledge of plant-based medicines. His views were corroborated by the plethora of foreign- and domestic-sponsored medical posters tacked onto clinic walls throughout Diégo that pictured happy, plump, two-child families visiting clinics, while scrawny and sickly looking, multiple-child families shied away. These posters bore no witness to Alicia's testimony, the nurse-midwife we met in chapter 1, whose government-supported medical clinic was infested with bats, had no electricity, and no proximate access to running water. Nor do these posters, or the organizations who sponsored them, take responsibility for the fact that a costly and subpar medical system is threatening to replace, rather than enhance, traditional Malagasy methods for healing the sick and then blaming mothers for its own shortcomings when children die.

No one would deny that Malagasy need more access to medicine, more vaccines, and safer venues for birthing their children, especially for high-risk pregnancies and when complications arise. Neither would anyone argue that the trend toward independent, charismatic, and Pentecostal forms of Christianity is likely to ebb, in Madagascar or in any part of the world, for that matter, anytime soon. That said, it would be equally irresponsible to deny the value of Malagasy efforts to conserve traditional religious customs and medicines. On the surface, food taboos, cold-water bathing, and ceremonial haircutting can appear arbitrary and antiquated. But Malagasy know that it is these very rituals that keep attention focused on mothers and children in their most vulnerable months. These ancestral rites build networks of support for mothers and babies, ensuring that children are made visible, declared worthy, and are firmly rooted in an extended family beholden to their care. It might seem ironic that Malagasy are both seeking deliverance from the ancestral past, burning the relics and medicines their forebears once relied on, and trying to preserve some of these same rituals and relics from the past, except that this tension is at the heart of every human effort to grow the next generation. Growing the next generation requires both preservation and innovation on the part of mothers, their families, and the specialists they consult to ensure their children thrive.

Visions for a Thriving Madagascar

As this chapter has demonstrated, not everyone has a reverence for their ancestors or prioritizes engagement with them upon the birth of a child. In urban cities like Diégo, there are many different kinds of communities—religious, familial, and otherwise—that people invest in to ensure the kind of belonging integral to their and their children's thriving. Some, like Marie, are turning away from ancestral customs, even though negotiating this is difficult given the cultural and religious interests of her daughter's paternal kin. Others, like Jacqueline, find value in more than one mode of spiritual engagement. Still others question what is being lost when people turn away from ancestral customs.

Abdel's perspective that something vital and dear is on the verge of extinction is worth giving voice to in this context. There exists a subset of the Malagasy population, whose demographics might surprise, who are growing concerned by a seeming loss of ancestral wisdom. These Malagasy are concerned about losing not just their ancestors' knowledge of medicinal plants but also some of the fady and fomba they inherited, which guide and constrain them to relate to God, their ancestors, to one another, and to the earth in mutually beneficial and life-supporting ways.

Amélie and Camellia's interest in preserving Nosy Lonjo, a story described in the second chapter of this book, is another example of this kind of conservation, where younger and highly educated urban Malagasy are taking an interest in customs that seem traditional, despite, or perhaps because of, their similar interest in being "modern." Traditional religious specialists and the people they serve are at an interesting juncture. Only time will tell whether or not traditional religious specialists will become more or less important in the increasingly competitive medical and religious economies of urban Madagascar. Will urban living highlight for Malagasy the need to preserve certain religious ideals, or, as Marie's story seems to indicate, will new religious ideals emerge in ways that make consultations with diviners, massage healers, and traditional midwives obsolete? In all likelihood, both trends will continue. In response to these seemingly opposing but concurrent shifts, Madagascar's traditional religious specialists are working hard to present themselves as vital human resources. They spend years earning a reputation as healers through experience-based training. They work tirelessly and without asking for payment in order that their work might honor the ancestors whom they serve and that they might cultivate intimate relations with their grandchildren that their knowledge might be passed down and embodied by them. Such traditional specialists may appear poor, like Bernadette and Hussein, whom we met in chapters 1 and 2, respectively, but this is precisely where their power lies, not in the shiny marketing images of new hospitals that sometimes fail to deliver what has been promised, but in the more unseen and carefully guarded spaces of their homes where their ancestors' spirits still dwell.

Traditional specialists' decision to live a bit under the radar might be a strategic political one, or it might be externally imposed by the gaze of authorities anxious to see such specialists disappear. Either way, the somewhat veiled nature of these practices parallels a general shift toward concealment with regard to all aspects of Malagasy Indigenous religions over the last several decades. As I have already stated, military invasions on the part of Merina during the late eighteenth and early nineteenth centuries prompted Sakalava and Antankarana polities in northern Madagascar to conceal formerly publicly displayed religious relics and to privatize public religious ceremonies.[33] Moreover, with the arrival of foreign Christian missionaries and French colonialists during the late nineteenth and early twentieth centuries, Christianity became conflated with notions of being civilized, as voiced by the sentiments expressed by mothers like Camellia, whom we met in chapter 3, and Marie from this chapter.

All of the aforementioned circumstances contribute to Malagasy endeavors to conceal certain kinds of healing therapies and even internalize the evolutionist view that their own Indigenous practices are inferior to the "more developed" religions of Christianity and Islam. But concealing does not necessarily mean disappearing. Concealment can also be about conservation. For just as all of the aforementioned historical circumstances have contributed to some people turning away from these practices, the same historical circumstances have also contributed to people like Camellia, Amélie, and Abdel's efforts to preserve traditional practices, in both cloaked and public ways. For centuries, Diégo has drawn a plethora of peoples to its shores. For a variety of reasons, including trade, slavery, colonialism, education, and economic opportunity, migrants have moved to Diégo and built lives for themselves. These migrants have brought with them a multitude of customs and religious practices. They have also left many things behind including relationships with people who are the keepers of key customs within their communities.

In such contexts, peoples' access to and relationship with ancestors will look different than it might among people who remain close to the lands on which their ancestors lived. But whether one is quietly turning away from ancestral customs for practical reasons, boldly burning relics from the ancestral past, or working hard to preserve customs and traditions that are at risk of fading away, ancestors in the lives of northern Malagasy pervade, especially in moments of birth, when aspects of the ancestors enter the world again in the lives of the newly born.

CONCLUSION

Birth, Loss, and Competing Moral Cosmologies

In this book, I have sought to describe the complexity behind the decisions that parents make around the birthing and raising of children and to explain the role of ancestors in Malagasy religions, in particular the role they play in shaping how parents welcome the newly born into the world. In Madagascar, children are evidence of the ancestors' blessings, evidence that in some kind of tangible way those who have come before us remain with us and continue on in the lives of our children. Given the sacred value of children in Malagasy society, childbirth can be one of the more important moments in a woman's life, a rite of passage like none other, and yet as the stories in this book make clear, childbirth can also be a struggle. It is, as some have described, women's spear battle, *their* battle with matters of life and death, and the process that turns girls into women and mothers. Women enter childbirth with the hope of crossing to the other side transformed and unscathed, but more often than not, women bring to their labors the struggles of their ancestors, some of whom lived through slavery and colonialism and experienced dislocations from their farmlands. Some women also bear the burdens of living in inescapable situations of poverty, all of which threaten their ability to bring children into the world in safe and dignified ways.

Women give birth at home with midwives, in government- and church-sponsored clinics, and in crowded hospitals, sometimes with too few doctors to properly attend their needs. Midwives, nurses, and doctors, for their part, strive to provide holistic care to women and babies during this fragile time period, care that not only addresses the biological needs of the birthing pair but also attends to the spiritual and cultural needs of women and their families. Given the religious pluralism of the region and the inadequacies of the current biomedical infrastructure, religious and traditional specialists must sometimes fill in the gaps in the healthcare system, even when they also recognize the limitations of their training. As Lesley Sharp has described, "The proliferation and professionalization of *tromba* mediums and other indigenous healers is, I believe, evidence of the limitations of clinical medicine in Madagascar."[1] In other words, tromba mediums and other kinds of healers, including midwives, proliferate in Madagascar today not just because it is tradition but also in part because of the profound need for more resources and more support personnel in areas of health and healing. Moreover, culturally sensitive care in matters of health, and in the event of childbirth, is not just a matter of respect; it ensures that more people, more resources, and more vigilance are directed to mothers and babies during this time.

The birth rituals that women observe, with the help of relatives and care providers, create protection around this critical juncture and draw women and babies into communities, ancestral and religious, so they might be held in safety by family and friends. The birth of a child highlights the need to remember one's heritage, to remember it correctly, and to remember it well on behalf of future generations. But as I have made clear in the chapters of this book, children do not automatically become worthy members of these sacred ancestral lineages. Rather, parents instill this sense of worthiness in them by observing fady during their pregnancies; by developing close relationships with midwives and healers; by performing ritual bathing and haircutting, alongside other kinds of religious blessing; and by mediating children's relationships to the spirit world, to harmful spirits and benevolent ones, all of which connects children to the resources they need to both flourish and belong. Within all of these contexts, there are choices to be made about which rituals to employ and which lineage-based customs will take precedent, and all of these choices have implications. A mother's decision to emphasize the customs of one lineage over another has implications for her and her children's worth and belonging. Similarly, a choice to engage in religious communities that emphasize connection with ancestors as opposed to those that encourage a dissolving of ancestral ties will have implications for children who may both lose and gain identities and resources based on the decisions of their parents.

Throughout this book, women's stories give us insight into the many challenges they face as mothers: the sadness of their dreams going unfulfilled when they give birth too young or without the support of their families; their struggles to merge their family's heritage with that of their partners' families; their stories of how unions around the birth of children do not always succeed and their stories of how they sometimes do. The birth of a child represents a new beginning, but babies also enter families in the midst of powerful and painful histories. As fragile members of society, their status is not well defined. Therefore, their spiritual and social identities must be carefully managed until they are sufficiently bathed into the powerful narratives of history their parents strive to produce. By remembering some traditional birthing practices and discarding others, Malagasy parents rebirth the parts of their heritages that they wish to preserve in their children and deliver themselves of the more painful or regrettable parts of their past they hope might fade away.

As I made clear in chapter 5, not all Diégo residents feel equally nostalgic about their ancestors' customs and not all religious leaders in Madagascar live according to the same ideals as do traditional midwives, massage healers, and diviners. Traditional religious specialists' habits of receiving compensation through gift giving and by taking informal vows of poverty are not shared by all religious specialists in Madagascar. This is true of some pastors of the burgeoning Pentecostal and charismatic churches in Madagascar, who often advertise their wealth as proof of their religious authenticity. Pastor André Mailhol, founder of the Apocalypse Church of Madagascar, is a prime example of this more parading style of leadership whose messages I heard frequently during my time in Madagascar. His sermons were broadcasted on radio and television stations throughout the island, and in the years since, he has undertaken a project to build a thirty-thousand-seat church in Antananarivo, the capital city of Madagascar. More recently, he was also a presidential candidate in the 2018 election, propped up by Russian officials who recruited him to split the opposition vote in the hope that the candidate who was most supportive of Russia's investment in chromium mining would win.[2] Thus, rather than being on the sidelines, some religious leaders, like Mailhol, take center stage in the media, in church planting, and in politics corrupted by Russian meddling.

Though the promise of prosperity is prevalent throughout Madagascar's Pentecostal and charismatic churches, it is also true that not all Pentecostal pastors are wealthy. Arguably the majority live modestly and serve house churches earning very little salary for doing so, but neither is the Apocalypse Church of Madagascar exceptional. Many Pentecostal churches, especially the larger ones, in Madagascar and globally promote a level of tithing that outsiders view as exploitative, especially given that so many followers of these churches are already suffering from extreme poverty. Church leaders nevertheless maintain that God returns wealth to those who give generously, citing versus from the Christian Bible like 2 Corinthians 9:6–7: "the one who sows sparingly will also reap sparingly, and the one who sows bountifully will also reap bountifully." While on the surface this style of giving to God in the hopes that one will receive something in return might appear similar to the kinds of reciprocal gift giving that clients of traditional specialists engage in. However, if one looks deeper, the latter is promising a kind of mutual care and concern while the former is promising an abundance that may never arrive. Moreover, while the reciprocity forged between traditional specialists and their clients creates an indebtedness that is personal and somewhat private, it's not clear that the bigger Pentecostal churches feel similarly indebted to their members in any kind of personal way.

In Madagascar, there are competing spiritual and moral ideas about how best to access divine powers and about how these divine blessings manifest among the living. Pentecostal pastors and traditional religious specialists share a common vision for a more thriving Madagascar, but whether that will materialize in the fall of the West and the rise of Madagascar, as Pentecostal pastor André Mailhol was predicting in the early decades of the twenty-first century, or a return to more equitable modes of sharing and exchanging, as traditional religious specialists like Hussein and Bernadette promote, remains to be seen. What is clear is that Malagasy parents live in a complex world full of competing religious and medical ideas about how best to raise healthy children and that mothers like Marie and Jacqueline, whom we meet in chapter 5, are navigating these worlds not without difficulty but creatively nonetheless and with the futures of not only themselves but also their children in mind.

With regard to the blessing and safeguarding of infants from spiritual harm, there are at least two dominant modes of thinking. One approach is rooted in a belief in "partial reincarnation," or ancestral continuation, and operates within a system of weighty engagement with ancestors, where ancestral power (hasina) is channeled through the work of religious specialists and impressed on the newly born. The other is what Britt Halvorson describes as a "re-enchantment of the body" toward ecstatic engagement with the Holy Spirit and is evidenced by Malagasy mothers' thirst for new kinds of spiritual healing for themselves and on behalf of their children.[3] The latter of these approaches are found in the abundance of shepherd-healing services at Lutheran churches and in Pentecostal services that offer people deliverance from both past and present-day spiritual ills. Sometimes parents find themselves on one side of this cosmological dichotomy, and other times individuals like Jacqueline, from chapter 5, find themselves in the middle of an internal struggle between the two. There is, on the one hand, a desire to teach children to connect with the spirits (or stories) of their past and, on the other hand, a struggle to help them avoid the kind of close contact with spiritual forces, ancestral or otherwise, that might be dangerous or too burdensome for children to bear.

Yet this discord in thinking is a unique and relatively recent religious phenomenon, stemming from very different systems of belief, one traditional and one derived from the growth of charismatic Christian thinking. The former asserts ancestors as an important and beloved part of the spiritual community. The latter sees the spiritual universe in bifurcated terms where God, Jesus, and the Holy Spirit are good, and every other spiritual entity is evil. Yet as we have seen, this tension between simultaneously celebrating and disengaging from ancestor spirits predates the emergence of charismatic Christianity in Madagascar. Malagasy have always had both a reverence for and a fear of their ancestors, who inspire while also pressing on and coercively interfering in the lives of the living. It is this tension between the maintaining of traditions to preserve the moral order and the invention of new traditions in order to construct a new future that makes the parenting of young children, and indeed all of life, so complex.

As I state in the introduction to this book, I have always felt drawn to the northern regions of Madagascar for its diversity, from my earliest solo adventures there as a student studying abroad to my most recent travels there to conduct research on birth rituals, ancestors, and religious pluralism. I have loved the diversity so palpable and confronting in the ways people dress, in the sambos and mango relishes and other kinds of food available on the streets, and in the various houses of worship that decorate the city. I have also loved the simultaneous urban and coastal feel of the city, where a walk from the graffitied main drag to one of the most gorgeous scenes of the bay takes only about a half an hour. But the cultural and religious landscape of the city is changing, and it is not yet clear how these changes will impact the generations growing up today. Childbirth in Madagascar is currently intricately entangled in healthcare agendas, changes in local religious climates, and in what Phillip

Jenkins describes as new modes of spiritual awareness among certain groups of African Christians, in the shifting gravity of global Christianity.[4] That said, birth rituals offer us a window, a preview, of these changes. Subtle shifts in the ways that parents bless, dedicate, and integrate the newly born both reflect and represent larger changes in the ways that Malagasy relate to their ancestors and seek various kinds of spiritual therapies and religious community. The full fruits of these shifts may not become apparent for a generation or two, when the rituals of one's childhood become the rituals that one's elders wish to instill in the lives of one's children, but change is nevertheless on the horizon.

The Constant Story of Religious Change

One evening offered a chance to simply sit and observe the city from afar. Together with Alicia, the midwife who served the island of Cap Diégo, a ten-minute boat ride from Diégo itself, I walked down to the edge of a small peninsula. We sat on an old military bench, near a flag stand. On one side of the peninsula, we watched as children swam on floating logs in the bay, jumping off the terribly broken concrete dock that jutted into the waters. On the other side, we saw a more pristine beach and some decaying military buildings. From this side was an excellent view of the opening of the bay into the Indian Ocean where larger cargo and cruise ships pass. Alicia and I watched a cruise ship leave the bay late that evening. We heard the vessel blow its horn and walked over to the ocean side with mangoes in our pockets. Mosquitos bit our ankles as we ate our mangoes and watched the ship depart. As the sun went down, we watched until we could see only the small lights of the departing ship. When our gaze shifted from afar to just beneath us on the shore, we caught site of a string of smaller pirogues and remarked on the juxtaposition of these different kinds of boats in the water before us.

Before Diégo, I had never before lived in place where things came together as they did in this place—where cruise ships sat beside hand-carved pirogues, where gatherings for births and deaths included a mixture of Christians and Muslims, and where stories about ghosts, mermaids, vampires, and crocodiles possessed by ancestor spirits circulated so widely. Upon first visiting, the city had an almost mythic feel to me, in ways that new places sometimes do. Over time though, it began to feel more normal, more like home. I grew accustomed to buying my rice and produce at the larger outdoor markets, and cooking my food in the aluminum pots with which locals cook. I learned to traverse the city by foot, by bicycle, and, when out past dark, by Renault taxi. I swam in the bay, listened to live salegy, witnessed possession, attended masses and funerals, and held many babies. I stayed long enough not to have to buy mangoes at the market, which locals say you should never do given the plethora of mango trees in the region, and long enough to be both a giver of and a recipient of *voandalana* (gifts, or, more literally, fruits from the road). Still the stories told in this book are but one perspective, and a limited one at that, a limited window into the changing religious landscape of the city, and into the rituals of birth and blessing that parents employ to integrate children into this landscape of human stories.

Diégo is alive with all kinds of cultural and religious diversity and fluctuation. However, because of their emphasis on religious exclusivism, the rise of Pentecostal and charismatic forms of Christianity, seems almost out of place in this region of the world where for centuries people have accepted each other's varying faiths and cultural traditions. That is not to say that tensions between varying groups have not also been a part of Diégo's history. Some of the stories in this book bear witness to these tensions. The religious landscape of Diégo Suarez has always been changing and is changing still today. In fact, change, religious and otherwise, is the only constant in the story of the northwestern tip of Madagascar whose culture was and is today a product of hundreds of years of cross-fertilization evidenced by the passing of ships both to and from its port cities. Still, there is something unique about this moment, religiously speaking. In northern Madagascar, Christians and Muslims live together as neighbors, relatives, and friends, and I trust that this episode of Pentecostal Christianity is not likely to eclipse that pluralism for the *longue durée*. But in the intervening years, it will be interesting to observe how the ever-evolving medical and religious infrastructures of the city shape the procreative strategies of mothers in their efforts to bear children who will come to know and embody the religious and ancestral traditions of their families.

Not yet mentioned in this book are practices related to caring for what Malagasy consider an unlucky baby, a baby born on a taboo day or in an unlucky way. Stories abound about these types of births and how people will leave babies like this to die by placing them in the footpath of a herd of cattle. In my experience, however, these stories came up more as lore than as ethnographic data. I never heard of a baby actually being killed in this manner. More often than not, parents use these rituals—placing an unlucky baby under the footpath of zebu—as a way to deliver a baby of its unlucky sentence of being born on a taboo day. By symbolically placing the child in a dangerous place, but not leaving the child too long, parents are then able to argue that God or the ancestors intervened. Divine forces did not let this child be trampled, and thus, the taboo placed on the child has been lifted. Rituals such as these may be hard for outsiders to understand. Moreover, they are sometimes seen as proof, especially by outsiders with limited knowledge of the island, that Malagasy are engaged in old, irrational rituals that are dangerous to mothers and children. This could not be further from the truth.

Rituals such as the one described here, to the extent that they are ever even practiced, are but one piece of the larger mosaic of rituals that parents use to discern who their children are, to connect them to the spirits that will sustain them, and to dissolve them of unhelpful, unlucky energies in order to prove that they are worthy and wanted and here in this world for a purpose. One thing I hope this book has done is unsettle the notion that Malagasy rituals around birth and death are exotic holdovers from a primitive past. They are in fact the very opposite. The rituals that Malagasy mothers, together with their families, employ on behalf of their children, in their earliest and most fragile days, are the very acts that enable children to grow bones, to have standing within their communities, and to belong. Birth rituals recall, reframe, and re-member complex histories even as they also uncover new possibilities and futures in the lives of children. They do this by connecting children to people and communities with powerful legacies, by rewriting an unlucky birth as a lucky one, and sometimes by severing ties to histories that are too burdensome to bear. Some of these strategies are weathered and some part of a newer religious emergence, but all are changing with the needs of mothers, babies, and the communities that support them.

Diégo is changing, and with that comes changes to the rituals parents use to bless, protect, and incorporate babies into their religious and lineage-based communities. The lives of women are changing as well, due in part to the larger religious and sociopolitical changes to the environment but also sometimes due to unique and unpredictable personal circumstances. This book offers a snapshot of the lives of several mothers in Madagascar, mothers whose lives have changed markedly since this research was conducted, and though it has not always been possible for me to stay in touch with all my informants through the years, I know that they are not the exact same mothers they once were. Neither has my life remained the same. My own transition to motherhood, which came after conducting this research, has deeply impacted this book and my understanding of the women whose stories I share.

A New Stage of Life

It was not until I returned from Madagascar to the United States to begin the postfieldwork writing process that I realized that pregnancy taboos and all the other behavioral restrictions around pregnancy and birth were not as unique to Madagascar as I had previously thought. Nor was it unique for expectant mothers to be suddenly more aware of their cultural and religious heritages prior to giving birth to their first child. I realized these things through my own pregnancy, which began shortly before I left Madagascar and returned to the United States. As I prepared for my first prenatal appointment with my midwife, I printed out several forms, including one that was to become my food journal. I was to record everything I ate, and I found myself reading about the foods I should avoid in American pregnancy books. These foods were prohibited either because they might contain harmful bacteria or because my baby simply might not enjoy them, things like spicy foods, which Americans believe babies cannot tolerate. And in my prenatal yoga classes, we shared complaints of heartburn and laughed about people's predictions that mothers with heartburn would produce babies with heads full of hair all the while secretly wondering whether there were any truths to these seemingly illogical predictions.

On a walk home from my prenatal yoga class one evening, I was startled when a perfect stranger slowed down in her sports utility vehicle to ask me whether I was having a boy or a girl. When I explained that I was not going to find out the sex of the baby, she paused, gave my belly a hard look, and then exclaimed, "It's a boy!" Just before leaving Madagascar, I remembered sitting in a Malagasy grandmother's living room, holding her newly born grandson. I listened as she excitedly interpreted her grandson's smiles toward me as an indication that he, the baby, also knew that I was carrying a boy. Thrilled by her interest in my pregnancy and intrigued by her predictions, I can remember feeling a little jealous of her belief that a baby of such a young age could know something like that. In those last few weeks in Madagascar, which were the first of my first pregnancy, I experienced several such startling encounters where strangers asked me if I was pregnant, not because my belly was swelling, because it wasn't, but because they simply "had a feeling." I could not recall ever having been asked that before in all my months of prior research on birthing-related topics. Did Malagasy know something I didn't? Were they more in tune with such matters than my Americans peers?

When I returned to the United States, I realized that Americans were just as curious and perceptive, albeit in different ways, about babies in utero. I had simply never noticed, because I had never before been the object of people's curiosity, advice, and scrutiny as pregnant women often are. Now, back in my home country and pregnant, I observed things I had never paid attention to before, like the amber teething necklaces that American babies sometimes wear, which suddenly seemed a lot more similar to the protective amulets and growth medicines babies in Madagascar wear to keep them safe and help them grow strong. Back at home in my own country, I was thrown a baby shower where I was gifted knitted blankets by the women in my congregation and baby clothes from my mom that had been passed down through the generations. I was invited to a friend's Blessingway, a traditional Navajo ceremony that has been appropriated by feminist-leaning white American women to bless their transition to motherhood. I was given an abundance of advice about childbirth and circumcision and was entrusted with stories about ancestors whose names I might consider upon the birth of my child.

Despite many more predictions by Malagasy and Americans alike that I was carrying a boy, I eventually gave birth to a baby girl whom we named Margaret at Martha Jefferson Hospital in Charlottesville, Virginia, who was welcomed into the world with all the medical rituals of the American birthing system. In the years that followed, I suffered two miscarriages, and gave birth to two more babies, both boys, both born at home under the care of midwives. Henry was born in a little white house on Lincoln Street in Englewood, Colorado, and Julian came to us swiftly, on a snowy winter morning, while I stood beside my bed in our house on Decatur Street, in Denver, Colorado. In my years of having babies, I participated in and helped orchestrate many rituals of blessing, including baby showers given to me by church members and friends, a baptism at Trinity Episcopal Church in Charlottesville, Virginia, and two dedications at South Broadway Christian Church in Denver. And when my Pentecostal Ghanaian friend wanted to perform an exorcism on my belly after my miscarriages, I allowed her to do so even though the practice felt unfamiliar and slightly uncomfortable to me. When I successfully became pregnant again after my miscarriages and returned to work after the summer, I was delighted to find an altar to Mary that my Jesuit Catholic friend and colleague had snuck into my office. I welcomed that same friend's offer to anoint my belly with prayers and holy oil in the company of my husband and two elder children before the birth of my third.

I was supported in each of my births by my husband, my midwives, my mother, and my sister, and when each of my children was born, my sister, who is an ordained minister, led us through prayers that enabled my husband and me to claim our children—to love them and to teach them to be a source of love in the world. I buried some of my daughter's hair and both my sons' placentas at the base of the fruit trees we planted in our yard, and in the years to come, I will likely lead them through many more rites of blessing and protection that will enable their sturdiness in the world. Like the women I interviewed, I, too, live in a world that is urban and diverse and the rituals I have used to bless and incorporate my children come to me by way of my ancestors, as well as through relatives, friends, and neighbors, and from a variety of religious and cultural traditions that intersect uniquely in my life and in the lives of my children. These rituals help ensure that they are protected, that they feel loved and worthy, and that they are held in the kinds of communities that will ensure their surviving and thriving. I cannot articulate precisely why I made all of the decisions I made. Sometimes they were mine alone, and many other times they were made in concert with those around me. Sometimes the rituals we performed were rooted in a specific religious tradition or theological orientation, sometimes in relationships, and sometimes there did not seem to be a meaning fully accessible to me. Sometimes the doing simply felt right.

At the time in which this book was published, the women I interviewed in 2011 and 2012 were in very different stages of their life than they are now. Many are no longer the new mothers they once were. Some are still in the thick of raising the newly born, but many more have children who are now halfway grown. Some have parted ways with their vady (partners), and some have remained together. Conducting research across the oceans makes it hard to go back and follow up on the lives of the women whose stories are shared on these pages. Three children into motherhood, my life has changed as well. I often though I have managed to keep up with a handful. I would be better suited to conduct this research now that I have my own experiences of motherhood and loss, of trying to find community for myself and my children, and of trying to discern which legacies and traditions I wish to pass on to them. On the other hand, the younger me, just as the older women in Madagascar intimated, was hungry for understanding and freer from the responsibilities of work and parenthood to wander the city, befriend neighbors, observe religious rituals, and soak in the language and culture with a presence of mind that seems all too far from me now.

While time—and the ability to give myself over to research—feels less available, what is available to me now is the acquired wisdom motherhood has granted me. Without passage into that stage of life, this book might have come to fruition sooner, but it would also be far more lacking in insight, the kind necessary to rightly frame the stories I was entrusted with in northern Madagascar in 2011 and 2012. It is my hope that the stories told in this book feel true to the women who took the time to share them with me. There are many more stories that could have been told, but perhaps this limited collection has unearthed some small but nevertheless rich portrayal of how Malagasy think, feel, and behave at the cosmological crossroads where the dying become the dead and the newly living become as flesh and bone.

As I come to the end of this book, what remains is a haunting, sobering memory of a hill where dead babies hang from baskets in trees. This research was an attempt to bear witness to the ways in which women, and mothers in particular, engage with ancestors and other kinds of religion upon the birth of a child—the ways in which women welcome new life from their bodies into their communities in urban landscapes where religious diversity and repro- ductive insecurities prevail. This book is about the rituals and other processes by which the newly born acquire bones in these contexts, but it is also about loss and the threat of loss and the ways in which the two—life and loss—are sometimes intertwined. Had Zafisoa and I never made it to this haunted hill, I do not think I could have fully, or even partially, understood the practice of laying babies to rest somewhere other than the family tomb. Had I not had my own losses, years later—miscarriages at twelve and thirteen weeks, babies- to-be I buried in the flower beds of two different houses—I do not think I could have understood this practice either. And so, I close with an image of this hill, a hill whose spirits speak to the precariousness that is the welcom- ing of new life into the world, and the rituals that accompany the special kind of loss that is the loss of a baby. For the rituals of birth, told throughout this book, would matter a whole lot less if loss were not a reality so many have had to reckon with.

Traces of Closure and Loss on the Hill

As Zafisoa and I made our way closer to the hill where babies' remains hang in baskets from the trees, we passed some aomby (cattle) and a security check- point where police officers wished us well on our "marche sur pieds." We passed others walking along the road, some carrying a basket on the head or in the hand. There were a couple of women washing in a portion of the bay water to the right of the road, and two migrant workers from Fianarantsoa repairing a section of broken pavement in the road. We walked, and the sun bore down. We drank some water.

Finally, we saw the hill. It was a haunting, sad place. There were many baskets, both in the trees and on the ground. They seemed to endure for a much longer time than the bodies of the babies who had been contained within them. There were remnants of nearly everything of what these young lives could have been: newborn clothes strewn about, pieces of lamba, baby blankets, a stuffed animal, and piles of rocks that looked like small tombstones. We saw the top of a sippy cup, a knitted sweater, two bottles, a mosquito net, a bag with some medicines and a syringe inside, and some bones. Most of the baskets had nothing in them, except the remaining lamba in which babies' bodies had been wrapped. There was one lamba on the ground that looked to still contain the remains of a baby. Another one tied to the branches of a tree had the shape of a swaddled baby and a pungent odor of decay wafted from it. Another basket contained bugs, shells, and tamarind fruit that the tree had shed into the basket, with no sign of a deceased infant. Many objects remained, but they were in disarray. The coastal winds blew everything about. The tide came in and out, leaving shells and taking all else that found its way down the hill, close enough to the water's edge to be consumed by the engulfing tide.

There was tangible loss on the hill, but much of the loss was simply alluded to by the absence of what should have been. There were no mothers, no fathers, no breasts with leaking milk, no warm coddling arms, no older siblings to coo at these little ones who had left their families too soon—just tattered underpants and broken toys, withered baskets and shreds of cloth along the sand. Baobabs, tamarind trees, and little spiny bushes scratched our legs. It was hot and sad, but not always terribly so. It was clear from how these babies had been placed and the assorted objects their families had left behind that these departed ones had been loved by someone, both in their living and in their dying. The hill was not proof that water babies (zaza rano) were not worthy of being buried in the family tomb; it was proof that the departure of a zaza rano was a different kind of loss—not of someone whose legacy would be remembered in their bones, but of potential. This kind of loss required a different kind of mortuary care and a different kind of mourning.

If our lives have meaning only by way of our being connected to others, symbolized by the heirloom jewelries we fasten around our children, then the

The hill on the way to Ramena Beach where babies who have died are laid to rest. *Photos by author.*

loss of a child whose birth had the potential to bring families together creates fractures in that journey, missing links in our webs of connection. When you lose a child your efforts to make bones from water, to create something enduring out of our otherwise fluid, ephemeral lives, are like warm murky water once more—pregnant with new possibilities, yes, but also pregnant with uncertainties—and heartache for what might have been. Families who carry the swaddled bodies of their lifeless babies to this hill are returning these young ones to the ancestors—not placing them in the family tomb, where their identities might become part of a larger collective, but returning them to the watery world of the ancestors, a world as fecund with possibility as it is fixed. By placing them in trees along the bay, there is hope that once engulfed by the tide, they might someday resurface in some inexplicable way, return to one's womb once again, as several mothers who lost children indicated that babies sometimes do.

Zafisoa remarked that people probably leave their babies here to try to forget and leave it all behind—the medicines with which they tried to heal their babies, the toys with which they tried to comfort their sick little ones, the mosquito nets with which they tried to protect them. The mother, or perhaps the mother and father, carefully and delicately wrap up these precious things and leave them in a tree, not in the ground or in a family tomb, where their bones could become part of an abiding community, but high up in a tree. Time and the earth's elements will dissolve the materials as well as some of the pain, but the loss will remain, scattered by the winds, eventually engulfed in the ocean's tide, but never forgotten. These lives have returned to the watery world of the ancestors, a world that holds our memories, our pains, our losses, and also our hopes that out of the murkiness something new will eventually emerge, from water into bones.

NOTES

Introduction

1. "There are those born at seven months/moons" (*misy miteraka fito fanjava*). Interview with Bernadette, January 17, 2012.

2. In Malagasy religions, coins have a symbolic spiritual value. Their roundness is associated both with the auspiciousness of full moons and with the open mouths of ancestors speaking. Royalty are buried with coins in their mouths, so that they may continue to speak to the living through spirit possession ceremonies. Families often have one or more coins they use during religious ceremonies to invoke ancestor spirits. Coins are also used to transmit ancestral power (hasina) to participants by mixing them in the mediums of water, sacred clays (kaolin), and in this case, an earthy medicine for babies that Bernadette described as fameno. For more on the significance of coins see Michael Lambek, "The Value of Coins in a Sakalava Polity," *Comparative Studies in Society and History* 43, no. 4 (October 2001): 735–762.

3. Kaolin clay is used in rituals throughout the African continent as well as in African diaspora communities in the Americas. In Madagascar, kaolin is also sometimes called *tanimalandy*, which means "white earth." For uses of kaolin in Madagascar, see Marie Pierre Ballarin, "Royal Ancestors and Social Change in the Majunga Area: Northwest Madagascar 19th–20th Centuries," in *Knowledge, Renewal and Religion: Repositioning and Changing Ideological and Material Circumstances among the Swahili on the East African Coast*, ed. Kjersti Larsten (Uppsala: Nordic Africa Institute, 2009), 73. Also see Marie Pierre Ballarin, "How Spirits Travel along the Western Indian Ocean Rims," *Azania: Archaeological Research in Africa* 42, no. 1 (July 2007): 53–67. For an example of

its usage in the diaspora, in particular among African Americans in Virginia, see Mark Leone and Gladys-Marie Fry, "Conjuring in the Big House Kitchen," *Journal of American Folklore* 112, no. 445 (Summer 1999): 372–403.

4. The work of remembering, caring for, and invoking the dead is gendered in interesting and complex ways, something that is discussed throughout the book. For more on gender and ancestors see Karen Middleton, introduction to *Ancestors, Power and History in Madagascar*, ed. Karen Middleton (Boston: Brill, 1999), 25–26.

5. Throughout this book, I refer to the city in which this research took place as "Diégo Suarez," or simply "Diégo," named after sixteenth-century Portuguese explorers Diégo Diaz and Fernando Suarez because this is the name most commonly used by northern Malagasy who both proudly appropriate the vazaha-ness (foreignness) of their historic port city and find European encroachment a contentious issue. However, it is important to note that the original Malagasy name of the city is Antsiranana, which is also the name of the northern province of which the city is a part. In the 1970s, following independence from French colonial rule, efforts were made to restore local names to cities and sacred sites, but residents of a few places informally kept their European names. Diégo is one such place (Solofo Randrianja and Stephen Ellis, *A Short History of Madagascar* [London: Hurst, 2009], 14). It is also important to note that there are multiple different dialects of Malagasy and sometimes multiple correct ways of spelling words. In my transcribing of interviews, I consulted with my research assistants on spelling, opting for spelling standards based on northern dialects of Malagasy.

6. See Pier M. Larson, "Desperately Seeking 'the Merina' (Central Madagascar): Reading Ethnonyms and Their Semantic Fields in African Identity Histories," *Journal of Southern African Studies* 22, no. 4 (December 1996): 521–560. Also see Rita Astuti, "'The Vezo Are Not a Kind of People': Identity, Difference and 'Ethnicity' among a Fishing People of Western Madagascar," *American Ethnologist* 22, no. 3 (August 1995): 464–482. Also for more on why ethnicity might not be the right translation for all people groups in Madagascar see Rita Astuti, "'It's a Boy,' 'It's a Girl!' Reflections on Sex and Gender in Madagascar and Beyond," in *Bodies and Persons: Comparative Perspectives from Africa and Melanasia*, ed. Michael Lambek and Andrew Strathern (Cambridge: Cambridge University Press, 1998), 33.

7. Michael Lambek and Andrew Walsh, "The Imagined Community of the Antankarana: Identity, History, and Ritual in Northern Madagascar," *Journal of Religion in Africa* 27, no. 3 (August 1997): 308.

8. Jorgen Ruud's research among the Sakalava of western Madagascar during the mid-twentieth century revealed that Sakalava often attributed a

woman's conception to the ancestors' favor on her, saying, "The ancestors have made her pregnant" (*ny razana nampitoe-zaza azy*). And expectant mothers were sometimes known to say, "My father (or grandfather) is inside myself" (*ny babako bababeko anatiko*) (Jorgen Ruud, *Taboo: A Study of Malagasy Customs and Beliefs* [London: Oslo University Press, 1960], 248).

9. Muarice Bloch, *From Blessing to Violence: History and Ideology in the Circumcision Ritual of the Merina of Madagascar* (Cambridge: Cambridge University Press, 1986), 41.

10. Jennifer Cole, *Forget Colonialism? Sacrifice and the Art of Memory in Madagascar* (Berkeley: University of California Press, 2001), 136.

11. See Ballarin, "Royal Ancestors and Social Change," 69–84; Michael Lambek, *The Weight of the Past: Living with History in Mahajanga, Madagascar* (New York: Palgrave Macmillan, 2003); Lesley A. Sharp, *The Possessed and the Dispossessed* (Berkeley: University of California Press, 1993); Gillian Feeley-Harnik, *A Green Estate: Restoring Independence in Madagascar* (Washington, DC: Smithsonian Institute Press, 1991); Lambek and Walsh, "Imagined." See David Graeber, "Dancing with Corpses Reconsidered: An Interpretation of Famadihana in Arivonimamo Madagascar," *American Ethnologist* 22, no. 4 (May 1995): 258–278. Also see Maurice Bloch, "Death, Women and Power," in *Death and the Regeneration of Life*, ed. Maurice Bloch and Jonathan Parry (Cambridge: Cambridge University Press, 1982), 211–230.

12. See Cole, *Forget Colonialism?*; Bloch, *From Blessing*; Sharp, *Possessed*.

13. For other sources on childbirth and its rituals in Madagascar see Bodo Ravololomanga, *Etre Femme et Mère à Madagascar: (Tañala d'Ifanadiana)* (Paris: L'Harmattan, 1992), 119–207; Maurice Bloch, "Zafimaniry Birth and Kinship Theory," *Social Anthropology* 1, no. 1b (February 1993): 119–132; Gillian Feeley-Harnik, "Childbirth and the Affiliation of Children in Northern Madagascar," *Taloha* 13 (2000): 135–172; Karen Middleton, "Tombs, Umbilical Cords, and the Syllable Fo," in *Cultures of Madagascar: Ebb and Flow of Influences*, ed. Sandra Evers and Marc Spindler (Leiden: International Institute for Asian Studies, 1995), 223–235; Astuti, "'It's a Boy,'" 29–52.

14. Ruud, *Taboo*, 248. Also see Robert Jaovelo-Dzao's comments on babies and their connection to ancestors and the ancestral realm in *Mythes, Rites et Transes à Madagascar: Angano, Joro et Tromba, Sakalava* (Analamahitsy: Éditions Ambozontany, 1996), 130.

15. Feeley-Harnik, *Green*, 52.

16. Middleton, "Tombs," 223–235.

17. Middleton, "Tombs," 225.

18. The full paragraph for this statement reads: "L'imaginal *sakalava* semble suggérer que le nouveau-né n'appartient plus au monde des Ancêtres d'une

part, il n'est pas tout à fait intégré encore dans le monde des vivants. Entre autres indices, on doit d'abord retenir la separation du cimetière des bébés-eaux (zaza rano). Tout nouveau-né, qui meurt avant l'apparition de la première dent, ne saurait être agrégé dans la cimetière ancestral. La naissance en elle-même présente une ambiguïté symptomatique: aucun enfant ne vient sur la terre sans qu'un deliver concomitant ne doive être enterré, ce qui équivaut symboliquement à l'inhumation d'un mort" (Jaovelo-Dzao, *Mythes*, 130).

19. See Kofi Asare Opoku, *West African Traditional Religion* (Singapore: FEP International Private Limited, 1978), 138; Margaret Drewal, *Yoruba Ritual: Performers, Play and Agency* (Bloomington: Indiana University Press, 1992), 39; Alma Gottlieb, *The Afterlife Is Where We Come From: The Culture of Infancy in West Africa* (Chicago: University of Chicago Press, 2004), 49; Paul Geissler and Ruth Jane Prince, *The Land Is Dying: Contingency, Creativity and Conflict in Western Kenya* (Oxford: Berghahn Books, 2012), 177–179; Jacob Olupona, *African Religions: A Very Short Introduction* (New York: Oxford University Press, 2014), 33.

20. Malagasy anthropologist Father Robert Jaovelo-Dzao described Malagasy beliefs in reincarnation as stemming from the religious beliefs of the island's early Indonesian inhabitants (interview with Jaovelo-Dzao, March 14, 2012). Another noteworthy informant described her belief that life and death were a cyclical process whereby aspects of the ancestors are reborn again in the next generation (interview with informant, January 2, 2011). Also see Rita Astuti and P. L. Harris, "Understanding Mortality and the Life of the Ancestors in Rural Madagascar," *Cognitive Science* 32, no. 1 (June 2008): 715; Jaovelo-Dzao, *Mythes*, 360; Theodore Besterman, "The Belief in Rebirth among the Natives of Africa (Including Madagascar)," *Folklore* 41, no. 1 (January 2012): 44–47.

21. Middleton, introduction, 26.

22. Middleton, introduction, 25–26.

23. Lambek, *Weight*, 2003; Graeber, "Dancing," 1995.

24. Sharp, *Possessed*, 1993; Parker Shipton, *Mortgaging the Ancestors: Ideologies of Attachment in Africa* (New Haven, CT: Yale University Press, 2009); Feeley-Harnik, *Green*; Nancy Jay, *Throughout Your Generations and Forever: Sacrifice, Religious and Paternity* (Chicago: University of Chicago Press, 1992).

25. Lambek, *Weight*, 25.

26. For more on the history of Islam in Madagascar, see S. von Sicard, "Malagasy Islam: Tracing the History," *Journal of Muslim Minority Affairs* 31, no. 1 (April 2011): 101–112.

27. See Laura M. Tilghman, "The Dead Are Dead/Ancestors Never Die: Migrants, Rural Linkages, and Religious Change in Northeastern Madagascar," *Journal of Religion in Africa* 48, no. 4 (2020): 347–375. Tilghman's research

on rural-urban linkages in the Tamatave region of Madagascar reveals that Protestants of all varieties (mainstream, millenarian, and charismatic) are more likely to see practices of ancestral engagement as more morally questionable than Catholics are.

28. Regardless of a person's particular religious orientation, there are certain religious beliefs and practices that undergird the fabric of Malagasy society. These include the belief in a creator god; belief in the power of other spiritual forces, both malevolent and benevolent; belief that those who have come before (razana) are still present and actively involved in the lives of the living; and an ethic of reciprocity called fihavanana, in line with other African societies' emphasis on "the communal ethos." Robert Jaovelo-Dzao notes that historically, in Madagascar, God (Zanahary) has been rather loosely defined by different people, and at different times, to be both one and many, male and female, mother and father. But as is true in most societies, beliefs about spirits, and about the origins of the life, are always evolving. With the introduction of Islam in the eleventh century and the arrival of British missionaries, who opened schools and churches and translated Malagasy from an Arabic to a Roman script and the Bible from English into Malagasy, in the early decades of the nineteenth century, understandings of the divine have changed.

29. Pastor Mailhol André Christian Dieu Donné founded the Apocalypse Church of Madagascar (Fiangonana Apokalypsy Maneran-tany) in 1996 after hearing a voice from God asking him to do so. More information about the church can be found on the church's website. ("Momba ny fiangonana," Fiangonana Apokalypsy Maneran-tany, accessed August 13, 2024, https://apokalypsy.com/mg/static/a-propos).

30. Mahilaka, a coastal town just south of Diégo Suarez, played an important role in Swahili trading networks and served as a main trading settlement in the region at the time. It is considered by some to be the first major port and urbanized city on the entire island of Madagascar. For more on northwestern Madagascar, and its Swahili culture, see Timothy Insoll, *The Archaeology of Islam in Sub-Saharan Africa* (New York: Cambridge University Press, 2003), 194. Also see Chantal Radimilahy, "Madagascar: From Initial Settlement to the Growth of Kingdoms," in *The Oxford Handbook of African Archaeology*, ed. Peter Mitchell and Paul Lane (Oxford: Oxford University Press, 2013), 943–956. Also see Adria La Violette, "The Swahili World," in *The Oxford Handbook of African Archaeology*, ed. Peter Mitchell and Paul Lane (Oxford: Oxford University Press, 2013), 901–914.

31. According to historians Randrianja and Ellis, "the clearest direct archaeological evidence of people living in Madagascar that can be dated with

some degree of accuracy comes from caves in the hills around what would later be called the bay of Diégo Suarez." Remains of animal bones and locally made pottery are carbon dated from roughly 685 to 745 CE and these dates cover an earlier level that may date back to 405 CE (Randrianja and Ellis, *Short*, 20).

32. *Sambos* is the Malagasy word for the fried treats originating from India known more commonly as samosas.

33. For comparative data on the poverty rates in various cities throughout Madagascar see "Madagascar—Area Database," Global Data Lab, accessed May 25, 2023, https://globaldatalab.org/areadata/profiles/MDGt/.

34. According to data from the World Bank, as recently as 2019, approximately 75 percent of people in Madagascar are living on less than $1.90 per day compared with only 1.2 percent of the population in the United States ("Living on Less Than $1.90 Per Day in Madagascar," Borgen Project, accessed May 25, 2023, https://borgenproject.org/tag/poverty-in-madagascar).

35. "Madagascar," UNICEF Data, accessed January 5, 2023, https://data .unicef.org/country/mdg/.

36. Sebastian Silva-Leander, "Multiple Deprivations in Children in Madagascar," UNICEF, October 2020, accessed May 25, 2023, https://www .unicef.org/esa/media/8456/file/UNICEF-Madagascar-Summary-Note-Child -Poverty-(MODA)-Study-2020-EN.pdf.

37. See Feeley-Harnik, "Childbirth and the Affiliation of Children in Northern Madagascar," 135–172.

38. Laura Tilghman noted something similar among residents of Tamatave. See Tilghman, "Dead Are Dead," 354.

39. See Eva Keller's discussion of how anchorage takes place over multiple generations in "The Banana Plant and the Moon: Conservation and the Malagay Ethos of Life in Masoala, Madagascar," *American Ethnologist* 35, no. 4 (November 2008): 651.

40. Diana Eck, *Encountering God: A Spiritual Journey from Bozeman to Banaras* (Boston: Beacon Press, 1993), 43, 190–197.

41. See Mabiala Justin-Robert Kenzo, "Religion, Hybridity, and the Construction of Reality in Postcolonial Africa," *Exchange* 33, no. 3 (January 2004): 244–268. Also see Eva Spies, "Being in Relation: A Critical Appraisal of Religious Diversity and Mission Encounter in Madagascar," *Journal of Africana Religions* 7, no. 1 (2019): 62–83, and Michelle Voss Roberts, "Religious Belonging and the Multiple," *Journal of Feminist Studies in Religion* 26, no. 1 (Spring 2010): 43–62.

42. Roberts, "Religious Belonging," 52.

43. Spies, "Being," 62–63.

44. Robbie Davis-Floyd, *Birth as an American Rite of Passage* (Berkeley: University of California Press, 1992), 8.

45. Pamela Klassen, *Blessed Events: Religion and Home Birth in America* (Princeton, NJ: Princeton University Press, 2001), 5.

46. Catherine Bell, *Ritual Perspectives and Dimensions* (Oxford: Oxford University Press, 1997), 94–95. Both Robbie Davis-Floyd and Pamela Klassen frame birth rituals in a similarly comprehensive way, affirming that the childbirth education classes, baby showers, and Blessingway ceremonies that precede birth, as well as the checkups, baptisms, brises, and other ceremonies that follow birth, add many layers of meaning to the birth experience (Davis-Floyd, *Birth as an American*; Klassen, *Blessed Events*).

47. Gottlieb, *Afterlife*, 38–49.

48. Kwame Appiah, *The Lies That Bind: Creed, Country, Color, Class, Culture* (London: Profile Books, 2018), 11.

49. Appiah, *Lies*, 11.

50. M. G. Vassanji, *Uhuru Street: Short Stories* (Portsmouth: Heinemann, 1991).

51. Ritu Tyagi, "Rethinking Identity and Belonging: 'Mauritianness' in the Work of Ananda Devi," in *Islanded Identities: Constructions of Postcolonial Cultural Insularity*, ed. Maeve McCusker and Anthony Soares (Leiden: Brill, 2011), 92.

52. Tyagi, "Rethinking," 97.

53. Pamela Feldman-Savelsberg, *Mothers on the Move: Reproducing Belonging between Africa and Europe* (Chicago: University of Chicago Press, 2016), 8.

54. In 1885, British missionary James Richardson translated *hasin-tanana* as "a present given to the *mpisikidy* [diviner], etc., after the cure of a disease, or to a midwife after the birth of a child" (*Malagasy Dictionary and Encyclopedia of Madagascar*, s.v. "hasin-tanana," accessed January 27, 2022, http://malagasyword .org/bins/homePage).

55. Marcel Mauss, *The Gift: The Form and Reason for Exchange in Archaic Societies*, trans. W. D. Halls (London: Routledge, 1990).

56. Marie Ignace de Loyola Rakotondramiadanirina, "Reimagining Solidarity in Post-Colonial Madagascar: An Historical, Cultural and Theological Examination of the Concept of Fihavanana in the Malagasy Context" (thesis, Boston College, 2015), 9.

57. Rakotondramiadanirina, "Reimagining," 10.

58. Richard Huntington discovered similar practices among the Bara of southern Madagascar: "If a very young child (*zaza mena*, 'red child') dies, there is no funeral or burial in the paternal tomb, nor can the father give the body to his in-laws for burial in their tomb as he might with an older child. The child is

not yet part of the social order connected to the father and the ancestors, and the bodies of such babies are simply abandoned in 'a wet place' (*tany le*)" (Richard Huntington, *Gender and Social Structure* [Bloomington: Indiana University Press, 1988], 31).

59. As of 2018, approximately 19 percent of people living in Madagascar were living in urban locations ("Madagascar en chiffres," INSTAT Madagascar, accessed May 25, 2023, https://www.instat.mg/madagascar-en-chiffres).

60. Feldman-Savelsberg, *Mothers*, 6.

61. Feldman-Savelsberg, *Mothers*, 6.

62. By open-ended interviews, I mean relatively unstructured conversations. As Charlotte Davies notes, "interviews carried out by ethnographers whose principal research strategy is participant observation are often virtually unstructured, that is, very close to a 'naturally occurring' conversation. However, even in such unstructured interviews ethnographers have in mind topics they wish to explore and questions they would like to pose; thus they tend to direct the conversation with the research in mind, without imposing much structure on the interaction" (Charlotte Aull Davies, *Reflexive Ethnography: A Guide to Researching Selves and Others* [New York: Routledge, 1998], 105). For the majority of interviews, I had at least one research assistant with me who helped me understand key Malagasy words and phrases, though my proficiency in Malagasy is such that I am conversational around topics covered in this book. When interviews were recorded, I also had help transcribing them. Four interviews were conducted in English. The remaining were conducted in Malagasy and less frequently in French, or in a combination of the two as residents in Diégo Suarez often switch between French and Malagasy.

63. Davies, *Reflexive*, 5.

64. According to the University of Chicago Divinity School's definition of the History of Religions, "[a] Western monotheisms should not be the only paradigms and/or objects of legitimate study, [b] religion cannot be reduced to belief, but also includes issues of practices, institutions, communities, habitus and other factors that often operate below the level of consciousness, and [c] interpretation involves critical probing and systematic interrogation of the idealized self-representations of any religious phenomenon." ("History of Religions," University of Chicago, accessed August 13, 2024, https://divinity.uchicago.edu/academics/committees-and-areas-study/history-religions.)

65. Michael Carrithers et al., "Is Anthropology Art or Science," *Current Anthropology* 31, no. 3 (June 1990): 263–282.

66. See Talal Asad, ed., *Anthropology and the Colonial Encounter* (London: Ithaca Press, 1973).

1. Birthing Babies in Diégo Suarez

1. As part of my informal affiliation with the University of Antsiranana, I agreed to help teach English classes. This enabled me to have fascinating interactions with a vibrant and intelligent group of Malagasy students.

2. Conversation with students, January 26, 2012.

3. Tension between highland Malagasy and coastal Malagasy can be attributed to many factors. Highlanders tend to have lighter skin phenotypes and trace their ancestry to present-day Indonesia and Malaysia, while coastal groups trace their ancestry to various places throughout East Africa and the Middle East. This tension is both racial and political, as memories of highland Merina invasions during the eighteenth century, when the Merina polity tried to exercise control over the entire island, linger in people's minds. Memories of the slave trade also contribute to the racial tension between coastal and highland groups, even though both coastal and highland kingdoms sold and purchased slaves.

4. In 2012, in an article published in the *New York Times* about high maternal mortality rates in Malawi, author Courtney Martin spoke of the need for "cultural" and "attitudinal change" in regard to the "tribal traditions" and "customs that have governed their lives for as long as anyone can remember." Martin maintained that "a massive cultural shift is needed" before Malawian women can realize their vision of lower maternal mortality rates. In another article published by the *Washington Post* in 2008, author Kevin Sullivan does argue that an alarmingly high maternal mortality rate in Sierra Leone can in part be blamed on the fact that "governments don't provide enough decent hospitals or doctors; families can't afford medications." He also writes, "A lack of education and horrible roads cause women to make unwise health choices, so that they often prefer the dirt floor of home to deliveries at the hands of a qualified stranger at a distant hospital." Both of these authors in part paint high maternal mortality rates in Africa as caused by women's refusal to give birth in hospitals, when in reality, poverty, lack of resources, and lack of proximate and well-maintained medical facilities should shoulder more of the blame. See Courtney Martin, "Malawi's Leader Makes Safe Childbirth Her Mission," *New York Times*, November 2, 2013, and Kevin Sullivan, "A Mother's Final Look at Life," *Washington Post*, October 12, 2008.

5. According to the World Health Organization's Global Statistics for 2012, 44 percent of all births in Madagascar are attended by skilled health personnel (World Health Organization, "World Health Statistics 2012," 102, accessed August 13, 2024, https://www.who.int/docs/default-source/gho-documents/world -health-statistic-reports/world-health-statistics-2012.pdf). By comparison,

in the United States that number is 99 percent (104). According to data collected between the years 1990 and 2010, the likelihood that a child will die in Madagascar before reaching the age of five is 62 per 1,000. By comparison, the figure in the United States is 8 per 1,000. The rate of stillbirths in Madagascar is 21 per 1,000. The overall infant mortality rate was 43 per 1,000 in 2010 compared with 97 per 1,000 in 1990 (57). By comparison in the United States, the still birth rate was 3 per 1,000, and the overall infant mortality rate was 8 per 1,000. Infant mortality rates in the United States are significantly lower than in Madagascar but still by no means low (59). According to data collected between 1990 and 2010, the maternal mortality rate in Madagascar is such that 240 per 100,000 women will die in childbirth or as a result of complications that occurred during childbirth. Comparatively, in the United States the maternal mortality rate is 21 per 100,000. In Europe there are twenty-six countries with maternal mortality rates lower than 10 per 100,000. Qatar, Japan, Singapore, and Australia also have maternal mortality rates lower than 10 per 100,000 for the same period (1990–2010) (21).

6. Margaret Andersen, "Creating French Settlements Overseas: Pronatalism and Colonial Medicine in Madagascar," *French Historical Studies* 33, no. 3 (June 2010): 427.

7. Also see Margaret Andersen, *Regeneration through Empire: French Pronatalists and Colonial Settlement in the Third Republic* (Lincoln: University of Nebraska Press, 2015), 22.

8. Andersen, "Creating," 431.

9. Andersen, "Creating," 421.

10. Andersen, "Creating," 428.

11. Andersen, "Creating," 431.

12. Mireille Rabenoro, "Motherhood in Malagasy Society: A Major Component in the Tradition vs. Modernity Conflict," *Jenda: A Journal of Culture and African Women Studies* 4, no. 1 (2003): 4.

13. Nancy Rose Hunt, *A Colonial Lexicon of Birth Ritual, Medicalization, and Mobility in the Congo* (Durham, NC: Duke University Press, 1999).

14. For more on the history of childbirth in the United States and globally, see Randi Epstein, *Get Me Out: A History of Childbirth from the Garden of Eden to the Sperm Bank* (New York: Norton, 2010); Phyllis Brodsky, *The Control of Childbirth: Women versus Medicine through the Ages* (Jefferson, NC: McFarland, 2008); Tina Cassidy, *Birth: The Surprising History of How We Are Born* (New York: Atlantic Monthly Press, 2006); Richard Wertz and Dorothy Wertz, *Lying-In: A History of Childbirth in America* (New Haven, CT: Yale University Press, 1989); Judith Leavitt, *Brought to Bed: Childbearing in America, 1750–1950*

(New York: Oxford University Press, 1986); Margarete Sandelowski, *Pain, Pleasure and American Childbirth: From the Twilight Sleep to the Read Method* (Westport, CT: Greenwood Press, 1984).

15. For more information on these programs, see Agnes Ramananarivo and Misa Rahantason, "Midwives Improve Access to Family Planning Services in Madagascar," USAID, accessed May 25, 2023, https://www.usaid .gov/madagascar/news/midwives-improve-access-family-planning-services -madagascar. Also see Eva Burke et al., "Youth Voucher Program in Madagascar Increases Access to Voluntary Family Planning and STI Services for Young People," *Global Health: Science and Practice* 5, no. 1 (March 2017): 33–43.

16. For an example of an environmental organization (Blue Ventures) employing an integrated health and environment program, see Vik Mohan and Tess Shellard, "Providing Family Planning Services to Remote Communities in Areas of High Biodiversity through a Population-Health-Environment Programme in Madagascar," *Reproductive Health Matters* 22, no. 14 (June 2014): 93–103.

17. Eva Keller, "The Banana Plant and the Moon: Conservation and the Malagay Ethos of Life in Masoala, Madagascar," *American Ethnologist* 35, no. 4 (November 2008): 659.

18. For more on spirit mediums, healer-diviners, and mpijoro, see, among others, Michael Lambek, *The Weight of the Past: Living with History in Mahajanga, Madagascar* (New York: Palgrave Macmillan, 2003); Lesley A. Sharp, *The Possessed and the Dispossessed* (Berkeley: University of California Press, 1993); Robert Jaovelo-Dzao, *Mythes, Rites et Transes à Madagascar: Angano, Joro et Tromba, Sakalava* (Analamahitsy: Éditions Ambozontany, 1996); John Mack, "Healing Words: Becoming a Spirit-Host in Madagascar," *Anthropology and Medicine* 18, no. 2 (January 2011): 231–243.

19. Exceptions include Hélène Quashie, Dolorès Pourette, Olivier Rakotomalala, and Frédérique Andriamaro, "Traditional Therapeutics, Biomedicine and Maternal Health in Madagascar: Paradoxes and Power Issues around the Knowledge and Practices of Reninjaza," *Health, Culture and Society*, 7, no. 1 (2014): 1–15; and Julia Bello-Bravo, "Preserving Tradition in the Here and Now: Barriers to the Preservation and Continuity of Traditional Healing Knowledge and Practices in Madagascar," *Social Sciences and Humanities Open*, 8, no. 1 (2023): 1–8. There are also at least two published student papers on the importance of traditional midwives that came out of the School for International Training's study abroad program in the capital city of Antananarivo. See Shenna Banish, "Don't Diss the Reninjaza: A Case for Integrating Traditional Birthing Attendants into the Allopathic System to Improve Prenatal Health

in Rural Madagascar," (Independent Study Project (ISP) Collection, School for International Training, 2014), 1–14, https://digitalcollections.sit.edu/isp_collection/1888. Also see Emma Tuttleman-Kriegler, "Birth in Madagascar: The Disreputable Portrayal of Traditional Birth Attendants in Madagascar's Past and Present" (senior thesis, Tulane University, 2015), 1–25, https://www.academia.edu/13906017/Birth_in_Madagascar_The_Disreputable_Portrayal_of_Traditional_Birth_Attendants_in_Madagascars_Past_and_Present.

20. To travel to Cap Diégo from Diégo Suarez, passengers board a small motorboat for the price of 1,000 ariary (the equivalent of around US$0.30 at the time).

21. The medicinal properties of these herbs, and information on the usage of them by northern Malagasy peoples, have been well documented by the international organization Jardin du Monde (https://www.jardinsdumonde.org/).

22. "Madagascar en chiffres," INSTAT Madagascar, accessed May 25, 2023, https://www.instat.mg/madagascar-en-chiffres.

23. "Madagascar en chiffres: Région Diana."

24. Martin, "Malawi's Leader," 2013.

25. This kind of prejudicial thinking is what Curtis Keim describes as American myths about Africans' cultural inferiority—myths that have replaced the older depictions of Africans' racial inferiority, but similarly serve as justification for Western dominance in the developing world (*Mistaking Africa: Curiosities and Inventions of the American Mind* [Boulder, CO: Westview Press, 1999], 8).

26. See Tracy J. Luedke and Harry G. West, introduction to *Borders and Healers: Brokering Therapeutic Resources in Southeast Africa*, ed. Tracy J. Luedke and Harry G. West (Bloomington: Indiana University Press, 2006), 6–11.

27. Robbie Davis-Floyd, *Birth as an American Rite of Passage* (Berkeley: University of California Press, 1992), 2.

28. Pamela Klassen, *Blessed Events: Religion and Home Birth in America* (Princeton, NJ: Princeton University Press, 2001), 64.

29. Feeley-Harnik was the first outside scholar to note the usage of the phrase *spear battle* as a description of childbirth in northern Madagascar, hypothesizing that the phrase enables Malagasy women to liken their experience of childbirth with the experience of male circumcision. See Gillian Feeley-Harnik, "Childbirth and the Affiliation of Children in Northern Madagascar," *Taloha* 13 (2000): 135–172.

30. Feeley-Harnik, "Childbirth," 145.

31. Interview with Jacqueline, December 23, 2011.

32. Michael Lambek's theory of sacrifice is somewhat relevant here. See Michael Lambek, "Sacrifice and the Problem of Beginning: Meditations from

Sakalava Mythopraxis," *Journal of the Royal Anthropological Institute* 13, no. 1 (March 2007): 19–38.

33. Feeley-Harnik, "Childbirth," 136, 142.

34. Bodo Ravololomanga, *Etre Femme et Mère à Madagascar: (Tañala d'Ifanadiana)* (Paris: L'Harmattan, 1992), 119.

35. Jane Turrittin, "Colonial Midwives and Modernizing Childbirth," in *Women in African Colonial Histories*, ed. Susan Geiger, Nakanyike Musisi, and Jean Mari Allman (Bloomington: Indiana University Press, 2002), 77.

36. Aoua Kéita, *Femme d'Afrique: La vie d'Aoua Kéita racontée par elle-même* (Paris: Présence Africaine, 1975), 261.

37. Maurice Bloch, *From Blessing to Violence: History and Ideology in the Circumcision Ritual of the Merina of Madagascar* (Cambridge: Cambridge University Press, 1986), 71.

38. In the context of her research in the Analava region of Madagascar, Gillian Feeley-Harnik notes that at haircutting ceremonies, "A mock battle is held in which the mother's kin sneak up on the father's village, where she is living, and try to steal the baby." Feeley-Harnik goes on to detail how the baby's father's kin must then pay a ransom for the baby, which will be used to fund the haircutting celebration. These contentious encounters, according to Feeley-Harnik, speak to the multiple layers of affiliation that children have with both paternal and maternal kin despite the popular claim that "men are the masters of children." According to Feeley-Harnik, the latter statement carried some irony for her informants, many of whom felt that in the contemporary context, the harder battle was fought not over which parent, or set of kin, would have greater influence but rather over how to get fathers to simply acknowledge and support their children (Feeley-Harnik, "Childbirth," 137).

In the case of boys' circumcision, Bloch describes several examples of mock fighting that occur within ceremonies performed by Malagasy Merina, including fights over the consumption of unripe bananas and stalks of sugar cane, which represent the untamed fertility of the uncircumcised. Bloch also describes a scene in which youth attempt to bang on and break down the door of the house where the to-be-circumcised boy is being held. These youth threaten the child with a spear until they are resisted by the child's father and other relatives inside the house. Bloch describes these episodes of violence as playful and exhilarating for participants and sees them as part of the symbolic violence needed to dissolve the child of his wild untamed essence and his more natural affinities with his maternal kin so that he might be transformed into a descendant of his father's lineage. See Bloch, *From Blessing*, 72.

39. Feeley-Harnik, "Childbirth," 159.

40. Feeley-Harnik also noted this in the 1990s in her research on birth rituals in the Analava region ("Childbirth," 158).

41. The history of midwifery as a spiritual vocation predominates in societies throughout the world. Among African American midwives in the southern United States, Gertrude Fraser documents the extent to which "there was a shared conviction that formal training, no matter how detailed, could not replace the need for the divine intervention of God to guide the midwife when she was attending a woman" (*African American Midwifery in the South* [Cambridge, MA: Harvard University Press, 1998], 26). See also Ina May Gaskin, *Spiritual Midwifery* (Summertown, TN: Book Publishing Company, 1975).

42. The transmission of healing practices through the medium of dream revelation is common in Madagascar. See Jennifer Cole, *Forget Colonialism? Sacrifice and the Art of Memory in Madagascar* (Berkeley: University of California Press, 2001), 138.

43. Interview with Bernadette, January 13, 2012.

44. SALFA is the biomedical arm of the Malagasy Lutheran Church (Fiangonana Loterana Malagasy [FLM]). There are SALFA clinics throughout the island of Madagascar offering medical services, and many of the clinics have places for women to give birth. Through its health ministry, the Lutheran church has also established midwife training schools in the central highlands. The privately funded clinics are sometimes better stocked than the government clinics, though they can also be more expensive. As one woman complained, the church-funded clinics do not really feel like "a mission" because they are too expensive.

45. Maurice Bloch demonstrates water as a medium of blessing most clearly in his work on the ritual of the royal bath whereby royal power is transmitted from royalty to subjects through an annual bathing rite (*From Blessing*, 1986).

46. For the last couple of decades, the Malagasy government has been collaborating with international organizations to increase training opportunities for midwifery students, and other medical personnel, but traditional midwives, like Bernadette, are rarely invited to participate in these training programs. More frequently, it is young students, who do not yet have any experience, who are recruited. For more on such programs see "Training Midwives in Madagascar to Bridge a Dangerous Gap in Maternal Healthcare," United Nations Population Fund, December 6, 2021, https://www.unfpa.org/news/training-midwives -madagascar-bridge-dangerous-gap-maternal-health-care. At the time in which this research was conducted, I knew of only one governmental initiative to offer continuing medical education to traditional midwives, which is not to say that there are not more, only that there are not many. Scholars have demonstrated the extent to which traditional midwives are often not opposed to further

medical training, so long as they are guaranteed the freedom to continue their spiritual approaches alongside medical technologies. Usually, however, they are not guaranteed this freedom to continue spiritual approaches as one kind of authority (religious/medical) is often perceived to threaten the other. See Klassen's discussion of Gertrude Fraser's research on how African American midwives' "spiritual authority" was derailed by "new secular medical authority" in *Blessed Events* (26). Also see Fraser, *African American*, 340, 36.

47. When Merina of the central highlands invaded northern Madagascar, threatening the autonomy of Sakalava and Antankarana polities that governed the northern part of the island during the late eighteenth and early nineteenth century, Merina officials prohibited northern community festivals centered on royal ancestors, fearing that such large gatherings around such powerful symbols of power might enable protestors of the Merina to further organize. In turn, northern groups took it upon themselves to further transform formerly public rituals into concealed ceremonies and to temporarily transfer their attention from the construction of royal tombs to the care of ancestral relics, which could be more easily moved and hidden (Gillian Feeley-Harnik, *A Green Estate: Restoring Independence in Madagascar* [Washington, DC: Smithsonian Institute Press, 1991], 103).

48. Luedke and West, *Borders and Healers*, 31.

49. Luedke and West, *Borders and Healers*, 8.

50. Interview with Françoise, January 11, 2012.

51. Though she did not explain what she meant by "injections," it was my assumption that she meant that traditional midwives did not have to rely on drugs like Pitocin to speed up women's labor; rather, they had other means of helping to move things along.

52. Bathing women in warm water is a customary practice used to help women relax during childbirth. When Françoise insisted on the need to use warm water, she was not referring to the lineage-based postpartum bathing that women observe when recovering from childbirth. She herself is ranginaly and performs cold-water bathing after childbirth.

53. Interview with Hélène, October 26, 2011.

54. Nearly a decade later, in September 2021, as I am completing this book, Diégo Suarez was being described in news articles as the new epicenter of the COVID-19 pandemic and the Hopitaly Manarapenitra as the primary reference for COVID-19 throughout the region (Sarah Tétaud, "Madagascar: Diégo-Suarez, New Epicenter of the COVID-19 Pandemic," *Teller Report*, September 14, 2020).

55. "Health in Madagascar Takes Turn for the Worse as $22m Hospital Abandoned," *The Guardian*, August 3, 2016.

56. "Hôpital Manara-Penitra d'Antsiranana: 629 patients accueillis en un mois," *Tribune de Diégo*, February 4, 2013.

2. Motherhood and Creative Confluences of Care

1. According to Tracy J. Luedke and Harry G. West, "periodic drought and environmental degradation"; "massage flows of refugees"; "the end of the Cold War," which meant the end of "Eastern bloc support for socialist regimes in southeast Africa"; "structural readjustments programs"; and the emergence of "neoliberal states which have largely abandoned the public projects of development" have together created devastating circumstances for Africans' health systems. They write, "In short, the interrelated catastrophes the region has suffered have been felt acutely in the realm of health and healing. Besides bringing about the collapse in many countries of health care networks constructed by post-independent states (Neil Andersson and Shula Marks, "The State, Class and the Allocation of Health Resources in Southern Africa," *Social Science and Medicine* 28, no. 5 (1989): 515–530; Julie Cliff and Abdul Razak Noormahomed, "Health as a Target: South Africa's Destablization of Mozambique," *Social Science and Medicine* 27, no. 7 (1988): 717–722; Julie Cliff and Abdul Razak Noormahomed, "The Impact of War on Children's Health in Mozambique," *Social Science and Medicine* 36, no. 7 (1993): 843–848; Steven Feierman, "Struggles for Control: The Social Roots of Health and Healing in Modern Africa," *African Studies Review* 28, no. 2/3 (1985): 73–147; James Pfeiffer, "African Independent Churches in Mozambique: Healing the Afflications on Inequality," *Medical Anthropology Quarterly* 16, no. 2 (2002): 176–199; Sjaak van der Geest, "Is There a Role for Traditional Medicine in Basic Health Services in Africa? A Plea for a Community Perspective," *Tropical Medicine and International Health* 2, no. 9 (1997): 903), these crises have placed the institutions of kinship and community, through which people might seek relief, under enormous strain. Under these desperate circumstances, residents of the region have been compelled to piece together disparate therapeutic resources in an attempt to meet their health needs" (introduction to *Borders and Healers: Brokering Therapeutic Resources in Southeast Africa*, ed. Tracy J. Luedke and Harry G. West [Bloomington: Indiana University Press, 2006], 3).

2. Interview with Nasreen, January 12, 2012.

3. The English name for rômba is African basil. For more on the medicinal properties of rômba and its uses in northern Madagascar, see Jean Pierre Nicolas, *Fahasalaman'ny Fianakaviana sy Zavamaniry Fatao Fanafody aty Amin'ny Tapany Avaratr'i Madagasikara* (Quimper: Jardins du Monde, Édition Mai, 2011), 214.

4. Ritu Tyagi, "Rethinking Identity and Belonging: 'Mauritianness' in the Work of Ananda Devi," in *Islanded Identities: Constructions of Postcolonial*

Cultural Insularity, ed. Maeve McCusker and Anthony Soares (Leiden: Brill, 2011), 92.

5. Ranginaly mothers occasionally place cold water on their babies' heads, but newborn babies do not bathe in the same ritual manner as do their mothers. That is, they do not bathe in cold water from head to toe thrice daily, though there will be occasions for them to practice this kind of ritual bathing as they get older.

6. Malagasy commonly wear silver bracelets around their wrists. They are given as gifts to children and are markers of many things. Some Malagasy have told me that if you want to find out who still practices fombandrazana (ancestral customs), look for people who are wearing the silver bracelets. Paul Congo, an informant who describes himself as Catholic, insisted that he could not abandon the traditions he was bathed in and then pointed to his bracelet as evidence that he continues to observe such ancestral customs (conversation with Paul Congo, February 6, 2012). In the case of Céline and Roland, they placed a silver bracelet around their infant son's wrist because they discovered that some of their Christian friends frowned on the black cotton bracelets containing ghost repellents. Céline and Roland nevertheless wanted to put some form of religious protection on their son, so they opted for a religious charm that seemed more widely accepted among their Catholic friends and family.

7. My research assistant Édith described arakaraka as a disease that occurs when a spirit follows a baby back to its house because the spirit wants to eat the food that was bought for the baby. Arakaraka is both the name of the disease and the name of the spirit that causes the disease. When someone becomes sick with the disease, you say they "caught" the spirits (*nazon'ny arakaraka*), she explained.

8. This healing remedy is modeled after similar Islamic practices where scriptures are ingested after having been washed off a chalkboard or dissolved in paper in an effort to offer someone healing or protection. These various forms of protection employed by Céline and Roland borrow from Christian, Islamic, and Indigenous religious practices and thus speak to the religious diversity of the area.

9. Interview with Antoinette, September 18, 2011.

10. Interview with Amélie, October 10, 2011.

11. For an interesting discussion of tin-roofed houses and what they represent in east Madagascar, insofar as they are associated with colonial wealth status, see Jennifer Cole, *Forget Colonialism? Sacrifice and the Art of Memory in Madagascar* (Berkeley: University of California Press, 2001), 194.

12. As discussed more thoroughly in chapter 4, haircutting ceremonies, called mangadoso faneva or mampiravaka tsaiky, cleanse babies of their birth and also serve a larger initiatory function. Haircutting ceremonies are often performed

when babies receive their first teeth and are poised to become full-fledged members of the human community. During the ceremony, ancestors are invoked to bless the mother and child, and the baby is given a special rice porridge and chicken leg.

13. Tsimihety are an ethnic group traditionally from the north-central coast of Madagascar. For more on Tsimihety and their cultural practices, see Michael Lambek, "Taboo as Cultural Practice among Malagasy Speakers," *Man* 27, no. 2 (June 1992): 245–266.

14. Nancy Jay, *Throughout Your Generations and Forever: Sacrifice, Religious and Paternity* (Chicago: University of Chicago Press, 1992), 1.

15. See Pamela Klassen's point that "while scholars focusing on North American birthing practices have emphasized the paternalistic, interventionist, and capitalist nature of obstetrics, many of those studying childbirth in nonindustrialized countries . . . have grappled most directly with the reality that 'in the world as a whole, every minute a woman dies as a result of complications during pregnancy and birth, and every minute eight babies die because of poor care for their mothers in pregnancy and birth'" (*Blessed Events: Religion and Home Birth in America* [Princeton, NJ: Princeton University Press, 2001], 31).

16. See Courtney Martin's framing of childbirth, and the dangers associated with it, in Malawi in "Malawi's Leader Makes Safe Childbirth her Mission," *New York Times*, November 2, 2013.

17. Conversation with Camellia and Amélie, May 26, 2012.

18. Camellia is working to preserve Nosy Lonjo as a cultural heritage site. Currently in Diégo, this religious site is threatened by the new construction of private homes along Diégo's bay front, which would block residents from walking down to the bay in order to perform their prayers and ritual bathing. Camellia was researching this problem and planned to make a case before city administrators that a portion of Diégo's bay front should be set aside for public ritual use.

19. Oyvind Dahl, *Meanings in Madagascar: Cases of Intercultural Communication* (Westport, CT: Bergin and Garvey, 1999), 104.

20. *Malagasy Dictionary and Encyclopedia of Madagascar*, s.v. "hasintanana," accessed January 27, 2022, http://malagasyword.org/bins/homePage.

21. *Malagasy Dictionary*, s.v. "hasintanana."

22. Marcel Mauss, *The Gift: The Form and Reason for Exchange in Archaic Societies*, trans. W. D. Halls (London: Routledge, 1990).

23. Robin Wall Kimmerer, *Braiding Sweetgrass: Indigenous Wisdom, Scientific Knowledge and the Teachings of Plants* (Minneapolis: Milkweed Editions, 2013), 23.

24. Henry W. Little, *Madagascar: Its History and People* (London: William Blackwood and Sons, 1884), 80.

25. See Parker Shipton, *Bitter Money: Cultural Economy and Some African Meanings of Forbidden Economies* (Washington, DC: American Anthropological Association, 1989); Cole, *Forget Colonialism?*; Steven Friedson, *Dancing Prophets: Musical Experience in Tumbuka Healing* (Chicago: University of Chicago Press, 1996).

26. Gillian Feeley-Harnik writes, "Wage labor—'getting a wage' (*mikarama*, *mangala karama*, from Swahili *gharama*, expense) or 'getting a day's work' (*mangala journée*, from French *journée de travail*, day's work)—was associated with the work of purchased slaves who worked for others with little benefit to themselves" (*A Green Estate: Restoring Independence in Madagascar* [Washington, DC: Smithsonian Institute Press, 1991], 250). Feeley-Harnik argues that Malagasy, particularly Sakalava, distinguish between the work of "'growing/ tending/nursing crops' (*mitsabo*) and 'working for people' (*miasa amin'olo*)," arguing that Sakalava associate wage labor "with the work of purchased slaves who worked for others with little benefit to themselves" (250).

27. Christiane Rafidinarivo Rakotolahy notes a conversation with a massage healer who indicated her preference for nonsalaried labor, because she equated salaried labor with slave labor. If one is salaried, one is not working for oneself but for another person or persons ("Le référent de l'esclavage dans les représentations transactionnelles marchandes à Madagascar," *Journal des Africanistes* 70, nos. 1–2 [2000]: 126).

28. Interview with Josette, November 15, 2011. Josette listed the price according to FMG (Franc Malgache). Madagascar switched back to its precolonial currency, the ariary (one ariary is equal to five FMG), in the year 2005, but most paper money still contains ariary and FMG denominations, and often people will still quote prices in FMG. Thus, the ability to multiply or divide by five on the spot and be able to guess whether or not someone has given you a price in FMG or ariary is crucial in places like markets.

29. Conversation with Sylvie, October 12, 2011.

30. The word *maditry* means naughty, and parents almost always playfully describe their children in this way.

31. Five dollars might not seem like much money but 10,000 ariary can buy a lot in Madagascar and is nearly five times what a Malagasy person might pay to have someone wash a small bag of clothing. Also, see note 28 about Malagasy currency.

32. The Hôpital FJKM is a privately funded clinic or medical dispensary run by a Protestant denomination, FJKM.

33. Lesley A. Sharp, *The Possessed and the Dispossessed* (Berkeley: University of California Press, 1993), 208.

34. Feeley-Harnik discusses the importance of children being situated in both maternal and paternal lines, reporting that Malagasy call those who are not properly situated in their paternal lineages "'a thing without a father' (*raha tisy baba*)." "Childbirth and the Affiliation of Children in Northern Madagascar," *Taloha* 13 (2000): 162.

35. Robert Thornton discusses something similar among South African healers. See Robert Thornton, *Healing the Exposed Being: A South African Ngoma Tradition* (Johannesburg: Wits University Press, 2018), 148.

3. Bathing and Seclusion

1. See, for example, Anita Hannig, "Spiritual Border Crossings: Childbirth, Postpartum Seclusion and Religious Alterity in Amhara, Ethiopia," *Africa* 84, no. 2 (April 2014): 294–313; Shih-Yu Lee, Yang, and Yang, "Doing-in-Month Ritual among Chinese and Chinese-American," *Journal of Cultural Diversity* 20, no. 2 (January 2013): 94–99; Barbara Ann Piperata, "Forty Days and Forty Nights: A Biocultural Perspective on Postpartum Practices in the Amazon," *Social Science and Medicine* 67, no. 7 (May 2008): 1094–1103; Nancy Rose Hunt, *A Colonial Lexicon of Birth Ritual, Medicalization, and Mobility in the Congo* (Durham, NC: Duke University Press, 1999), 276–280; and Gertrude Fraser, *African American Midwifery in the South* (Cambridge, MA: Harvard University Press, 1998).

2. Interview with Nadima, May 22, 2012.

3. Mireille Rabenoro, "Motherhood in Malagasy Society: A Major Component in the Tradition vs. Modernity Conflict," *Jenda: A Journal of Culture and African Women Studies* 4, no. 1 (2003): 2.

4. Historian Nancy Rose Hunt also notes similar sentiments of nostalgia with regard to the increasing disappearance of a postpartum period of rest among women in the Congo (*Colonial*, 313).

5. Hannig, "Spiritual," 2014; Astrid Blystad, Ole Bjorn Rekdal, and Herman Malleyeck, "Seclusion, Protection and Avoidance: Exploring the Metida Complex among the Datoga of Northern Tanzania," *Africa* 77, no. 3 (2007): 331–350; Rebecca Popenoe, *Feeding Desire: Fatness, Beauty and Sexuality among a Saharan People* (New York: Routledge, 2004).

6. Bodo Ravololomanga, *Etre Femme et Mère à Madagascar: (Tañala d'Ifanadiana)* (Paris: L'Harmattan, 1992), 148–149.

7. Rita Astuti, "'It's a Boy,' 'It's a Girl!' Reflections on Sex and Gender in Madagascar and Beyond" in *Bodies and Persons: Comparative Perspectives from Africa and Melanasia*, ed. Michael Lambek and Andrew Strathern (Cambridge: Cambridge University Press, 1998), 35–36.

8. In her research on the "forty days and forty nights" postpartum practices among Ribeirinha women in eastern Amazon, Barbara Piperata offered similar

ideas about women being open and vulnerable as an explanation for why they needed to undergo this period of *resguardo* (rest). Interestingly, however, she notes that women who were undergoing resguardo never described themselves as feeling weak or vulnerable but instead described it as a joyful period and welcomed the new status they experienced and "the alternations to their daily routine" (Piperata, "Forty," 1102; also see Popenoe, *Feeding*, 145).

9. Blystad, Rekdal, and Malleyeck, "Seclusion," 335.

10. Karen Middleton, "How Karembola Men Became Mothers," in *Cultures of Relatedness: New Approaches to the Study of Kinship*, ed. Janet Carsten (New York: Cambridge University Press, 2000), 108.

11. Middleton, "How Karembola Men Became Mothers," 114.

12. Marilyn Strathern, *The Gender of the Gift: Problems with Women and Problems with Society in Melanesia* (Berkeley: University of California Press, 1988). Also see Blystad, Rekdal, and Malleyeck, "Seclusion," 335.

13. For more on tethering infants to their ancestral roots in a different context (in the southern region of Madagascar), see Karen Middleton, "Tombs, Umbilical Cords, and the Syllable Fo," in *Cultures of Madagascar: Ebb and Flow of Influences*, ed. Sandra Evers and Marc Spindler (Leiden: International Institute for Asian Studies, 1995), 223–235.

14. Middleton, "How Karembola Men Became Mothers," 117.

15. Maurice Bloch, "The Ritual of the Royal Bath in Madagascar: The Dissolution of Death, Birth and Fertility into Authority," in *Rituals of Royalty: Power and Ceremonial in Traditional Societies*, ed. David Cannadine and Simon Price (Cambridge: Cambridge University Press, 1987), 284.

16. See Bloch, "Ritual," 1987. Also see Maurice Bloch, *From Blessing to Violence: History and Ideology in the Circumcision Ritual of the Merina of Madagascar* (Cambridge: Cambridge University Press, 1986) and Maurice Bloch "Death, Women and Power," in *Death and the Regeneration of Life*, ed. Maurice Bloch and Jonathan Parry (Cambridge: Cambridge University Press, 1982), 211–230.

17. Bloch, "Death," 221.

18. Bruce Routledge, *Archaeology and State Theory: Subjects and Objects of Power* (New York: Bloomsbury Academic, 2014), 56.

19. Gillian Feeley-Harnik, *A Green Estate: Restoring Independence in Madagascar* (Washington, DC: Smithsonian Institute Press, 1991), 103.

20. See Feeley-Harnik, *Green*, 103–105; Michael Lambek and Andrew Walsh, "The Imagined Community of the Antankarana: Identity, History, and Ritual in Northern Madagascar," *Journal of Religion in Africa* 27, no. 3 (August 1997): 308–333; and Karen Middleton, *Ancestors, Power and History in Madagascar* (Leiden: Brill Academic Publishers, 1999), 184–185.

21. Interview with Dr. Hanitra, October 27, 2011.

22. Nancy Rose Hunt describes similar postnatal practices among Congolese women. In particular, parturients have hot water splashed on them by female relatives similar to what Malagasy described (*Colonial*, 278–279).

23. Interview with Nadima, May 22, 2012.

24. Kwame Appiah, *The Lies that Bind: Creed, Country, Color, Class, Culture* (London: Profile Books, 2018), 8–10.

25. When I refer to Sakalava peoples I am referring to an ethnic/identity group with many different subclans. Sakalava can also refer to the polity/monarchy that ruled over much of western Madagascar from the sixteenth through the eighteenth centuries. They began to lose power to the emerging Merina polity in the eighteenth century. Sakalava remember and reclaim their lost power in a variety of ways including through the ritual reburial of their kings. See Feeley-Harnik, *Green*, 1991.

26. Lesley Sharp, *The Possessed and the Dispossessed* (Berkeley: University of California Press, 1993), 110.

27. Ranginaly is a way of life with customs and dietary restrictions beyond the cold-water bathing practices that women observe postpartum. That said, most people of ranginaly ancestry do not worry about observing these customs except during vulnerable periods. Thus, generally speaking, cold-water bathing refers to a particular style of bathing post-childbirth and not to a more general manner of bathing. Almost all residents in Diégo bathe with cold water on a daily basis because few families have hot water in their homes, but people do sometimes warm water over a stove for use in bathing on particularly cold days or when someone is ill. If, however, a person is ranginaly, it would be dangerous to use warm water during a time of illness or during the time of one's recovery from childbirth.

28. Gillian Feeley-Harnik, "Childbirth and the Affiliation of Children in Northern Madagascar," *Taloha* 13 (2000): 137.

29. Michael Lambek, *The Weight of the Past: Living with History in Mahajanga, Madagascar* (New York: Palgrave Macmillan, 2003), 103; Sharp, *Possessed*.

30. Interview with Therese, January 2, 2012.

31. According to Blystad, Rekdal, and Malleyeck, most Datoga believe that certain kinds of death, and certain kinds of experiences which cause people to come close to death (like childbirth), can anger spirits. To calm the spirits, various rituals are prescribed which are said to cool the ancestors' anger ("Seclusion," 335). While cold-water bathing likely serves other purposes, the reader should note that Malagasy also have complex ideas about hot and cold, not only in relation to healing and biomedicine but also in relation to spirits

and other religious ideas, and that these associations about temperature vary regionally.

32. Interview with Amélie, November 17, 2011.

33. I posed this question in Malagasy using the phrasing "Anao mivavaka? Anao Silamo, Chrétienne sa Gasy fo?" which literally means "Do you pray? Are you Muslim, Christian or only Malagasy?" I learned to ask questions about religious affiliation in this way after hearing informants self-identify as "Gasy fo" which literally means "only Malagasy" and indicates that they practice Malagasy customs (fombagasy) or ancestral customs (fombandrazana) exclusively and do not adhere to any Christian or Muslim religious observances.

34. Hannig, "Spiritual," 305–306.

35. Hannig, "Spiritual," 308.

36. Jennifer Cole, Forget Colonialism? Sacrifice and the Art of Memory in Madagascar (Berkeley: University of California Press, 2001), 158.

37. See Gwyn Campbell's chapter "Female Bondage in Imperial Madagascar, 1820–95," in Women and Slavery: Africa, the Indian Ocean World, and the Medieval North Atlantic, vol. 1, ed. Suzanne Miers and Joseph C. Miller (Athens: University of Ohio Press, 2007), 237–258.

38. This is true for two reasons. First, the northern region of Madagascar is more cosmopolitan than other regions, which makes it harder to tell where people are from or the histories from which they descend. Second, in Madagascar at large, no single ethnicity or identity group was exclusively associated with enslaving, which means that it is not always possible to identify the descendants of slaves based on appearance, ethnicity, or lineage anywhere throughout the island.

39. Campbell, "Female Bondage," 240.

40. Campbell, "Female Bondage," 251.

41. I regret not posing more questions about women's efforts to remember slave ancestry in the lives of their children but hope to pursue this in a later project.

42. Interview with Camellia, December 23, 2011.

43. He wrote, "[the observance of fady in Madagascar] might be understood as a responsible act: one indicating the deeply felt willingness of individuals to be grouped among some and in 'contraposition' to others" (Andrew Walsh, "Responsibility, Taboos, and 'The Freedom to do Otherwise,'" Journal of the Royal Anthropological Institute 8, no. 3 [September 2002]: 453).

44. See my discussion of Alma Gottlieb's ethnography The Afterlife Is Where We Come From in the introduction to this volume.

45. She wrote, "Much of what a pregnant woman encounters in her daily life—the air she breathes, the food and drink she consumes, the emotions she

feels, the chemicals she's exposed to—are shared in some fashion with her fetus. They make up a mix of influences as individual and idiosyncratic as the woman herself. The fetus incorporates these offerings into its own body, makes them part of its flesh and blood. And, often, it does something more: it treats these maternal contributions as information, as biological postcards from the world outside" (Annie Paul, *Origins: How the Nine Months before Birth Shape the Rest of Our Lives* [New York: Free Press, 2008], 6).

46. Cole, *Forget Colonialism?*, 107.

47. Ravintsôha is an herbal infusion made with lemon leaves.

48. As Camellia described this two-week period of relative postpartum seclusion, flashbacks of scenes I had seen at the Dispensaire ran through my mind. I remembered seeing women leaving the Dispensaire with babies wrapped in such a way that they were completely obscured. One woman walked out of the facility with her baby tied around her abdomen. She was wearing a lamba, and had I not been sitting outside of the birthing room of the Dispensaire, I might not have suspected that the bulge within the lamba tied around her waist contained a baby. On another occasion, I saw a woman buying vegetables with what appeared to be a fully swaddled and hidden baby wrapped snug around her. She also had her toddler daughter by her side. Other babies who left the Dispensaire appeared completely covered, sometimes with a tiny face showing, other times not, and it's hot in Diégo, so surely this method of covering was not exclusively meant to keep them warm.

49. Lamaka are the woven mats that Malagasy use to eat, sleep, or to sit on during special ceremonies.

50. In Madagascar, women who do not ordinarily wear headscarves will often don one during a special occasion, or as part of a traditional religious ceremony. This practice is common among both Muslims and Christians. Additionally, and for different reasons, there are some Pentecostal churches in Diégo that require women to wear headscarves during services. The former example has more to do with declaring the formality of the occasion while the latter has more to do with modesty.

51. Interview with Adeline, January 12, 2012.

52. It is common in Madagascar to refer to one's mother's mother or one's aunts of one's grandmother's generation with the common word for grandmother, *dady*.

53. *Rasazy* is one of the many Malagasy words for midwife. It is a combination of the Malagasy word *renin-jaza*, used to refer to traditional midwives, with the French word *sage-femme*, which Malagasy use to refer to medically trained midwives. The word *rasazy* is often used to describe retired nurse-midwives who now practice out of their homes, as renin-jaza do.

54. Rabenoro, "Motherhood," 8.

55. Abortions are illegal in Madagascar. They are, however, readily available at clinics and hospitals. They are expensive, but women know where to go to obtain them. Because they are illegal, the procedures are often not explained in detail. For example, one woman was given pills to terminate her very early pregnancy. The doctor, however, never used the word *abortion* or confirmed or denied her pregnancy. She simply performed a sonogram and wrote her a prescription. Other young women told me that doctors would agree to perform abortions, but requested that women arrive at the clinic or hospital after hours.

56. Rabenoro, "Motherhood," 2.

57. Arnold van Gennep, *The Rites of Passage*, 2nd ed. (1909; Chicago: University of Chicago Press, 1960).

58. Bloch, *From Blessing*, 1986.

59. See Caroline Walker Bynum, "Women's Stories, Women's Symbols: A Critique of Victor Turner's Theory of Liminality," in *Readings in Ritual Studies*, ed. Ronald Grimes (New Jersey: Prentice Hall, 1996), 77–79. Also see Bruce Lincoln, *Emerging from the Chrysalis: Studies in Rituals of Women's Initiation* (Cambridge, MA: Harvard University Press, 1981).

60. Lincoln, *Emerging*, 57.

61. See chap. 1. Also see Feeley-Harnik, "Childbirth," 142.

62. Rôm-patsa are a type of small shrimp that women give to other women who have just given birth, as they are understood to help a woman's milk come in faster. Rôm-patsa can also refer to any type of gift given to women post-childbirth.

63. See Michael Lambek's theory on sacrifice as one of the means by which we consecrate new beginnings in "Sacrifice and the Problem of Beginning: Meditations from Sakalava Mythopraxis," *Journal of the Royal Anthropological Institute* 13, no. 1 (March 2007): 19–38.

4. Turning "Water Babies" into "Real Human Beings"

1. Most generically, lamba refers to the clothes that people wear. There are many different kinds of lamba throughout Madagascar; thus, the word is often accompanied by a modifier. Historically, lamba were handwoven from raw materials including from "raffia leaf, bast, cotton, or indigenous 'wild' silk (Borocera)." See Sarah Fee, "The Shape of Fashion: The Historic Silk Brocades (*akotifahana*) of Highland Madagascar," *African Arts* 46, no. 3 (Autumn 2013): 26. Today, lamba are made of both local and imported dyes and materials. Different kinds of lamba were and are still used today as everyday clothing, to wrap the dead, as gifts from royalty and esteemed political figures to foreigners, by women

to carry babies on their backs, and, last, in the example I provide in this article, to wrap around the bodies of young infants who die prematurely. For more on the history of cloth/clothing in northern Madagascar, see Gillian Feeley-Harnik, "Cloth and the Creation of Ancestors in Madagascar," in *Cloth and the Human Experience*, ed. A. Weiner and J. Schneider (Washington, DC: Smithsonian Institution Press, 1989). Also see Gillian Feeley-Harnik, "Number One— Nambawani—Lambaoany: Clothing as an Historical Medium of Exchange in Northwestern Madagascar," in *Lova/Inheritance: Past and Present in Madagascar*, ed. Z. Crossland, G. Sodikoff, and W. Griffin (Ann Arbor: University of Michigan Scholarly Publishing Office, 2003), 63–103; Rebecca Green, "Lamba Hoany Proverb Cloths from Madagascar," *African Arts* 36, no. 2 (Summer 2003): 30–46; and Lesley Sharp's description of various regional garbs throughout Madagascar, including details about clothing styles in coastal and northern parts of the island (*The Possessed and the Dispossessed* [Berkeley: University of California Press, 1993], 57).

2. Interview with Zafisoa, October 29, 2011. Her words in the original French were "c'est parce que ce n'est pas plein de l'os." Richard Huntington discovered similar practices among the Bara of southern Madagascar: "If a very young child (zaza mena, 'red child') dies, there is no funeral or burial in the paternal tomb, nor can the father give the body to his in-laws for burial in their tomb as he might with an older child. The child is not yet part of the social order connected to the father and the ancestors, and the bodies of such babies are simply abandoned in a 'a wet place' (tany le)" (*Gender and Social Structure* [Bloomington: Indiana University Press, 1988], 31). Rita Astuti also notes that among Vezo populations, babies are similarly considered not fully human until they have bones and are thus protected in various ways. She also notes that young babies who die prematurely cannot be buried in the family tomb because they are understood to not have bones, and tombs are for bones. See Astuti, "'It's a Boy,' 'It's a Girl!' Reflections on Sex and Gender in Madagascar and Beyond," in *Bodies and Persons: Comparative Perspectives from Africa and Melanasia* (Cambridge: Cambridge University Press, 1998), 35–37.

3. Gillian Feeley-Harnik, "Childbirth and the Affiliation of Children in Northern Madagascar," *Taloha* 13 (2000): 150.

4. In Malagasy, there is no variation in spelling between plural and singular nouns. Thus, depending on the context, I will translate zaza rano to mean both "water baby" and "water babies."

5. It is well documented that Malagasy in other regions, including in central and southern Madagascar, describe newborn babies in similar ways. See Maurice Bloch, "Zafimaniry Birth and Kinship Theory," *Social Anthropology* 1, no. 1b (February 1993): 123. Also see Huntington, *Gender*, 31.

6. Michael Lambek, *The Weight of the Past: Living with History in Mahajanga, Madagascar* (New York: Palgrave Macmillan, 2003), 92.

7. Lambek, *Weight*, 92.

8. This story was first told to me by Heriniaina and later by other members of his family, including his sister Zafisoa and their mother, Madame Serafina, with whom I have stayed on multiple occasions on my many trips to Madagascar.

9. *Moisy* is most often translated to mean "diviner" or "spiritual healer." There are other Malagasy words for healer-diviners, including *ombiasy* and *mpisikidy*.

10. *Angano* is often translated to mean a "fable" or "tale," and these stories are not meant to be taken literally.

11. This story can be read for its political implications as well. For in the delta of the Mahavavy River lies the SIRAMA sugar plantation and factory, a formerly French-owned, now state-owned, operation whose owners and employers frequently disregard the region's fady with regard to working the land. See Andrew Walsh, "Preserving Bodies, Saving Souls: Religious Incongruity in a Northern Malagasy Mining Town," *Journal of Religion in Africa* 32, no. 3 (January 2002): 459. Also see Michael Lambek and Andrew Walsh, "The Imagined Community of the Antankarana: Identity, History, and Ritual in Northern Madagascar," *Journal of Religion in Africa* 27, no. 3 (1997): 315. Although the company does make financial contributions to the royal ceremonies performed by the Antankarana as a way of mitigating their disregard of the "Tuesday taboo," a contentious relationship nevertheless exists between the company and the landowners, called *tompon-tany*. Given these circumstances, it is possible to infer that the contemporary telling of this fable serves as a warning to employers of the company, migrant workers, and landowners alike about the possible ramifications of breaking fady.

12. Jennifer Cole, *Sex and Salvation: Imagining the Future in Madagascar* (Chicago: University of Chicago Press, 2010), 74; Lambek, *Weight*; Bloch, "Zafimaniry Birth," 119–132; Maurice Bloch, *Placing the Dead: Tombs, Ancestral Villages and Kinship Organization in Madagascar* (New York: Seminar Press, 1971); Huntington, *Gender*.

13. Bloch, *Placing*; Lambek, *Weight*.

14. The phrase *acquiring bones* is one I borrow from Maurice Bloch in his discussion of house building among Zafimaniry couples. However, it is also an emic concept since Bloch's informants described a process by which their houses acquired "bones" through marriage and the procreation of children. Similarly, in the context of my own research, Diégo residents spoke of babies acquiring bones when teeth emerge, and babies are then subsequently given ceremonial haircuttings and initiated as "real human beings" (*vrais humains*) into their families (Bloch, "Zafimaniry Birth").

15. Bloch, "Zafimaniry Birth"; Maurice Bloch, *From Blessing to Violence: History and Ideology in the Circumcision Ritual of the Merina of Madagascar* (Cambridge: Cambridge University Press, 1986); Maurice Bloch, "Death, Women and Power," in *Death and the Regeneration of Life*, ed. Maurice Bloch and Jonathan Parry (Cambridge: Cambridge University Press, 1982), 211–230; Bloch, *Placing*; Huntington, *Gender*.

16. Maurice Bloch expresses this view in his famous theory of ritual, as does Nancy Jay in her seminal book on the role of sacrifice rituals in the establishing of paternal orders. Both accurately portray rituals as remedies for the transience of human existence. However, in my view, both also portray women as symbols rather than as agents of their own life course and as active participants in rituals—participants who likely construct their own meanings within the confines of ritual activities. See Maurice Bloch, *Prey into Hunter: The Politics of Religious Experience* (New York: Cambridge University Press, 1992). Also see Nancy Jay, *Throughout Your Generations and Forever: Sacrifice, Religious and Paternity* (Chicago: University of Chicago Press, 1992).

17. In recent years, scholars working in Madagascar have attempted to stress the ambiguity of life trajectories (Lambek, *Weight*), the role of gender (Cole, *Sex and Salvation*), and the importance of birth rituals and future-oriented, as opposed to strictly remembrance-oriented, practices. See also Bloch, "Zafimaniry Birth," and Feeley-Harnik, "Childbirth." Nevertheless, aside from a few notable exceptions (Feeley-Harnik, "Childbirth"; Bloch, "Zafimaniry Birth"), birth rituals (fomba fiterana) are underrepresented in the literature on Madagascar, despite the importance of life-stage rituals at all junctures in the life cycle.

18. What I mean by "normative" is that Bloch offers a description of that ritual that women are "supposed" to observe. He does not discuss how many women actually observe these rituals or how perfectly or imperfectly they perform rites according to the prescribed dictates ("Zafimaniry Birth").

19. Bloch, "Zafimaniry Birth."

20. Bloch, "Zafimaniry Birth," 131. In this article, Bloch offers a very useful correction/qualification to the overly binary distinction that James Fox makes between "tomb based" and "birth based" kinship systems. Fox argues that as compared with African societies, people in Austronesian societies belong to a kinship only in their death. See James Fox, "The House as a Type of Social Organization on the Island of Roti," in *De la hutte au palais: Sociétés 'à maison' en Asie du Sud-Est Insulaire*, ed. C. Macdonald (Paris: CNRS, 1987), 171–178. Bloch admits to making a similar argument about the highland Merina of Madagascar. See Bloch, *Placing*. Rita Astuti also makes this claim with regard to Vezo who

live along Madagascar's southwest coast. See Rita Astuti, "Learning to Be Vezo: The Construction of the Person among Fishing People of Western Madagascar" (PhD diss., London School of Economics and Political Science, 1991). However, Bloch now proposes that such a dichotomy be qualified to include "house-based" systems such as the case of Zafimaniry who predominantly live in the southern-central highlands of Madagascar.

21. Bloch, "Zafimaniry Birth," 122.

22. Bloch, "Zafimaniry Birth," 123. Albeit in a different context, Rita Astuti echoes this point made by Bloch that birth matters little for what she calls "'creating' the social person. What it means to be Vezo is to learn to embody the habits of being Vezo thus birth alone is not enough to grant inclusion into the category of Vezo." See Astuti, "'It's a Boy,'" 37. By contrast, Karen Middleton argues that kindedness, at least among Karembola of southern Madagascar, is not shaped only or finally in the tomb. She writes, "Karembola believe that living people are kinded, and that ancestry shapes the living person in important ways" ("How Karembola Men Became Mothers," in *Cultures of Relatedness: New Approaches to the Study of Kinship*, ed. Janet Carsten [New York: Cambridge University Press, 2000], 113).

23. Interview with Roger, January 3, 2012.

24. According to Feeley-Harnik, northern Malagasy understand the health and well-being of their children to be critically tied to their inclusion among both patrilineal and matrilineal kinship networks. It is through "mock battles" performed at haircutting ceremonies that relatives from both sides vie for influence in their children's lives (Feeley-Harnik, "Childbirth," 136).

25. Lambek, *Weight*; Rita Astuti, "'The Vezo Are Not a Kind of People': Identity, Difference and 'Ethnicity' Among a Fishing People of Western Madagascar," *American Ethnologist* 22, no. 3 (August 1995): 464–482; Bloch, *Placing*.

26. See William Ellis, *History of Madagascar* (London: Fisher, Son, 1838). Also see Chase Salmon Osborn, *Madagascar: Land of the Man-Eating Tree* (1924; repr., Somerville, MA: Heliograph, 2012), 279.

27. For more on haircutting and other birth rituals in Madagascar, see Feeley-Harnik, "Childbirth"; Bloch, "Zafimaniry Birth."

28. See the ethnographic works Lambek, *Weight*; Jennifer Cole, *Forget Colonialism? Sacrifice and the Art of Memory in Madagascar* (Berkeley: University of California Press, 2001); David Graeber, "Dancing with Corpses Reconsidered: An Interpretation of Famadihana in Arivonimamo Madagascar," *American Ethnologist* 22, no. 4 (May 1995): 258–278; and Lesley A. Sharp, *The Possessed and the Dispossessed* (Berkeley: University of California Press, 1993).

29. The term *vady* is used colloquially to refer to a boyfriend, girlfriend, or partner. It is used casually and less often between people who are married. When people marry or have been together a long time, couples use more weighted and respectful terms such as *ramose* (for men) or *madame* (for women).

30. Although the context differs significantly, Nancy Rose Hunt addresses the giving of a chicken at birth rituals in the Congo. She discusses the symbolism behind a father giving chickens to their fathers-in-law at the end of their wife's postpartum period. She notes that the purpose of the gift is to give blood (from the chicken) to replace the blood lost by the mother in childbirth. I am not aware of any connection between the chicken's loss of blood and the mother's loss of blood in the case of haircutting ceremonies in Madagascar, but that does not mean that such an association does not exist. See Nancy Rose Hunt, *A Colonial Lexicon of Birth Ritual, Medicalization, and Mobility in the Congo* (Durham, NC: Duke University Press, 1999), 278.

31. Karen Middleton notes that in southern Madagascar, among Karembola, kindedness is revealed rather than constructed. In other words, people are not exactly born with ethnic or ancestral identities, nor do they construct them through performance; rather, they become revealed over time through a person's actions in the world. Though northerners do not necessarily have the same ideas about kindedness, it is true that babies' multiple paternal and maternal affiliations are understood to be both shaped and strengthened by rituals and relationships and that these same rituals to some extent also reveal what is already there ("How Karembola Men Became Mothers," 107).

32. Interview with Genevie, February 10, 2012.

33. Interview with Zafisoa, February 4, 2012.

34. FJKM (Fiangonan'i Jesoa Kristy eto Madagasikara), the Church of Jesus Christ in Madagascar, is considered to be the largest Protestant denomination in Madagascar. It was founded in 1968 and is the successor body of the London Missionary Society, the Paris Missionary Society, and the Friends Foreign Missionary Association. FJKM is a reformed Protestant denomination and Malagasy raised in this church often describe themselves simply as "Protestante." The term *Protestante* is not used to refer to other mainline churches in Madagascar such as Anglicans or Lutherans.

35. See Arnold van Gennep, *The Rites of Passage* (1909; Chicago: University of Chicago Press, 1960). Also see Victor Turner, *The Ritual Process: Structure and Anti-Structure* (New York: Routledge Taylor & Francis Group, 1969).

36. In describing the sacred, Jonathan Z. Smith writes, "This is a most important point, one that is only recently gaining acceptance among historians of religions although it was already brilliantly described by Van Gennep in *Les*

Rites de passage (1909) as the 'pivoting of the sacred.' That is, there is nothing that is inherently sacred or profane." Jonathan Z. Smith, "The Bare Facts of Ritual," *History of Religions* 20, no. 1/2 (November 1980): 115.

37. Eva Keller, "The Banana Plant and the Moon: Conservation and the Malagay Ethos of Life in Masoala, Madagascar," *American Ethnologist* 35, no. 4 (November 2008): 659.

38. Andrew Walsh, "Responsibility, Taboos, and 'The Freedom to do Otherwise,'" *Journal of the Royal Anthropological Institute* 8, no. 3 (September 2002): 453.

39. Astuti, "Vezo Are Not a Kind of People," 464–482. Also see Lambek and Walsh, "Imagined Community of the Antankarana," 308.

40. Hunt, *Colonial*, 76.

41. See Ellis, *History of Madagascar*. Also see Osborn, *Madagascar*, 279.

42. Feeley-Harnik, *Green*, 47.

43. See Ellis, *History of Madagascar*. Also see Osborn, *Madagascar*, 279.

44. Paul Connerton, *How Societies Remember* (New York: Cambridge University Press, 1989), 48.

45. See Vanessa Ochs, *Inventing Jewish Ritual* (Philadelphia: Jewish Publication Society, 2007). Also see Margaret Drewal, *Yoruba Ritual: Performers, Play, and Agency* (Bloomington: Indiana University Press, 1992).

46. Peter Metcalf and Richard Huntington, *Celebrations of Death: The Anthropology of Mortuary Ritual* (Cambridge: Cambridge University Press, 1991), 113.

47. Bloch "Death, Women and Power," 211–230; Huntington, *Gender*; Metcalf and Huntington, *Celebrations of Death*, 113–122.

48. See Bloch, *From Blessing*; Bloch, "Zafimaniry Birth"; Bloch, "Death, Women and Power"; Bloch, *Placing*; Huntington, *Gender*; and Lambek, *Weight*.

49. Lambek, *Weight*, 103.

50. The majority of northern coastal Malagasy are ranginaly as compared with the mafana of the central highlands. As such, they observe thrice-daily rituals of cold-water bathing postpartum lest they or their children experience fatigue, seizures, or even death. Described as a dominant practice, stronger than the custom of mafana, ranginaly is an identity one either marries into or inherits through one's parents. Because it is considered a dominant trait, practicing ranginaly can be the means by which mothers assert influence over their children despite a father's more principal claim. See Sharp, *Possessed*, 110. Also see chapter 3.

51. In this story told to Feeley-Harnik in the 1990s in the Analalava (northern) region of Madagascar, God asked a woman, "Who should be killed, you or your child?" She replied, "The child." When God asked a man who should be killed, he replied, "Myself." God therefore declared that men, rather than

women, would be masters over their children. Women in the Analalava region note the irony of this story, given that women, rather than men, sacrifice more on behalf of their children, including in childbirth, where they sometimes nearly die in order to give their children life. See Feeley-Harnik, "Childbirth," 1.

5. Bearing Babies in Dynamic Religious Landscapes

1. Parker Shipton, *Mortgaging the Ancestors: Ideologies of Attachment in Africa* (New Haven, CT: Yale University Press, 2009), 227.

2. Jennifer Cole and Karen Middleton, "Rethinking Ancestors and Colonial Power in Madagascar," *Africa: Journal of the International African Institute* 71, no. 1 (February 2001): 2.

3. Gillian Feeley-Harnik, *A Green Estate: Restoring Independence in Madagascar* (Washington, DC: Smithsonian Institute Press, 1991).

4. Nancy Rose Hunt, *A Colonial Lexicon of Birth Ritual, Medicalization, and Mobility in the Congo* (Durham, NC: Duke University Press, 1999).

5. The maîtrise degree is the equivalent of the master's degree in the American school system but is based on the French model of education.

6. Interview with Marie, May 12, 2012.

7. Marie referred to her partner and father of her daughter with the word *boyfriend* (*garcon, copin*) on some occasions and the word *husband* (*mari*) on other occasions. They had, however, not yet legally married, something she discusses later in the story.

8. Malagasy sometimes refer to the capital of Madagascar, Antananarivo, by its abbreviated name, Tana.

9. For more on Malagasy youth turning away from ancestral customs in order to forge new ways of living in Madagascar's cities, see Jennifer Cole, *Sex and Salvation: Imagining the Future in Madagascar* (Chicago: University of Chicago Press, 2010); and Laura Tilghman, "City Livelihoods and Village Linkages: Rural-Urban Migrants in Tamatave, Madagascar" (PhD diss., University of Georgia, 2014).

10. Jennifer Cole also notes this tendency among urban Malagasy to associate ideas about modernity and progress with lightness as opposed to the darkness of the countryside (*Sex*, 65).

11. Laura M. Tilghman, "The Dead Are Dead/Ancestors Never Die: Migrants, Rural Linkages, and Religious Change in Northeastern Madagascar," *Journal of Religion in Africa* 48, no. 4 (2020): 347–375.

12. The movement was originally known as Students/Disciples of the Lord but eventually became known as Fifohazana—related to the Malagasy word *mifoha*, which means "to wake up." See Cynthia Holder Rich, *Indigenous Christianity in Africa* (New York: Peter Lang, 2011), 23. As Rich notes, "[The

movement] features a number of traditional emphases of Christian ecstatic movements the world around, including evangelism and Bible study, and one that is less standard: care for people with mental illness" (23).

13. See Britt Halvorson, "Translating the *Fifohazana* (Awakening): The Politics of Healing and the Colonial Mission Legacy in African Christian Missionization," *Journal of Religion in Africa* 40, no. 4 (Jan 2010): 417–418.

14. The words *iraka* and *mpiandry* refer to those who are sent out and those who wait, respectively. Iraka (disciples) were trained to travel and spread the gospel, while mpiandry were trained to offer healing and spiritual guidance to communities within the camps (toby). Originally, iraka were called *apostoly* (apostles), but movement leaders changed the title of those sent out from apostoly to iraka under pressure from mission churches, whose leaders were concerned with the use of the words *apostles* and *disciples* within a movement not officially sanctioned by them. The office of mpiandry (shepherd-healers) emerged during this same context (Rich, *Indigenous*, 45).

15. For more on the history of this movement, see Halvorson, "Translating," 417–418.

16. See Roger Rafanomezantsoa, "The Contribution of Rainisoalambo to the Indigenization of the Protestant Churches in Madagascar," in *The Fifohazana: Madagascar's Indigenous Christian Movement*, ed. Cynthia Holder Rich (Amherst: Cambria Press, 2008), 14.

17. In 1869, after several decades of missionionization from the missionaries of the London Missionary Society, Merina Queen Ranavalona II officially converted to the religion and had all talismans (sampy) burned publicly.

18. Shepherd-healer missionaries from Madagascar serve in a Lutheran church in Minneapolis/St. Paul, Minnesota. See Halverson, "Translating."

19. Halvorson, "Translating," 417–420.

20. According to Halvorson, in the 1960s, foreign missionaries and the leadership of the Malagasy Lutheran Church (FLM) were concerned by the activities of shepherd-healers, who they considered overly emotional and syncretic and no doubt a threat to their institutional church power. This began to change in the late 1970s / early '80s, though the processes by which this change occurred are not entirely clear. It seems the FLM slowly began to accept the movement and now claims the movement as an integral part of its ministry ("Translating," 417–420).

21. Rainsoalambo and his followers wore white robes modeled after an Indigenous style of dress called *didy mananjara*. See Rafanomezantsoa, "Contribution."

22. See Halvorson, "Translating," 418; Phillip Jenkins, *The Next Christendom: The Rise of Global Christianity* (New York: Oxford University Press, 2002),

143; Lesley Sharp, *The Possessed and the Dispossessed* (Berkeley: University of California Press, 1993), 270; G. C. Oosthuizen, *The Healer Prophet in Afro-Christian Churches* (New York: Brill, 1992), 71; and Birgit Meyer, "'Praise the Lord:' Popular Cinema and Pentecostalite Style in Ghana's New Public Sphere," *American Ethnologist* 31, no. 1 (January 2004): 92–110.

23. See Girish Daswani, "On Christianity and Ethics: Rupture as Ethical Practice in Ghanaian Pentecostalism," *American Ethnologist* 40, no. 3 (August 2013): 467–479.

24. Oosthuizen, *Healer*, 75.

25. Rich, *Indigenous*, 18.

26. Rich, *Indigenous*, 18; Céline Ratovoson, "La femme malgache responsable de son environnement physique et systèmes religieux," in *Centre d'information et de Documentation Scientifique et Technique* (Antananarivo: L'Académie Malgache, 1989), 128; Mariette Razivelo, "Women and the Formation of a Malagasy Theology" (thesis, Wartburg Theological Seminary, 1980), 2–3.

27. See Cynthia Hoehler-Fatton's discussion of this, albeit in a different context (western Kenya), *Women of Fire and Spirit: History, Faith and Gender in Roho Religion in Western Kenya* (New York: Oxford University Press: 1996), 206.

28. Interview with Jacqueline, December 4, 2011.

29. The restriction against eating pork, common in northern Madagascar, is likely a residual practice that stems from people's ancestors' Muslim heritage, though many of the descendants who observe this fady no longer practice Islam.

30. At the time of this research, there were two kings of the Antankarana, an ethnic group residing in northern Madagascar, and a dispute as to who is the legitimate heir to the throne. The king Jacqueline was referring to is the elder of the two, who lives in Ambilobe.

31. See Sharp, *Possessed*.

32. Interview with Abdel Cadère, February 1, 2012.

33. Feeley-Harnik, *Green*, 103.

Conclusion

1. Lesley Sharp, *The Possessed and the Dispossessed* (Berkeley: University of California Press, 1993), 208.

2. Michael Schwirtz and Gaelle Borgia, "How Russia Meddles Abroad for Profit: Cash, Trolls and a Cult Leader," *New York Times*, November 11, 2019.

3. Britt Halvorson, "Translating the *Fifohazana* (Awakening): The Politics of Healing and the Colonial Mission Legacy in African Christian Missionization," *Journal of Religion in Africa* 40, no. 4 (January 2010): 426.

4. Philip Jenkins, *The Next Christendom: The Rise of Global Christianity* (New York: Oxford University Press, 2002).

BIBLIOGRAPHY

Andersen, Margaret. "Creating French Settlements Overseas: Pronatalism and Colonial Medicine in Madagascar." *French Historical Studies* 33, no. 3 (Summer 2010): 417–444.

Andersen, Margaret. *Regeneration through Empire: French Pronatalists and Colonial Settlement in the Third Republic.* Lincoln: University of Nebraska Press, 2015.

Andersson, Neil, and Shula Marks. "The State, Class and the Allocation of Health Resources in Southern Africa." *Social Science and Medicine* 28, no. 5 (1989): 515–530.

Anzaldúa, Gloria. *Light in the Dark/Luz en lo Oscuro: Rewriting Identity, Spirituality, and Reality.* Durham, NC: Duke University Press, 2015.

Appiah, Kwame. *The Lies That Bind: Creed, Country, Color, Class, Culture.* London: Profile Books, 2018.

Asad, Talal, ed. *Anthropology and the Colonial Encounter.* London: Ithaca Press, 1973.

Astuti, Rita. "'It's a Boy,' 'It's a Girl!' Reflections on Sex and Gender in Madagascar and Beyond." In *Bodies and Persons: Comparative Perspectives from Africa and Melanesia,* edited by Michael Lambek and Andrew Strathern, 29–52. New York: Cambridge University Press, 1998.

Astuti, Rita. "Learning to Be Vezo: The Construction of the Person among Fishing People of Western Madagascar." PhD diss., London School of Economics and Political Science, 1991.

Astuti, Rita. "'The Vezo Are Not a Kind of People': Identity, Difference and 'Ethnicity' among a Fishing People of Western Madagascar." *American Ethnologist* 22, no. 3 (August 1995): 464–482.

Astuti, Rita, and P. L. Harris. "Understanding Mortality and the Life of the Ancestors in Rural Madagascar." *Cognitive Science* 32, no. 4 (June 2008): 713–740.

Ballarin, Marie Pierre. "How Spirits Travel along the Western Indian Ocean Rims." *Azania: Archaeological Research in Africa* 42, no. 1 (July 2007): 53–67.

Ballarin, Marie Pierre. "Royal Ancestors and Social Change in the Majunga Area: Northwest Madagascar 19th–20th Centuries." In *Knowledge, Renewal and Religion: Repositioning and Changing Ideological and Material Circumstances among the Swahili on the East African Coast*, edited by Kjersti Larsten, 69–84. Uppsala: Nordic Africa Institute, 2009.

Banish, Shenna. "Don't Diss the Reninjaza: A Case for Integrating Traditional Birthing Attendants into the Allopathic System to Improve Prenatal Health in Rural Madagascar." Independent Study Project (ISP) Collection, School for International Training, 2014. https://digitalcollections.sit.edu/isp_collection/1888.

Bell, Catherine. *Ritual Perspectives and Dimensions*. Oxford: Oxford University Press, 1997.

Bello-Bravo, Julia. "Preserving Tradition in the Here and Now: Barriers to the Preservation and Continuity of Traditional Healing Knowledge and Practices in Madagascar." *Social Sciences and Humanities Open* 8, no. 1 (2023): 1–8.

Besterman, Theodore. "The Belief in Rebirth among the Natives of Africa (Including Madagascar)." *Folklore* 41, no. 1 (January 2012): 44–47.

Blier, Suzanne. *African Vodun: Art, Psychology, and Power*. Chicago: University of Chicago Press, 1995.

Bloch, Maurice. "Death, Women and Power." In *Death and the Regeneration of Life*, edited by Maurice Bloch and Jonathan Parry, 211–230. Cambridge: Cambridge University Press, 1982.

Bloch, Maurice. *From Blessing to Violence: History and Ideology in the Circumcision Ritual of the Merina of Madagascar*. Cambridge: Cambridge University Press, 1986.

Bloch, Maurice. *Placing the Dead: Tombs, Ancestral Villages, and Kinship Organization in Madagascar*. New York: Seminar Press, 1971.

Bloch, Maurice. *Prey into Hunter: The Politics of Religious Experience*. New York: Cambridge University Press, 1992.

Bloch, Maurice. "The Ritual of the Royal Bath in Madagascar: The Dissolution of Death, Birth and Fertility into Authority" In *Rituals of Royalty: Power and Ceremonial in Traditional Societies*, edited by David Cannadine and Simon Price, 271–297. Cambridge: Cambridge University Press, 1987.

Bloch, Maurice. "Zafimaniry Birth and Kinship Theory." *Social Anthropology* 1, no. 1b (February 1993): 119–132.

Blystad, Astrid, Ole Bjorn Rekdal, and Herman Malleyeck. "Seclusion, Protection and Avoidance: Exploring the *Metida* Complex among the Datoga of Northern Tanzania." *Africa* 77, no. 3 (2007): 331–350.

Boddy, Janice. "Barbaric Custom and Colonial Science: Teaching the Female Body in the Anglo-Egyptian Sudan." *Social Analysis* 47, no. 2 (2003): 60–81.

Brodsky, Phyllis. *The Control of Childbirth: Women versus Medicine through the Ages.* Jefferson, NC: McFarland, 2008.

Brown, Margaret. "Reclaiming Lost Ancestors and Acknowledging Slave Descent: Insights from Madagascar." *Comparative Studies in Society and History* 46, no. 3 (July 2004): 616–645.

Burke, Eva, Judy Gold, Lalaina Razafinirinasoa, and Anna Mackay. "Youth Voucher Program in Madagascar Increases Access to Voluntary Family Planning and STI Services for Young People." *Global Health: Science and Practice* 5, no. 1 (March 2017): 33–43.

Bynum, Caroline Walker. "Women's Stories, Women's Symbols: A Critique of Victor Turner's Theory of Liminality." In *Readings in Ritual Studies*, edited by Ronald Grimes, 71–85. New Jersey: Prentice Hall, 1996.

Campbell, Gwyn. "Female Bondage in Imperial Madagascar, 1820–95." In *Africa, the Indian Ocean World, and the Medieval North Atlantic*, vol. 1 of *Women and Slavery*, edited by Gwyn Campbell, Suzanne Miers, and Joseph C. Miller, 237–258. Athens: Ohio University Press, 2007.

Carrithers, Michael, Andrew Barry, Ivan Brady, Clifford Geertz, Roger M. Keesing, Paul A. Roth, Robert A. Rubinstein, and Elvi Whittaker. "Is Anthropology Art or Science." *Current Anthropology* 31, no. 3 (June 1990): 263–282.

Cassidy, Tina. *Birth: The Surprising History of How We Are Born.* New York: Atlantic Monthly Press, 2006.

Cliff, Julie, and Abdul Razak Noormahomed. "Health as a Target: South Africa's Destablization of Mozambique." *Social Science and Medicine* 27, no. 7 (1988): 717–722.

Cliff, Julie, and Abdul Razak Noormahomed. "The Impact of War on Children's Health in Mozambique." *Social Science and Medicine* 36, no. 7 (1993): 843–848.

Cole, Jennifer. *Forget Colonialism? Sacrifice and the Art of Memory in Madagascar.* Berkeley: University of California Press, 2001.

Cole, Jennifer. *Sex and Salvation: Imagining the Future in Madagascar.* Chicago: University of Chicago Press, 2010.

Cole, Jennifer, and Karen Middleton. "Rethinking Ancestors and Colonial Power in Madagascar." *Africa: Journal of the International African Institute* 71, no. 1 (February 2001): 1–37.

Connerton, Paul. *How Societies Remember.* New York: Cambridge University Press, 1989.

Dahl, Oyvind. *Madagasckar, midt i brenningene.* Oslo: Luther, 1976.

Dahl, Oyvind. *Meanings in Madagascar: Cases of Intercultural Communication.* Westport, CT: Bergin and Garvey, 1999.

Daswani, Girish. "On Christianity and Ethics: Rupture as Ethical Practice in Ghanaian Pentecostalism." *American Ethnologist* 40, no. 3 (August 2013): 467–479.

Davies, Charlotte Aull. *Reflexive Ethnography: A Guide to Researching Selves and Others.* New York: Routledge, 1998.

Davis-Floyd, Robbie. *Birth as an American Rite of Passage.* Berkeley: University of California Press, 1992.

Drewal, Margaret. *Yoruba Ritual: Performers, Play and Agency.* Bloomington: Indiana University Press, 1992.

Eck, Diana. *Encountering God: A Spiritual Journey from Bozeman to Banaras.* Boston: Beacon Press, 1993.

Ellis, William. *History of Madagascar.* London: Fisher, Son, 1838.

Epstein, Randi. *Get Me Out: A History of Childbirth from the Garden of Eden to the Sperm Bank.* New York: Norton, 2010.

Fee, Sarah. "The Shape of Fashion: The Historic Silk Brocades (*Akotifahana*) of Highland Madagascar." *African Arts* 46, no. 3 (Autumn 2013): 26–39.

Feeley-Harnik, Gillian. "Childbirth and the Affiliation of Children in Northern Madagascar." *Taloha* 13 (2000): 135–172.

Feeley-Harnik, Gillian. "Cloth and the Creation of Ancestors in Madagascar." In *Cloth and the Human Experience,* edited by A. Weiner and J. Schneider, 75–117. Washington, DC: Smithsonian Institution Press, 1989.

Feeley-Harnik, Gillian. *A Green Estate: Restoring Independence in Madagascar.* Washington, DC: Smithsonian Institute Press, 1991.

Feeley-Harnik, Gillian. "Number One—Nambawani—Lambaoany: Clothing as an Historical Medium of Exchange in Northwestern Madagascar." In *Lova/Inheritance: Past and Present in Madagascar,* edited by Z. Crossland, G. Sodikoff, and W. Griffin, 63–103. Ann Arbor: Scholarly Publishing Office, University of Michigan, 2003.

Feierman, Steven. "Struggles for Control: The Social Roots of Health and Healing in Modern Africa." *African Studies Review* 28, no. 2/3 (1985): 73–147.

Feldman-Savelsberg, Pamela. *Mothers on the Move: Reproducing Belonging between Africa and Europe.* Chicago: University of Chicago Press, 2016.

Fox, James. "The House as a Type of Social Organization on the Island of Roti." In *De la hutte au palais: Sociétés 'à maison' en Asie du Sud-Est Insulaire,* edited by C. Macdonald, 171–178. Paris: CNRS, 1987.

Fraser, Gertrude. *African American Midwifery in the South.* Cambridge, MA: Harvard University Press, 1998.

Friedson, Steven. *Dancing Prophets: Musical Experience in Tumbuka Healing.* Chicago: University of Chicago Press, 1996.

Gaskin, Ina May. *Spiritual Midwifery.* Summertown, TN: Book Publishing Company, 1975.

Geissler, Paul, and Ruth Jane Prince. *The Land Is Dying: Contingency, Creativity and Conflict in Western Kenya*. Oxford: Berghahn Books, 2012.

Gottlieb, Alma. *The Afterlife Is Where We Come From: The Culture of Infancy in West Africa*. Chicago: University of Chicago Press, 2004.

Graeber, David. "Dancing with Corpses Reconsidered: An Interpretation of Famadihana in Arivonimamo Madagascar." *American Ethnologist* 22, no. 4 (May 1995): 258–278.

Green, Rebecca. "Lamba Hoany Proverb Cloths from Madagascar." *African Arts* 36, no. 2 (Summer 2003): 30–46.

Halvorson, Britt. "Translating the *Fifohazana* (Awakening): The Politics of Healing and the Colonial Mission Legacy in African Christian Missionization." *Journal of Religion in Africa* 40, no. 4 (January 2010): 413–441.

Hannig, Anita. "Spiritual Border Crossings: Childbirth, Postpartum Seclusion and Religious Alterity in Amhara, Ethiopia." *Africa* 84, no. 2 (April 2014): 294–313.

Hoehler-Fatton, Cynthia. *Women of Fire and Spirit: History, Faith and Gender in Roho Religion in Western Kenya*. New York: Oxford University Press: 1996.

Hunt, Nancy Rose. *A Colonial Lexicon of Birth Ritual, Medicalization, and Mobility in the Congo*. Durham, NC: Duke University Press, 1999.

Huntington, Richard. *Gender and Social Structure in Madagascar*. Bloomington: Indiana University Press, 1988.

Insoll, Timothy. *The Archaeology of Islam in Sub-Saharan Africa*. New York: Cambridge University Press, 2003.

Jaovelo-Dzao, Robert. *Mythes, Rites et Transes à Madagascar: Angano, Joro et Tromba, Sakalava*. Analamahitsy: Éditions Ambozontany, 1996.

Jay, Nancy. *Throughout Your Generations and Forever: Sacrifice, Religious and Paternity*. Chicago: University of Chicago Press, 1992.

Jenkins, Philip. *The Next Christendom: The Rise of Global Christianity*. New York: Oxford University Press, 2002.

Johnson-Hanks, Jennifer. *Uncertain Honor: Modern Motherhood in an African Crisis*. Chicago: University of Chicago Press, 2005.

Jordan, Brigitte, and Robbie Davis-Floyd. *Birth in Four Cultures: A Crosscultural Investigation of Childbirth in Yucatan, Holland, Sweden, and the United States*. Prospect Heights, IL: Waveland Press, 1993.

Keim, Curtis. *Mistaking Africa: Curiosities and Inventions of the American Mind*. Boulder, CO: Westview Press, 1999.

Kéita, Aoua. *Femme d'Afrique: La vie d'Aoua Kéita racontée par elle-même*. Paris: Présence Africaine, 1975.

Keller, Eva. "The Banana Plant and the Moon: Conservation and the Malagay Ethos of Life in Masoala, Madagascar." *American Ethnologist* 35, no. 4 (November 2008): 650–664.

Kenzo, Mabiala Justin-Robert. "Religion, Hybridity, and the Construction of Reality in Postcolonial Africa." *Exchange* 33, no. 3 (January 2004): 244–268.

Kimmerer, Robin Wall. *Braiding Sweetgrass: Indigenous Wisdom, Scientific Knowledge and the Teachings of Plants*. Minneapolis: Milkweed Editions, 2013.

Klassen, Pamela. *Blessed Events: Religion and Home Birth in America*. Princeton, NJ: Princeton University Press, 2001.

Kus, Susan, and Victor Raharijaona. "Matters of Life and Death: Mortuary Rituals as Part of a Larger Whole among the Betsileo of Madagascar." *Archaeological Papers of the American Anthropological Association* 10, no. 1 (January 2001): 56–68.

Lambek, Michael. "Sacrifice and the Problem of Beginning: Meditations from Sakalava Mythopraxis." *Journal of the Royal Anthropological Institute* 13, no. 1 (March 2007): 19–38.

Lambek, Michael. "Taboo as Cultural Practice among Malagasy Speakers." *Man* 27, no. 2 (June 1992): 245–266.

Lambek, Michael. "The Value of Coins in a Sakalava Polity." *Comparative Studies in Society and History* 43, no. 4 (October 2001): 735–762.

Lambek, Michael. *The Weight of the Past: Living with History in Mahajanga, Madagascar*. New York: Palgrave Macmillan, 2003.

Lambek, Michael, and Andrew Walsh. "The Imagined Community of the Antankarana: Identity, History, and Ritual in Northern Madagascar." *Journal of Religion in Africa* 27, no. 3 (August 1997): 308–333.

Larson, Pier M. "Desperately Seeking 'the Merina' (Central Madagascar): Reading Ethnonyms and Their Semantic Fields in African Identity Histories." *Journal of Southern African Studies* 22, no. 4 (December 1996): 541–560.

La Violette, Adria. "The Swahili World." In *The Oxford Handbook of African Archaeology*, edited by Peter Mitchell and Paul Lane, 900–914. Oxford: Oxford University Press, 2013.

Leavitt, Judith. *Brought to Bed: Childbearing in America, 1750–1950*. New York: Oxford University Press, 1986.

Lee, Shih-Yu, Shunyu Yang, and Yu-O Yang, "Doing-in-Month Ritual among Chinese and Chinese-American." *Journal of Cultural Diversity* 20, no. 2 (January 2013): 94–99.

Leone, Mark, and Gladys-Marie Fry. "Conjuring in the Big House Kitchen." *Journal of American Folklore* 112, no. 445 (Summer 1999): 372–403.

Lincoln, Bruce. *Emerging from the Chrysalis: Studies in Rituals of Women's Initiation*. Cambridge, MA: Harvard University Press, 1981.

Little, Henry W. *Madagascar: Its History and People*. London: William Blackwood and Sons, 1884.

Luedke, Tracy J., and Harry G. West. Introduction to *Borders and Healers: Brokering Therapeutic Resources in Southeast Africa*, edited by Tracy J. Luedke and Harry G. West, 1–20. Bloomington: Indiana University Press, 2006.

Mack, John. "Healing Words: Becoming a Spirit-Host in Madagascar." *Anthropology and Medicine* 18, no. 2 (January 2011): 231–243.

Mauss, Marcel. *The Gift: The Form and Reason for Exchange in Archaic Societies*. Translated by W. D. Halls. London: Routledge, 1990.

Metcalf, Peter, and Richard Huntington. *Celebrations of Death: The Anthropology of Mortuary Ritual*. Cambridge: Cambridge University Press, 1991.

Meyer, Birgit. "'Praise the Lord': Popular Cinema and Pentecostalite Style in Ghana's New Public Sphere." *American Ethnologist* 31, no. 1 (January 2004): 92–110.

Middleton, Karen. *Ancestors, Power and History in Madagascar*. Leiden: Brill Academic Publishers, 1999.

Middleton, Karen. "How Karembola Men Became Mothers." In *Cultures of Relatedness: New Approaches to the Study of Kinship*, edited by Janet Carsten, 104–127. New York: Cambridge University Press, 2000.

Middleton, Karen. "Tombs, Umbilical Cords, and the Syllable Fo." In *Cultures of Madagascar: Ebb and Flow of Influences*, edited by Sandra Evers and Marc Spindler, 223–235. Leiden: International Institute for Asian Studies, 1995.

Mohan, Vik, and Tess Shellard. "Providing Family Planning Services to Remote Communities in Areas of High Biodiversity through a Population-Health-Environment Programme in Madagascar." *Reproductive Health Matters* 22, no. 14 (June 2014): 93–103.

Nicolas, Jean Pierre. *Fahasalaman'ny Fianakaviana sy Zavamaniry Fatao Fanafody aty Amin'ny Tapany Avaratr'i Madagasikara*. Quimper: Jardins du Monde, Édition Mai, 2011.

Ochs, Vanessa. *Inventing Jewish Ritual*. Philadelphia: Jewish Publication Society, 2007.

Olupona, Jacob. *African Religions: A Very Short Introduction*. New York: Oxford University Press, 2014.

Oosthuizen, G. C. *The Healer Prophet in Afro-Christian Churches*. New York: Brill, 1992.

Opoku, Kofi Asare. *West African Traditional Religion*. Singapore: FEP International Private Limited, 1978.

Osborn, Chase S., *Madagascar: Land of the Man-Eating Tree*. 1924. Reprint, Somerville, MA: Heliographic, 2012.

Paul, Annie. *Origins: How the Nine Months before Birth Shape the Rest of Our Lives*. New York: Free Press, 2008.

Pfeiffer, James. "African Independent Churches in Mozambique: Healing the Afflications on Inequality." *Medical Anthropology Quarterly* 16, no. 2 (2002): 176–199.

Piperata, Barbara Ann. "Forty Days and Forty Nights: A Biocultural Perspective on Postpartum Practices in the Amazon." *Social Science and Medicine* 67, no. 7 (May 2008): 1094–1103.

Popenoe, Rebecca. *Feeding Desire: Fatness, Beauty and Sexuality among a Saharan People.* New York: Routledge, 2004.

Quashie, Hélène, Dolorès Pourette, Olivier Rakotomalala, and Frédérique Andriamaro. "Traditional Therapeutics, Biomedicine and Maternal Health in Madagascar: Paradoxes and Power Issues around the Knowledge and Practices of Reninjaza." *Health, Culture and Society* 7, no. 1 (2014): 1–15.

Rabenoro, Mireille. "Motherhood in Malagasy Society: A Major Component in the Tradition vs. Modernity Conflict." *Jenda: A Journal of Culture and African Women Studies* 4, no. 1 (2003): 135–172.

Radimilahy, Chantal. "Madagascar: From Initial Settlement to the Growth of Kingdoms." In *The Oxford Handbook of African Archaeology*, edited by Peter Mitchell and Paul Lane, 943–956. Oxford: Oxford University Press, 2013.

Rafanomezantsoa, Roger, "The Contribution of Rainisoalambo to the Indigenization of the Protestant Churches in Madagascar." In *The Fifohazana: Madagascar's Indigenous Christian Movement*, edited by Cynthia Holder Rich, 11–26. Amherst: Cambria Press, 2008.

Rakotolahy, Christiane Rafidinarivo. "Le référent de l'esclavage dans les représentations transactionnelles marchandes à Madagascar." *Journal des Africanistes* 70, nos. 1–2 (2000): 123–144.

Rakotondramiadanirina, Marie Ignace de Loyola. "Reimagining Solidarity in Post-Colonial Madagascar: An Historical, Cultural and Theological Examination of the Concept of Fihavanana in the Malagasy Context." Thesis, Boston College, 2015.

Randrianja, Solofo, and Stephen Ellis. *A Short History of Madagascar.* London: Hurst, 2009.

Ratovoson, Céline. "La femme malgache responsable de son environnement physique et systèmes religieux." In *Centre d'information et de Documentation Scientifique et Technique.* Antananarivo: L'Académie Malgache, 1989.

Ravololomanga, Bodo. *Etre Femme et Mère à Madagascar: (Tañala d'Ifanadiana).* Paris: L'Harmattan, 1992.

Razivelo, Mariette. "Women and the Formation of a Malagasy Theology." Thesis, Wartburg Theological Seminary, 1980.

Rich, Cynthia Holder. *Indigenous Christianity in Africa.* New York: Peter Lang, 2011.

Roberts, Michelle Voss. "Religious Belonging and the Multiple." *Journal of Feminist Studies in Religion* 26, no. 1 (Spring 2010): 43–62.

Routledge, Bruce. *Archaeology and State Theory: Subjects and Objects of Power*. New York: Bloomsbury Academic, 2014.

Ruud, Jorgen. *Taboo: A Study of Malagasy Customs and Beliefs*. London: Oslo University Press, 1960.

Sandelowski, Margarete. *Pain, Pleasure and American Childbirth: From the Twilight Sleep to the Read Method*. Westport, CT: Greenwood Press, 1984.

Sargent, Carolyn. *Maternity, Medicine and Power: Reproductive Decisions in Urban Benin*. Berkeley: University of California Press, 1989.

Sharp, Lesley. *The Possessed and the Dispossessed*. Berkeley: University of California Press, 1993.

Shipton, Parker. *Bitter Money: Cultural Economy and Some African Meanings of Forbidden Economies*. Washington DC: American Anthropological Association, 1989.

Shipton, Parker. *Mortgaging the Ancestors: Ideologies of Attachment in Africa*. New Haven, CT: Yale University Press, 2009.

Silva-Leander, Sebastian. "Multiple Deprivations in Children in Madagascar." United Nations Children's Fund Briefing Note, October 2020. https://www.unicef.org/esa/media/8456/file/UNICEF-Madagascar-Summary-Note-Child-Poverty-(MODA)-Study-2020-EN.pdf.

Smith, Jonathan Z. "The Bare Facts of Ritual." *History of Religions* 20, no. 1/2 (1980): 112–127.

Spies, Eva. "Being in Relation: A Critical Appraisal of Religious Diversity and Mission Encounter in Madagascar." *Journal of Africana Religions* 7, no. 1 (2019): 62–83.

Strathern, Marilyn. *The Gender of the Gift: Problems with Women and Problems with Society in Melanesia*. Berkeley: University of California Press, 1988.

Thomas, Lynn. *Politics of the Womb: Women, Reproduction, and the State in Kenya*. Berkeley: University of California Press, 2003.

Thornton, Robert. *Healing the Exposed Being: A South African Ngoma Tradition*. Johannesburg: Wits University Press, 2018.

Tilghman, Laura. "City Livelihoods and Village Linkages: Rural-Urban Migrants in Tamatave, Madagascar." PhD diss., University of Georgia, 2014.

Tilghman, Laura. "The Dead Are Dead/Ancestors Never Die: Migrants, Rural Linkages, and Religious Change in Northeastern Madagascar." *Journal of Religion in Africa* 48, no. 4 (2020): 347–375.

Turner, Victor. *The Ritual Process: Structure and Anti-Structure*. New York: Routledge Taylor & Francis Group, 1969.

Turrittin, Jane. "Colonial Midwives and Modernizing Childbirth." In *Women in African Colonial Histories*, edited by Susan Geiger, Nakanyike Musisi, and Jean Mari Allman, 71–91. Bloomington: Indiana University Press, 2002.

Tuttleman-Kriegler, Emma. "Birth in Madagascar: The Disreputable Portrayal of Traditional Birth Attendants in Madagascar's Past and Present." Senior thesis, Tulane University, 2015. https://www.academia.edu/13906017 /Birth_in_Madagascar_The_Disreputable_Portrayal_of_Traditional_Birth _Attendants_in_Madagascars_Past_and_Present.

Tyagi, Ritu. "Rethinking Identity and Belonging: 'Mauritianness' in the Work of Ananda Devi." In *Islanded Identities: Constructions of Postcolonial Cultural Insularity*, edited by Maeve McCusker and Anthony Soares, 91–108. Leiden: Brill, 2011.

van der Geest, Sjaak. "Is There a Role for Traditional Medicine in Basic Health Services in Africa? A Plea for a Community Perspective." *Tropical Medicine and International Health* 2, no. 9 (1997): 903–911.

van Gennep, Arnold. *The Rites of Passage*. 2nd ed. Chicago: University of Chicago Press, 1960. First published in French as Les Rites de Passage in 1909.

Vassanji, M. G. *Uhuru Street: Short Stories*. Oxford: Heinemann, 1991.

von Sicard, S. "Malagasy Islam: Tracing the History." *Journal of Muslim Minority Affairs* 31, no. 1 (April 2011): 101–112.

Walsh, Andrew. "Preserving Bodies, Saving Souls: Religious Incongruity in a Northern Malagasy Mining Town." *Journal of Religion in Africa* 32, no. 3 (January 2002): 366–392.

Walsh, Andrew. "Responsibility, Taboos, and 'The Freedom to do Otherwise.'" *Journal of the Royal Anthropological Institute* 8, no. 3 (September 2002): 453.

Wertz, Richard, and Dorothy Wertz. *Lying-In: A History of Childbirth in America*. New Haven, CT: Yale University Press, 1989.

INDEX

Adeline, 126–129, 131–132, 135, 195

ady antsaboa, 46, 134. *See also* spear battle.

affiliation: childhood/affiliation of children, 15, 49, 170–171, 173, 219, 222, 229, 236, 238, 242, 254; familial and ancestral, 62, 142; religious, 24, 30, 142, 155, 167, 239; competing/multiple affiliations, 142, 149–150, 170–171, 246; patrilineal, 133, 170–171, 246; matrilineal, 150, 170–171, 246; with the University, 225

Africa/African, 3, 8, 11, 14, 21, 25, 35, 37, 39, 40, 43, 45, 47–48, 103, 107, 109, 115, 119–120, 145, 175, 177, 186, 188, 191, 206, 217, 218, 220–223, 225–226, 228–232, 235–237, 239, 241–244, 248–260, 263

Afro-Arab, 118

Alicia 41, 42, 43, 44, 48, 50, 60, 96, 197, 206

Allah, 71, 73

Ambanja, 71, 101, 122, 126, 193, 195

Ambobatany, 57

Ambatoreny, 187

Ambilobe, 2, 57–58, 146, 193, 250

Ambohitra 52

Amélie, 27, 80–88, 91–92, 97, 100, 103, 175, 195, 198–199, 233–234, 239

American(s), 2, 3, 11, 14, 25, 28, 45–46, 52–53, 55–56, 86, 98, 129–130, 135, 209–210, 218–219, 222–223, 227–228, 230–231, 234–236, 245, 247–248, 250–251, 254–257, 259

ancestor(s): and partial reincarnation, 8, 168, 204; the continuation of, 5, 7, 114, 123, 168, 174, 195, 204; and their relationship to midwives, 1, 41, 51, 53, 56, 92, 94, 96

Andersen, Margaret, 226, 251

Andry Rajoelina, 11, 33, 40, 62, 181, 187–189, 191, 194–195, 249

Anglican, 11, 182, 185, 246

Anjanahary, 125. *See also* Zanahary.

Anjoaty, 10, 88, 117–119, 123

Anjozorobe, 2

Ankarana National Park, 28, 140

Antananarivo, 36, 92, 162, 178, 182, 227, 248, 250, 258. *See also* capital.

Antandrano, 140

Antankarana, 2, 4, 6, 10, 28, 140, 167, 193, 199, 218, 231, 237, 243, 247, 250, 256

Antsiranana, viii, 9, 16, 28, 33–34, 62, 81, 87, 122, 137, 178, 195, 218, 225, 232

Antsiravibe, 28

aody be (growth medicines), 53, 84, 85, 87, 146

aomby (cows, cattle), 13, 117, 118, 140, 212

Apocalypse Church of Madagascar, 203, 221

aqiqa(s), 10, 72, 145, 157, 160, 162, 164

Arab, 11, 13, 47–48, 70, 72–74, 101, 118, 134, 145, 221

Arab Muslim, 11, 13, 70, 72, 145

arakaraka, 79, 233

ariary, 98, 100, 228, 235

Asia, 3, 10, 11, 13, 21, 103, 169, 218–219, 236–237, 242, 257

Asmara, 147–154, 172

Astuti, Rita, 108, 167, 218–220, 236, 242, 244–245, 247, 251

aunt(s), 25, 29, 58, 96, 128, 147, 148, 150, 166, 173, 175, 195, 212–213, 240

Auoa Keita, 48

Bambara, 48

baptize/baptism, 5, 10, 29, 79–80, 83, 87, 103, 114, 120, 126, 132, 135–136, 143, 145, 166, 173, 182–183, 210, 223

Bara, 48, 58, 170–171, 223, 236, 242, 258

baskets, 99, 137, 212–213

bear: as in childbearing, 5, 24–25, 28, 35, 37, 48, 118–121, 126–127, 133, 179, 226, 248, 256; as in to bear continuity with the past, 140, 169, 172, 185; a special connection to the ancestors, 7–8, 139; as in to carry, or bear the burden of, or bear witness to, x, 73, 122, 173, 175, 201, 205, 207–208, 212

Belgian, 168, 178

Bell, Catherine, 19, 223, 252

belonging, ix, 2, 4, 8, 15, 17, 20–23, 30–31, 45, 50, 62, 69, 70, 72–75, 78, 85, 102–103, 105–107, 111, 116, 124, 126, 132, 136, 143–144, 147, 155, 168, 170, 174–176, 185, 195, 198, 202, 222–223, 232, 254, 259–260

Bernadette, 1–2, 43, 48, 50–56, 60, 92, 96, 199, 204, 217, 230

Betsileo, 186–187, 256

Betsimisaraka, 5

biomedical, 41, 49, 53, 100, 102, 115, 118, 138, 202, 230

birth rituals, 1–4, 6, 10, 12, 15, 19, 20–21, 23, 28–32, 41–42, 45–50, 56, 59, 61, 68, 73, 78, 80, 83, 87, 102–103, 106–111, 115, 118, 120, 122, 124–126, 128–133, 135–136, 139, 142–145,

156, 163, 169–172, 176, 180, 182–183, 185, 195, 197, 202, 205–208, 210–212, 219, 223, 230–231, 237–238, 241, 244–247, 252, 256

black: as a social category, 151, 161–162; religious and/or material objects, 56, 79, 233

blessing(s), 2, 5, 8, 15, 19, 28–29, 40–42, 49–50, 53, 56, 58–59, 78–80, 85, 87, 91, 96, 100, 102, 104–105, 107, 111–113, 118, 122, 124–125, 129–130, 134–135, 139, 141–143, 145, 147–148, 150, 152–153, 155, 157, 161, 166–169, 173–174, 180, 186, 190, 201–202, 204, 207, 210, 211, 219, 223, 229–230, 237, 241, 244, 247, 252. *See also* tsodrano.

Bloch, Maurice, 5, 48, 111, 113, 143–144, 149, 167, 219, 229–230, 237, 241–245, 247, 252

blood, 109, 120, 140, 141, 160, 170–171, 240, 246

Bobaomby, 117–118

Bobo, 48

body, 2, 14, 18–19, 28–29, 31, 45, 103, 105, 108, 109–110, 115, 121–122, 130, 132–133, 135–136, 138, 141, 153, 171, 204, 207, 223, 240, 242, 245–246, 253

bone filled/bone-filled, x, 12, 74, 101, 138, 141, 145, 166, 171, 172

bones: as physical objects, 8, 22, 29, 40, 142, 213, 216, 222; instilling/acquiring bones, 3–4, 31, 45, 59, 69, 80, 101, 104, 139, 142–145, 150, 157, 170–172, 174, 176, 243; and belonging, ix, 3–4, 17, 23, 30, 50, 80, 139, 152, 155, 168, 170–172, 174, 208, 212; as a metaphor for that which endures, 3–4, 17, 23, 30–31, 139–140, 150, 155, 215; of ancestors, 8, 40, 140, 142; of babies, 3–4, 7, 22, 137–139, 141–145, 150, 216, 242; in relationship to teeth and social hardening/shaping, 7, 29, 141,168; related to healing and bonesetters, 93, 102

bori, 51, 52, 120, 186, 188

breast milk, 47, 107, 109, 213

breastfeed, 27, 53, 81, 126

British, 10, 38, 94, 221, 223

burial, 8, 99, 172, 223, 238, 242

Bynum, Caroline Walker, 241, 253

Cadère, Abdel, 195, 250

calling, 6, 43, 51, 56, 82, 96, 188

Camellia, 88, 91–92, 97, 122–126, 128–129, 132, 135–136, 195, 198–199, 234, 239–240

Cameroon/Cameroonian, 23

Campbell, Gwyn, 121, 239, 253

Cap Diégo, 12, 14, 30–32, 35–37, 40, 42–44, 52, 100, 122, 144, 155–156, 162, 175, 178, 182, 203, 206–207, 228, 234

capital: of Madagascar, 14, 36, 40, 92, 162, 178–179, 182, 203, 227, 248; of the northern most province of Madagascar, 12; social, 22, 104, 156. *See also* Antananarivo.

capitalistic/m/capitalist, 94, 96, 234

Catholic, 10, 24, 83, 87–88, 103, 126, 186, 210, 221, 233

cattle, 87, 184, 207, 212. *See also* aomby.

Céline, 74–80, 102–103, 191, 195, 233, 250, 258

central highlands, 4, 6, 10, 15, 34, 112, 143, 157, 187, 230–231, 245, 247

chains, 170

charismatic: forms of Christianity, 10, 31–32, 176–179, 185–186, 188, 191–192, 197, 203, 205, 207, 221. *See also* Pentecostal.

chicken leg, 78, 79, 96, 127, 149, 153, 234

childbirth, 19, 25–26, 28, 30, 35–40, 43, 45–50, 56–57, 59–61, 65, 68, 78, 80, 82, 84, 86, 106–109, 111, 114, 117–118, 120, 124–125, 132–135, 144, 150, 169, 195–196, 201–202, 205, 210, 219, 222–223, 225–231, 234, 236, 238, 241–242, 244–246, 248, 253–255, 259–260

Chinese, 3, 86, 169, 236, 256

Christianity, 10, 31–32, 120, 176–179, 186–188, 191, 199, 205–207, 248–250, 254–255, 258

Christian(s), 3, 10–11, 15, 24, 28, 31–32, 71, 78–80, 96, 103, 119–120, 139, 154, 156–157, 163, 166, 176–179, 186–188, 191, 194, 199, 204–207, 210, 221, 233, 235, 239–240, 248–250, 254–255, 257–258

church, x, 10–11, 19, 29, 83, 99, 126, 155–156, 174, 177, 182, 184–186, 188–189, 191–192, 194, 201, 203–205, 210, 221, 230, 232, 240, 246, 249–250, 257–258

churchyard, 155, 189

circumcision, 5, 46–47, 49, 111–113, 118, 132–134, 145, 152, 163, 173, 194, 210, 219, 228–229, 237, 244, 252

clay(s), 1, 53, 217

coastal, 28, 33–35, 40, 113, 122, 162, 178, 205, 213, 221, 225, 242, 247

coin(s), 1, 53, 88, 94, 113, 148, 169, 217, 256

cold–water bathing, 5, 19, 30, 72, 78, 105, 109, 114–117, 143, 171, 197, 231, 238, 247

Cole, Jennifer, 5, 98, 120, 124, 177, 219, 230, 233, 235, 239–240, 243–245, 248, 253

colonial(ism): medicine, 35, 37–40, 65, 226, 229, 236, 238, 246–249, 251, 255, 260; interventions (economic, political, cultural, religious), 22–23, 49, 87, 96, 168, 175, 178, 199, 218–219, 224, 230, 233, 235, 239–240, 245, 248, 250–251, 253, 255; in the academy, 29; during the period of, 52, 62, 194, 201; post–, 142, 145, 222–223, 256, 258; neo–, 22, 178. *See also* medicine.

colonization, 10, 193

communion, 29

community: importance of religious, x, 7, 32, 71–74, 102, 111, 139, 157, 160–161, 163, 186–187, 194–195, 206; the importance of lineage–based or ancestral, 5, 7, 9, 19, 21, 45, 50, 74, 85, 92, 102, 111, 121, 136, 139, 144–145, 167, 177, 194, 205, 216

Comorian, 72, 157, 161–163

Comorian Muslims, 157, 161–163

confluence(s), 21, 30, 59, 68–69, 81, 101, 103, 232

Congo, 39, 168, 178, 226, 233, 236, 238, 246, 248, 255

Congolese, 168, 178, 238

conversion, 11, 119, 172, 186–187

Corpus Christi, 28

countryside, 23, 49, 76, 147, 154–156, 185, 248

couvade, 110

cross–fertilization, 17, 207

custom(s): religious and ancestral, 6, 11–12, 14, 16, 18, 20, 22, 24, 30–31, 35, 38, 41–43, 45, 50, 53–54, 56–59, 61, 70, 72, 74–75, 79–80, 82–85, 94, 97, 103–106, 108, 110–111, 113–120, 122, 125–126, 131, 133, 135, 139, 142, 144–147, 149, 151–152, 154, 160, 167–173, 177–186, 195, 197–200, 202–203, 206, 219, 225, 231, 233, 238–239, 247–248, 253, 259

Dahl, Oyvind, ix, 92–93, 234, 253

Dar es Salam, 20–21, 52, 101

Datoga, 108, 236, 238, 252

Davis–Floyd, Robbie, 18, 45–46, 223, 228, 254–255

dead: as in the dead, 2–3 7–8, 27, 85, 93, 107, 150, 174, 178, 187, 212, 218, 220, 222, 241, 243, 248, 252, 259; babies, 99, 137, 212

death: responses to, 2; of infants and children, 99–100, 135, 174, 196; as a life stage, 3, 5, 9, 12, 19, 135, 142, 144, 147, 171, 20:, 206, 208, 219–220, 237, 244, 247, 252, 256, 257; activities that risk and/or bring people close to death, 48, 83, 114, 118, 134, 238

demon/demonic/devil/devoly, 1, 11, 19, 30, 69–70, 79–80, 101, 104, 110–111, 132, 134, 138, 143, 147, 150, 152, 172–173, 181, 188–189, 192–194, 195–196, 198, 230

Diégo Suarez, 3–5, 11–16, 20–26, 28, 30, 32–37, 40, 42, 43–44, 49, 51–52, 57, 62–64, 66, 68, 80, 84, 86–87, 97, 101, 112, 114, 127, 130, 137, 140, 163, 175, 195, 207, 218, 221–222, 224–225, 228, 231

Diola, 48

Dispensaire, 36–37, 42, 114, 129, 240

dispensary: medical, 34, 42, 50, 53–54, 97, 235

doctor(s), vii, 19, 27, 36, 47, 49, 53, 55–56, 59–60, 77, 97, 103, 114, 117, 131, 195–196, 201, 225, 241

domestic: rituals, 6, 54, 112–113, 146, 179; labor, 121; realm 146; as opposed to international, 197

East Africa/East Africans, 3, 8, 35, 45, 103, 119, 145, 175, 217, 225, 252

eating: in ritual contexts, 106, 133, 149, 161, 163; as part of lineage–based, 76, 80, 123, 146, 151, 192, 194, 250

economic: diversity, 12, 14–16; hub, 13; depression, decline or instability, 14, 35, 40, 76; circumstances or decision–making based on, 39, 50, 59, 86, 101, 156, 175, 245, 251; opportunity and/or success, 170, 199

Édith, 9–10, 27, 52, 57, 79, 94, 115, 127–130,

161, 233

English: language, viii, 22–23, 27, 33, 42, 98, 161, 221, 224–225, 232

Episcopal, 185, 210

Ethiopia, 119–120, 236, 255

ethnicity, 17, 116, 162–163, 218, 239, 245, 251

ethnography, 20, 24, 26, 224, 239, 254

Europeans, 25, 35, 38, 61, 88, 197, 218

evangelical/evangelism/evangelist, 11, 83, 249

exhumation, 2, 6, 104

exorcised/exorcism, 177, 186, 194, 210

fady (taboo(s)), 3–6, 24, 30–31, 46, 56, 61, 76, 78, 85, 91, 100, 103, 105, 110–111, 114, 116, 122–126, 128, 132–134, 136, 138, 140–141, 143, 146, 151, 167, 171–173, 180–181, 192, 194, 198, 202, 239, 243, 250. See also taboo.

fahasalamana (health), 52, 101. See also health.

famadihana, 2, 6, 8, 112, 219, 245, 255. See also exhumation.

fameno, 1, 53, 56, 217

fanafody (medicine), 1, 85, 92, 187, 189, 232, 257

fanafody–gasy, 187, 189

fathers, 23, 29, 84, 110, 154, 168–169, 173, 178, 184, 229, 246

Feeley–Harnik, Gillian, 7, 15, 113, 118, 144, 169, 172, 178, 219, 222, 228–231, 235–238, 241–242, 244–245, 247–248, 250, 254

Feldman–Savelsberg, Pamela, 21, 23, 223–224, 254

Fiangonana Loterana Malagasy (FLM), 188, 230

Fiangonan'i Jesoa Kristy eto Madagasikara (FJKM), 99, 155, 188, 246

Fifohazana, 186, 188, 191, 248–250, 255, 258

fihavanana, 22, 93, 168, 221, 223, 258

Fita, 27, 186, 188–189

Fitahiana, 27

fomba (customs): 6, 11, 24, 31, 57–58, 79, 82–83, 91, 100, 105, 114–116, 120, 138–139, 146–147, 151–152, 155–156, 166–168, 170, 179–182, 184–185, 191, 198, 233, 239, 244; fomba fiterana (birthing customs), 57, 244; fombagasy (Malagasy customs), 58, 83, 151–152, 179, 181, 184, 239; fombandrazana (ancestral customs), 11, 116, 139, 146–147, 155–156, 166, 168, 170, 191, 233, 239

food: growing, 5, 175, 194; eaten in ceremonies, 14, 106–109, 139, 145–146, 149–150, 153, 160, 166, 170; related to pregnancy and/or lineage customs, 6, 53, 69, 76, 78, 80, 105, 107, 111, 123, 125, 128, 133, 146, 154, 166, 170, 197, 209, 233, 239

foreigners, 13, 24–25, 130, 137, 194, 241. *See also* vazaha.

France, 25, 36, 38, 60, 179, 183

Françoise, 57–59, 86, 231

Fred, 93–96, 102

French: language, 23, 161, 224, 235, 240, 242, 260; people, 3, 25, 37–38, 60, 87, 96, 199; government or settlement, 10, 38, 49, 52, 54, 87, 178, 194, 218, 226, 243, 251

funerary rituals/customs/gatherings, 6, 8, 11, 146

gang(s), 14, 44

gender/ gender norms, 8, 17, 20, 25, 93, 104, 141, 161, 193, 218, 224, 236–237, 242–244, 247, 250–251, 255, 259

Genevie, 147, 148, 150–152, 172, 195, 246

Germany, 23, 38

gift giving, 21–22, 48, 92, 94–97, 135, 149, 170, 196, 203–204, 246

gift(s), ix, 21–22, 47–48, 51, 54–56, 74, 87, 91–97, 108, 113, 135, 149, 170, 193, 203–204, 207, 210, 223, 233–234, 237, 241, 246, 257, 259

God(s), 15, 24, 29, 41, 71–72, 79–80, 100, 122, 125, 151, 156, 163, 167, 173, 181–182, 198, 204–205, 208, 221–222, 230, 247, 254. *See also* Allah, Zanahary and Anjanahary.

Gottlieb, Alma, 19, 20, 220, 223, 239, 255

government: sponsored medical clinics/ initiatives, 34, 36, 42, 54, 59, 86, 97, 197, 201, 230; French colonial, 37, 178; U.S., 55; move towards neoliberalism, 23; in Sierra Leone, 225

grandfather(s), 9, 10, 27, 80, 153–154, 169, 219

grandmother(s), 43, 51, 57–58, 70, 83, 110, 124–125, 128–130, 136, 151–153, 173, 192–194, 209, 240

grandparents, 7, 27, 29, 55, 83, 166, 185, 195

grow/growth/growing: growing up, ix, 16, 18, 70, 79, 100, 205, 211; food crops, x, 5, 82, 194, 235; growing babies, 1, 7–8, 40, 49–50, 53, 79, 84, 110, 124, 134, 138, 141, 166–167, 172–173, 195, 197, 208; growth of Christianity/Pentecostalism, 10, 31–32, 177, 188, 205; population growth, 38–40; growing number of specialist, 96. *See also* aody be (growth medicines).

haircutting, x, 2–5, 7, 10, 15, 19, 28, 31, 47–50, 72–73, 82, 87, 103, 106, 112, 125, 132, 136, 139, 142–152, 154–155, 157–158, 160–163, 166–169, 171–173, 194, 197, 202, 229, 233, 243, 245–246

Hakim, 157, 160, 161–162, 164

Halvorson, Brit, 204, 249–250, 255

Hannig, Anita, 119–120, 236, 239, 255

hasina, 1, 2, 5–6, 53, 94–95, 102, 112–113, 167, 175, 177, 204, 217

hasin-tanana, 22, 94–95, 223

healer–diviner(s), 41, 47–48, 85, 94–95, 102, 180–181, 186–187, 191, 195, 198, 203, 223, 227, 243. *See also* mpisikidy.

healing, 1, 6, 70, 92, 94, 102–103, 107, 118, 124, 129, 168, 186–189, 192, 194–195, 197, 199, 202, 205, 227, 230, 232–233, 235–236, 238, 249–250, 252, 254–255, 257–259

health, 34–39, 45, 53, 55, 60–62, 68, 86, 91, 96–97, 101–104, 109, 114, 118, 125, 178, 184, 187, 195, 202, 204–205, 225, 227, 230–232, 245, 251–254, 257–258, 260

healthcare systems, 45, 101, 205

heirloom, 8–9, 139, 145, 150, 152, 154, 166–167, 169, 213

Hélène, 61, 227, 231, 258

herbal medicines, 43, 56, 92, 109, 135, 191, 195, 197

herbalist, 180–181, 191, 195

highlands, 4, 6, 10, 15, 34, 112, 114, 143, 157, 187, 230–231, 245, 247 hijab, 74, 160–161

holistic, 53, 57, 61, 101, 201

Holy Spirit, 188, 192, 204–205

Hôpital Be, 36–37, 43, 62, 77, 86, 99, 124, 128, 232, 235

Hopitaly Manarapenitra, 62, 65, 231

hospital, 12, 14, 33–37, 43, 46, 49, 54, 58–59, 62, 77, 79, 86, 92, 94, 97, 114–115, 118, 128, 169, 196, 199, 201, 210, 225, 231, 241

hot–water bathing, 114, 118–119

Hunt, Nancy Rose, 6, 38, 168, 178, 226, 236, 238, 246–248, 255

Huntington, Richard, 170, 223–224, 242–244, 247, 255, 257

Hussein, 88, 91–93, 96, 102, 199, 204

hybrid/hybridity/hybridized, 3–4, 13, 17–18, 29, 74, 80, 103, 157, 222, 256

identity: with regard to belonging, ix, 2, 17, 20–21, 29, 116, 122, 132, 136, 147, 154–155, 167, 185, 195, 223, 232, 260; with regard to infants and children, 2, 3, 19, 29, 80, 103–104, 109, 125, 141, 143–144, 147, 157, 160, 167, 195; of mothers, 2, 109, 122, 125, 147; religious, ix, 10, 80, 103, 162–163, 251; lineage–based, 80, 93, 103, 109, 125, 141, 143–144, 167, 183, 247; national, 113; ethnic, 4, 17, 218, 237–239, 243, 245, 256

illness: spiritual and biomedical, 14, 41, 59, 100, 114–115, 138, 140, 142, 188, 194, 238, 249

Imerina, 4, 33

indebtedness: social, 21, 30, 35, 56, 93, 95, 104, 204

independent: churches, 10, 191, 197, 258

Indian Ocean, 3, 12, 15, 20–21, 39, 175, 206, 217, 239, 252–253

indigenous: religions, 10–11, 24, 91, 103, 185, 191, 194, 199, 233, 234, 241, 258; to the land, to a place, 4, 15, 37, 169, 178; Christian healing movement (Fifohazana), 186–187, 191, 194, 248–250, 258; with regard to birthing customs and personnel, 52

Indo–Pakistani, 13, 162

infants, 7, 12, 19, 38, 105, 119, 123, 132, 138–139, 143, 145, 204, 237, 242

insecurity: reproductive, 23; existential, 30, 35, 41, 44, 56; economic, 35, 41, 56

instability: political, 14, 30, 35, 62

interfaith, 15, 157

invocation, 41, 79, 104–105, 112

Islam, 10, 12, 56, 71–73, 120, 145, 163, 199, 220–221, 233, 250, 255, 260

Jacqueline, 147, 151, 152, 172, 177, 186, 191–194, 198, 204, 228, 250

Jaovelo–Dzao, Robert, 219–221, 227, 255

Jesus, 19, 99, 187–189, 205, 246

jewel(s): heirloom and/or related to ancestors, 8, 13, 139–140, 145, 150, 166–167, 213

Joffreville, 1, 42, 51–52, 54, 56

joro, 7, 41, 79, 84, 91, 105, 112, 125, 128–130, 132, 135, 139, 142, 144–145, 147–148, 153, 161, 166, 169, 219, 227, 255. See also speech–prayer.

Joseph Gallieni, 37–38

kaolin, 1, 217

karazana (kindedness), 4, 123

Karembola, 108, 237, 245–246, 257

Kassonke, 48

kin: maternal kin, 108, 118, 142, 170–171, 173, 229, 245; paternal, 31, 105, 110, 117–118, 142, 150, 170–171, 173, 229; as in relatives, collective/extended kin, and kinship networks, 45, 110–112, 154, 172–177, 219, 232, 237, 242–245, 252, 257; kin–based obligations, 31, 69, 105, 108, 111, 117; creating links with, 142; and identity, 143

king: and the royal bath 112; of the Antankarana, 193, 250

kingdom: Merina, 33, 177, 225; Malagasy, 221, 258

kisaly, 148

Klassen, Pamela, 19, 46, 50, 223, 228, 231, 234, 256

knives, 47, 163, 169

Lake Anivorano, 140

lamaka, 28, 125, 149, 153, 161, 240

lamba, 49, 79, 88, 95, 117, 125, 137, 148, 169, 213, 240–242, 254–255

Lambek, Michael, 4, 118, 140, 167, 171, 217–220, 227–228, 234, 236–238, 241, 243–245, 247, 251, 256

land: ancestral, 5–7, 9, 23, 31, 39–40, 54, 95, 110, 141–142, 146, 156–157, 167–169, 175–178, 185, 194, 200–201, 243; related to indigeneity, 4, 95, 178; related to protection and/or conservation, 39, 141, 220, 243, 255

landowners, 3, 243

landscape(s): of birth, 30; of poverty and medical scarcity, 85; religious, v, 32, 35, 175–176, 192, 205, 207, 248; fertile, 100, 141; of the city (Diégo Suarez), 155, 207; of human stories, 207; urban, 212

libeli, 168

liminal/liminality, 7, 48, 133–134, 166, 241, 253

Lincoln, Bruce, 133, 134, 210, 226, 241, 251, 256

lineage, 2, 3, 5, 17, 23, 28, 30–31, 47, 81, 83, 85, 88, 100–101, 103, 110, 114, 116, 120–121, 125–126, 132, 136, 142, 144–146, 150, 154, 156, 167, 169, 171–173, 176–177, 202, 208, 229, 231, 236, 239

lolo (ghosts), 48, 107, 219, 229, 236, 258

London Missionary Society (LMS), 169, 187, 246, 249

loss: related to ancestors, 9, 12; related to losing infants and children, 99, 101, 138, 174, 201, 212–213, 215–216; reproductive, 100–101, 211; as a result of changing times, 106, 168, 201; of self, 210; of traditional knowledge, 196, 198; of blood, 246

Luedke, Tracy, 45, 228, 231–232, 257

Lutheran, 52, 188, 192, 194, 205, 230, 246, 249

Madame Serafina, 16, 243

mage, 11, 55, 60, 88, 108, 134, 181, 199, 212

Mahajanga, 140, 146, 219, 227, 238, 243, 256

Mahavavy, 140–141, 243

Mailhol, André, 11, 203–204, 221

maishetani, 186

maiz–maizana, 154

malaria, 14, 38

Malinke, 48

mampiboaka tsaiky (infant outing ceremony), 78, 125, 136

mampiravaka tsaiky (to be jewel the child), 139, 145, 233

mangadoso fagneva (haircutting), 139. See also haircutting.

Marc Ravalomanana, 33, 40

Marie, 177–185, 195, 198, 199, 204, 248

Marie Stopes International, 39

marriage, 12, 15, 108, 142–143, 146, 162, 174, 180–181, 184–185, 243

hasin–tanana, 22, 94–95, 223, 234

Masoala National Park, 39

massage–healer, 22. See also mpanindry.

maternal: health outcomes, 35, 38, 44–45, 225–227, 229–230, 258; kin and lines of descent, 9, 49, 78, 83, 108, 116, 118, 141–142, 145, 150–152, 172–173, 175, 236, 240, 246

maternity ward(s), 34, 36–37

matri–/matrilineal, 31, 81, 110, 120, 245

matron(s), 41, 51. See also midwife, renin-jaza, mpampivelona and sage-femmes.

Mauritian, 21, 74, 223, 232, 260

Mauritius, 21, 36

Mauss, Marcel, 22, 95, 223, 234, 257

medical: clinics and infrastructure, 24, 34, 35–38, 40–43, 46, 49–50, 53, 55, 60, 68, 77, 196–198, 202, 207, 225, 235; resources and support, 17, 22, 30, 35, 41–43, 55, 59–60, 62, 69, 77, 87, 97; personnel and specialists, 24, 35–36, 39, 41–43, 45, 48, 53, 55, 58–59, 62, 68, 87, 96–97, 101, 123, 145, 195, 230, 240; scarcity or lack of, 41, 45, 55, 85, 100, 225

medicalization: of childbirth, 30, 35–39, 54, 57 226, 236, 246, 248, 255

medicine: ancestral, traditional and herbal, 1, 19, 31, 43, 53, 56, 59, 84–86, 92, 95, 103, 109, 135, 146, 175, 178, 187, 189, 191, 195, 197, 210, 216–217, 227, 232, 236, 257, 260; colonial, 40, 65, 226; access to, 14, 35–36, 86, 97, 169, 197, 232, 251, 253, 258; biomedicine, 52, 54–55, 102, 169, 175, 196–197, 202, 213, 216, 226–227, 236, 238, 253, 258–259

mediumship, 186

meeta, 108

Merina/Imerina, 3–4, 6, 10, 33, 37, 49, 54, 95, 111–113, 140, 162, 177, 187, 199, 218–219, 225, 229, 231, 237–238, 244, 249, 252, 256. *See also* Imerina.

mermaid(s), 13, 140, 206

metida, 108, 236, 252

Middle East, 3, 12, 21, 48, 103, 178, 220, 225, 245, 248, 257

Middleton, Karen, 7, 108, 110, 177, 218–220, 237, 245–246, 248, 253, 257

midwife/midwifery, 1, 28, 36, 41–44, 48, 50–53, 55–60, 73, 86, 92, 94, 96, 101–102, 118, 124–125, 129, 196–197, 206, 209, 223, 230, 236, 240. *See also* matron, sages–femmes, mpampivelona, and renin–jaza.

migrant(s)/immigrants, 10, 13–16, 23, 155, 162, 199, 213, 220, 243, 248, 259

mijoro, 169

milk, 47, 57, 107–109, 123, 125, 147, 160, 163, 169, 213, 234, 241, 256

miscarriage, 23, 60, 100, 210, 212

missionaries, 10–11, 25, 91, 187, 193–194, 199, 221, 249

moasy, 56, 95, 140, 180–181

mock battles, 48–49, 245

modern: as in medicine, 33, 38, 55, 102, 196–197, 229, 260; as in updated or contemporary and/or related to modernity, 113, 146, 154, 157, 168–169, 178, 185, 198, 226, 232, 236, 248, 255, 258

Montagne D'Ambre National Parc, 1, 52, 140

moon: importance of, 113, 147, 217, 222, 227, 247, 255

Morandava, 180–181

mortality rate: related to mothers and infants, 14, 35, 38, 44, 106, 225, 226

mortuary: as in rituals, 171, 213, 247, 256–257

motherhood, v, ix, 21, 25–26, 28, 31, 60, 68–69, 73–74, 81, 86, 107, 110, 116, 122, 124, 130–135, 150–152, 160, 179, 183, 210, 211–212, 226, 232, 236, 241, 255, 258

mothers, v, ix, x, 2, 8, 10, 12, 14–16, 18–32, 35, 38–39, 41–43, 47–54, 56–62, 65, 68–71, 73–74, 78, 80–87, 92, 96–111, 114–117, 119–120, 122–126, 128–136, 141–142, 144, 146–147,

149–153, 155–156, 160, 162, 166, 168–171, 173, 175–176, 178–180, 182–184, 192–199, 201–202, 204, 207–213, 216, 219, 221, 223–226, 229, 232–234, 236–237, 240–241, 243, 245, 246–247, 254–255, 257–258

mpampivelona, 41, 51. See also matron, midwife, renin–jaza and sages–femmes.

mpanindry, 86, 95. *See also* massage–healer.

mpiandry, 11, 187–189, 191, 194–195, 249. See also shepherd–healer.

mpijoro, 41, 112, 142, 227

mpisikidy, 94, 186, 223, 243. *See also* healer–diviner.

Muslims, 3, 10–12, 70, 79, 119–120, 139, 157, 160–163, 206–207, 240

Nadima, 106, 115, 117–120, 236, 238

naming ceremonies, 5, 19, 29, 38, 78, 80, 143, 145

Nasreen, 69–74, 102, 160–161, 163, 195, 232

neocolonial, 22, 178

neoliberal, 23, 62, 65, 145, 193, 232

newborn/newly born, 3, 10, 20, 29, 102–103, 131, 139, 160, 213, 233, 242/2–3, 7–9, 12, 20, 27, 30, 38, 41, 49, 53, 69, 73, 104, 107, 145, 160, 166–167, 173, 200–201, 204, 206, 209, 211–212

Noémi, 188–189

nonaffiliated: religiously nonaffiliated, 10, 139

North American(s): cultural practices, 2, 234; as in the people, 25, 135; as in the place, 38. *See also*, Americans.

northern Madagascar, iii, 1, 3, 5, 7, 10, 12–13, 15–17, 21, 24, 30, 45, 54–55, 57, 87, 105, 118, 120–121, 139–140, 157, 161–162, 171, 173, 178, 199, 205, 207, 212, 218–219, 222, 228, 231–232, 236–239, 242–243, 245–247, 250, 253–254, 256, 260

northwestern Madagascar, 2, 7, 10, 12–13, 207, 221, 242, 254

Nosy Be, 10–11, 87–88, 91, 102–104, 112, 137, 140, 147, 155, 198, 234

Nosy Lonjo, 11, 87–89, 91, 102–104, 112, 137, 140, 155, 198, 234

nurse, 36–37, 49–50, 59, 81, 118, 124, 179, 183,
    197, 201, 240
ny fitohy raza, (the ancestor's continuation)
    5, 7, 123, 168, 174

Orthodox(y): as in Christian, 119–120, 163
Osman, 161

Pain du Sucre, 87
Paris, 74, 184, 219, 225–226, 236, 244, 246,
    254, 256, 258
partial reincarnation, 8, 204
paternal: as in relatives and lines of descent,
    31, 49, 83, 105, 110, 117–118, 142, 145, 147–
    148, 150, 152–154, 170–171, 173, 175, 198, 223,
    229, 234, 236, 242, 244, 246
patri–/patrilineal, 9, 120, 133, 142–143, 245
Pentecostal(s)/Pentecostalism, 10–11, 24, 31,
    176–177, 179, 185–186, 188, 191, 197, 203–205,
    207, 250, 254. See also charismatic.
Peul, 48
pirates, 13
placenta(s), 77, 103, 108, 110, 124, 142, 146, 211
pluralism, 2–3, 17, 31–32, 45, 55, 139, 146, 202,
    205, 207
pluralistic, 3, 17, 80, 144, 156–157, 163, 174, 195
politics/political: tensions between
    highlanders and coastal groups, 33, 35,
    40, 113, 140, 178, 225; instability, 14, 30,
    50, 63; corruption, 65, 203; of healing
    and religious experience, 244, 249–250,
    252, 255; of the womb, 54, 259; and the
    authoritarian gaze, 54; agendas, 35, 38, 40,
    113, 199
poor/poverty, 14, 45, 72, 81, 92, 160, 169, 199,
    234/2, 14, 17, 22, 30, 39, 44–45, 61, 68, 85, 91,
    100–101, 201, 203–204, 222, 225, 259
Popenoe, Rebecca, 108, 236–237, 258
Portuguese, 3, 12–13, 218
postpartum: rituals (including bathing), 5,
    19, 30, 56, 61, 69, 72–73, 78, 80, 83, 85, 87,
    103, 107–111, 114–116, 118, 120, 122, 125–126,
    130–133, 135–136, 171–173, 231, 238, 247;
    practices and customs, 31, 53, 106, 114–115,
    143, 236, 258; time period following birth,

43, 49, 82, 87, 111, 122, 126, 166, 170, 236,
    246; rest and seclusion, 105–108, 133, 236,
    240, 255; care that mothers receive, 107,
    110, 130, 172; mothers in Ethiopia, 119
pregnancy/pregnant, 5, 19, 21, 23, 26, 28, 40,
    46, 56, 59, 61, 69, 71, 75–78, 82, 85–87, 103,
    108, 110–111, 117, 122–128, 130–132, 146–147,
    149, 166–167, 171–173, 179, 183–184, 195,
    209, 234, 241
procreate/procreative, 19, 46, 50
pronatalist/pronatalism, 37, 226, 251/226,
    251
prophet, 72–73, 161, 189, 191, 235, 250, 255, 257
Protestant, 2, 10, 24, 28, 185–188, 221, 235, 246,
    249, 258

queen Ranavalona II, 95, 249

Rabenoro, Mireille, 106, 226, 236, 241, 258
Rabo, 147–149, 169
race, 29, 35, 37–39, 61, 78–79, 131, 142, 188, 191,
    212, 225, 233
racial: policies, 37; hierarchies, 38, 49, 162,
    225, 228; categories, 20; pride, 162
Rainisoalambo, Dada, 186–187, 249, 258
Rajoelina, Andry, 33–34, 40, 62
Ramena, 137, 215
ranginaly, 5, 30, 72–73, 78, 80, 102–103, 105,
    109, 111, 114–120, 122, 124–125, 129, 135, 136,
    143, 171, 173, 183, 231, 233, 238, 247
rano, x, 4, 7, 12, 22, 33, 111, 123, 128, 137–140,
    167, 169, 213, 220, 242. See also water.
Ravalomanana, Marc, 33, 40
ravintsôha, 43, 72, 78, 109, 115, 125, 129, 240
Ravololomanga, Bodo, 219, 229, 236, 258
raza/razana, viii, 4, 6, 7, 11, 40, 116, 123, 125,
    139, 146–148, 155–156, 166–170, 174–175,
    185, 191, 219, 221, 232, 233, 239, 253. See also
    ancestors.
reciprocity: the importance of, 17, 21, 30, 35,
    56, 69, 93, 103, 168, 221; between mothers
    and midwives, 22, 30, 35, 56, 92, 96, 143;
    with other kinds of religious and medical
    specialists, 95–96, 204; between people
    and ancestors, 53, 95, 104

relics: from birth, 7; from the ancestral past, 114, 197, 199, 200, 231

renin–jaza, 41, 50–51, 53–54, 57–59, 196, 240. See also midwife, matron, and mpampivelona.

reproduction/reproductive, 21, 23, 38–39, 65, 110, 168, 195, 227, 257, 259

rice: farming, 5; as an offering to ancestors, 11, 87–88, 95; as a staple food, 16, 206; as a gift of payment to midwives, 22, 94, 96; as part of special food given to mothers, 76, 107; in ceremonies, 125, 147, 149, 153–154, 160–161, 163, 234; as chicken food, 127; mofogasy, 138; sorting, 160

Rich, Cynthia Holder, 191, 248, 249, 250, 258

ritualized/ritualizing: forms of care, 12; worlds, 18; birth, 19, 45; haircuttings and first outings, 50, 105; blessings and speeches, 79, 139, 169. See also birth ritual(s).

Roland, 74–80, 102–103, 233

rôm–patsa, 47–48, 135, 241

rômba, 43, 72, 82, 115, 129, 232

root(s): relating to children and ancestors, 7, 40, 81, 101, 108, 143, 155, 237

rova, viii, 57, 95

royal/royalty, 2, 5–7, 10, 22, 28, 87, 95, 111–114, 156, 187, 217, 219, 229–231, 237, 239, 241, 243, 247, 252, 256, 260

royal bath, 5–6, 87, 95, 111–114, 156, 230–231, 237, 247, 252

rural, 23, 28, 40, 42, 152, 154, 157, 185, 220–221, 228, 248, 251–252, 259

Russia, 70, 203, 250

Ruud, Jorgen, 218–219, 259

sabeda, 76, 125, 147–149

sacred: places, 3, 11, 13, 88, 102–103, 112, 137, 140, 155, 218; knowledge, wisdom (ancestral or otherwise), 181, 202; objects, actions, moments, meals, 29, 83, 135, 163, 167, 169, 217; thresholds, 56; journeys, 68; value or power, 94, 141, 175–177, 201; person, 103; theories of, 246–247

sacrifice: rituals of, 6–8, 41, 145–146, 162–163, 219–220, 228, 230, 233–234, 239, 241,

244–245, 253, 255; that women make, 140–141, 248

sages–femmes, 41, 51, 55, 59. See also midwife, renin–jaza, matron, and mpampivelona.

Saharan, 108, 221, 236, 255, 258

Sakalava, 6–7, 10, 38, 116, 118–119, 123, 156, 169, 186, 199, 217–219, 227, 229, 231, 235, 238, 241, 255–256

salovana, 148, 153

Samo, 48, 128, 222

Sampan'asa Loterana Momba ny Fahasalamana (SALFA), 52, 230

sampy, 187, 249

Sarakole, 48

scissors, 47, 153–154, 160, 162–163, 169

semen, 52, 85, 170

Sera, 16, 172, 243

Sere, 48

sex work/sex workers, 7, 121, 209, 218, 243, 243–244

Sharp, Lesley, 47, 101, 116, 118, 193, 202, 219–220, 227, 235, 238, 242, 245, 247, 250, 259

shepherd–healer, 11, 118, 190, 249. See also mpiandry.

shepherd–healing, 186, 189, 192, 194, 205

Shipton, Parker, 175, 220, 235, 248, 259

Silamo, 119, 156, 172, 239

slave/slavery, 10, 12, 96, 121–122, 178, 199, 201, 225, 235, 239, 253

social: worlds, networks and ties (of babies and children), 2–3, 12, 15, 18, 20–21, 68, 92, 101–102, 106, 146, 170, 174; and spiritual awareness, 20; capital, status and worth (of babies and children), 19, 22–23, 31, 53, 59, 104, 119, 139, 155–156, 179; resources and support, 14, 15, 22–23, 30, 35, 45, 59, 70, 82, 85, 87, 97, 101, 103, 176, 178, 185, 189, 242, 255; norms, 8, 15, 46, 179; hardening/fixity, 139, 143–144, 155, 170–171

socializing, 19–20

Sonrai, 48

Southeast Asians, 3

spear battle: as a description of childbirth, 45–50, 60, 65, 134, 201, 228–229 spears: as religious instruments, 47, 49, 163

specialists: religious and medical, 2, 21, 22, 35–36, 40–41, 45, 54–56, 58–59, 68, 87, 92, 94–97, 102, 175, 177–178, 195–196, 198–199, 202–204

speech–prayer, 7, 79, 105. *See also* joro.

Spies, Eva, 17, 222, 259

spirit medium(s), 1, 7, 41, 53, 91–92, 112, 139–140, 142, 150–151, 156, 174, 186, 191–194, 202, 217, 227, 230, 254

spirit possession, 6, 140, 146, 189, 193, 217. *See also* tromba.

spirit(s): ancestor, 2, 6, 9–11, 13, 51, 53, 87, 101, 104, 112, 138, 140, 147, 155, 176, 192–193, 199, 202, 205–206, 208, 217, 238; harmful, bad or evil, 8–9, 11, 38, 79, 81, 188, 191, 193–194, 199, 202, 205; Holy, 188, 192, 205. See *also* maishetani, bori, ancestors, spirit possession and tromba.

spiritual: illness(es), 59, 100, 115, 138, 188; therapies, 32, 68, 87, 101–102, 186, 199, 206; awareness, 20, 29, 52, 206; and religious leaders, 24, 41, 87, 92, 187–188, 191, 203–204, 249. *See also* therapy/therapies and illness.

sun/sunrise: importance of, 78, 112, 125, 152

Swahili, 3, 12–13, 15, 157, 161, 169, 186, 217, 221, 235, 252, 256

Sylvie, 97–100, 195, 235

taboo(s), 3, 6, 19–20, 24, 30–31, 46, 53, 69, 80, 85, 105, 111, 167, 172, 181, 194, 197, 207–209, 219, 234, 239, 243, 247, 256, 259–260. *See also* fady.

tanindrazana (ancestral lands), 40, 167, 175

Tanzania, 20, 236, 252

taxi–brousse/taxis–brousses, 11, 36, 51, 57

teeth: in babies, 7, 79, 82, 137–138, 144–145, 147, 149, 151, 234, 243; as a sign of wealth, 82, 91–92; grandfathers', 154, 169

teknonym, 120

therapy/therapies: medical and spiritual, 32, 34, 68, 87, 101–102, 186, 199, 206

Tilghman, Laura, viii, 186, 220, 222, 248, 259

toby, 187, 249

tolotra harina, 149

tomb(s), 2, 6, 79, 112–113, 124, 137, 141–143, 170–172, 174, 212–213, 215–216, 219, 223, 231, 237, 242–245, 252, 257

traditional: healing and medicine, 1, 55–56, 86, 93, 95–97, 102, 178, 187, 189, 191, 195–197, 227, 232, 252, 258, 260; customs, religions, and religious practices, 2–3, 31, 42–43, 47, 49, 79–80, 82, 84, 87–88, 91, 103, 106, 114, 152, 154–155, 161, 168–170, 177–179, 184, 189, 191, 193, 197–199, 205, 210, 220, 237, 240, 249, 252, 257; traditionalist, 3, 56, 58, 86, 91, 93, 95–97, 102, 177, 187, 196, 198–199, 202–205, 227; midwives, 1, 36, 41–44, 50–51, 54, 58–59, 101–102, 198–199, 203–204, 227–228, 230–231, 252, 260

trano, 33, 128

tromba, 6, 41, 140, 174, 186, 192–194, 202, 219, 227, 255. *See also* spirit possession.

tsaiky, 78, 101, 115, 125, 128, 136, 139, 145, 233. *See also* zaza rano.

tsangantsainy, 6

Tsimihety, 84, 103, 234

tsingy, 4, 28

tsodrano, 111. *See also* blessing.

tsy mivavaka, 24, 156

Turner, Victor, 241, 246, 253, 259

Turrittin, Jane, 48, 229, 260

umbilical cord(s), 7, 108, 219, 237, 257

ummah, 72

uncle(s), 29, 49, 108, 145, 166, 173, 184, 195

UNICEF, 14, 222, 259

United States, 14, 25–26, 36, 39, 45, 54–55, 84, 96, 98, 188, 209–210, 222, 226, 230, 255

University of Antsiranana, viii, 9, 16, 28, 33–34, 62, 81, 122

urban/ urbanites/ urbanization, 3, 13–14, 20, 23, 29, 31, 34, 40, 42, 49, 144–146, 152, 154–157, 169, 174–175, 177–178, 185, 193–195, 198, 205, 211–212, 221, 224, 248, 259

USAID, 39, 227

272 INDEX

vao–teraka, 139
vazaha, 24–25, 42, 55, 83, 94, 100, 130, 137, 168, 194, 197, 218
Vazimba, 113
Vezo, 4, 108, 167, 218, 242, 244–245, 247, 251
village/villagers/village life, 2–3, 5, 16, 39, 42, 44, 140, 144, 180, 185, 187, 229, 243, 248, 252, 259
Viviane, 16
voandalana, 207
vocation, 43, 52, 68, 95, 230
Vohemar, 117–118, 155
vonjy, 79

Walsh, Andrew, 4, 123, 167, 218–219, 237, 239, 243, 247, 256, 260
water: rivers, waterfalls, and bodies of, 3, 11, 13–14, 87–88, 91, 112, 114, 140–141, 152, 206, 213; related to babies, x, 3–4, 7, 19, 118, 132, 134, 137–139, 150, 152, 166, 215–216; related to bathing, blessing, and birthing, 5, 11, 19, 30, 53, 58–59, 72, 78–79, 87–88, 91, 93, 105, 109, 111–119, 124–125, 129, 135, 143, 145, 148, 150, 152–153, 166, 169, 171–172, 183, 195–197, 217, 230–231, 233, 238, 247; related to the Malagasy life course, 3–4, 17, 30, 139, 171–174, 215–216; access to, and related to environmental pollution, 27, 34, 42, 44, 60, 127, 153, 155, 197; watering plants, 28; spiritual properties of, 140–141
water babies, x, 3–4, 7, 19, 30, 132, 134, 137–139, 152, 213, 241–242. See also zaza rano.

wealth, 14, 16, 25, 54–55, 96, 156, 168, 203–204, 233
West: as a geographic/cultural reference, 11, 25, 204; referring to Western culture, 19, 26, 224, 228; referring to Westerners, 81; and to the process of Westernization, 35, 38
West Africa(n), 8, 186, 188, 220, 257
West, Harry, 45, 55, 231, 232
white: as a social category, 2, 24–28, 38, 55–56, 151, 210; related to religious objects/attire, 1, 47, 160, 169, 189, 217, 249; white teeth, 91–92
Wolof, 48
womb(s), 6, 31, 54, 60, 73, 76, 96, 100, 123–124, 139, 141–142, 170, 172, 174, 216, 259
World Health Organization (WHO), 37, 39, 225, 230

Yemen(i), 13, 70

Zafimaniry, 143–144, 219, 242–245, 247, 252
Zafisoa, 16, 42, 79–80, 93–94, 137–138, 152–156, 172, 188–189, 212, 216, 242–243, 246
Zanahary, 24, 41, 167, 221. See also Anjanahary.
zanaka, 99
zaza kely, 139
zaza mena, 137, 139, 223, 242
zaza rano, x, 4, 7, 12, 123, 137–139, 167, 213, 220, 242. See also water baby.
zebu, 87, 207. See also aomby.

Erin K. Nourse is Associate Professor of Religious Studies at Regis University. She has published an article in the *Journal of Religion in Africa* and contributed chapters to the *Oxford Research Encyclopedia of African History* and to *Africa Every Day: Fun, Leisure, and Expressive Culture on the Continent.*

For Indiana University Press

Sabrina Black, Editorial Assistant
Lesley Bolton, Project Manager/Editor
Anna Francis, Assistant Acquisitions Editor
Anna Garnai, Production Coordinator
Katie Huggins, Production Manager
Bethany Mowry, Acquisitions Editor
Dan Pyle, Online Publishing Manager
Pamela Rude, Senior Artist and Book Designer
Stephen Williams, Assistant Director of Marketing

www.ingramcontent.com/pod-product-compliance
Lightning Source LLC
Chambersburg PA
CBHW031351290326
41932CB00044B/975